11/April'

IRISH
EDUCATIONAL
POLICY

IRISH EDUCATIONAL POLICY

Process & Substance

EDITED BY D.G. MULCAHY & DENIS O'SULLLIVAN

INSTITUTE OF PUBLIC ADMINISTRATION

First published 1989
Institute of Public Administration
57-61 Lansdowne Road
Dublin, Ireland.
Tel: (01) 697011 (Publications)
Fax: (01) 698644

Cataloguing in Publication Data
Irish educational policy: process and substance
    1. Ireland (Republic). Education. Policies of government
    I. Mulcahy, D.G. *1943-*
    II. O'Sullivan, Denis
    III. Institute of Public Administration. Dublin. Ireland
        379.417

ISBN 0 906980 96 8 hbk
ISBN 0 906980 91 7 pbk

Cover and title pages designed by Gerry Doherty
Book designed by Sarah O'Hara
Index by Helen Litton

Typeset in 11/12 Times Roman by Printset & Design Ltd
Printed by Criterion Press Ltd

Contents

Acknowledgements

In bringing this book to publication we have become indebted to many people. In particular, we would like to thank the following:

the contributing authors for agreeing to participate in the project and for maintaining their commitment to it. Such is the uniqueness of their contributions that we feel confident they will come to be regarded as benchmarks in Irish educational policy studies;

Jim O'Donnell, Assistant Director General, Institute of Public Administration, for his advice at various stages of the project, Sarah O'Hara who copy-edited the typescript, Helen Litton who compiled the index, and Kathleen Harte for helping to expedite the publishing process;

Mary Morrison and Claire Butler, Education Department, University College, Cork who did the lengthy secretarial work in connection with the project.

To all of these we wish to express our deeply felt gratitude and appreciation.

D.G. MULCAHY AND DENIS O'SULLIVAN
January 1989

Notes on Contributors

DAVID BARRY   Principal, St Caimin's Community School, Shannon, County Clare.

PATRICK CLANCY   Statutory Lecturer, Department of Sociology, University College, Dublin.

JOHN COOLAHAN   Professor of Education, St Patrick's College, Maynooth, County Kildare.

JOHN HARRIS   Principal, Newpark Comprehensive School, Dublin.

THOMAS KELLAGHAN   Director, The Educational Research Centre, St Patrick's College, Drumcondra, Dublin.

D.G. MULCAHY   Professor of Education, Eastern Illinois University, USA.

TIMOTHY J. OWENS   Teacher, St Aidan's Community College, Dublin Hill, Cork.

DENIS O'SULLIVAN   Statutory Lecturer, Department of Education, University College, Cork.

Introduction

D. G. Mulcahy and Denis O'Sullivan

Education is a major area of state investment, and not just financially — although that is the most publicised aspect — but occupationally, morally and politically. It represents a repository of the aspirations of a people with regard to their future, their view of their heritage, their definition of worthwhile and useful knowledge, and the standards which they consider appropriate in human relationships. Alone among social institutions outside of the family, the school system has the obligatory audience of the future adult population during its most formative years. Ultimately, the stability and growth of the state depends on the school system performing its functions, particularly in relation to socialisation, cultural transmission, and selection.

In Ireland, the study of education has responded to these realities with the expansion of education departments in universities and of colleges of education to encompass a wide range of specialists in such areas as psychology, sociology, evaluation and curriculum, the establishment of the Educational Research Centre and the formation of the Educational Studies Association of Ireland. A growing scholarly literature in educational studies is available in the *Irish Journal of Education* and *Irish Educational Studies* as well as in international journals, which reflects the interests of these specialists and their post-graduate students. Of their nature, these studies focus on specific educational issues or confine their analysis to the perspective of a particular discipline. In this development, policy making as an area of inter-disciplinary enquiry

1

remains neglected. It represents an anomaly that, despite considerable social investment in the widest sense, the structures and processes involved in establishing priorities for educational development have not undergone sustained scholarly analysis. This volume attempts to correct for this inadequacy.

In chapter 1, The Policy-Making Role of the Department of Education, Dr John Harris draws on his experiences as a former special adviser to Ministers for Education, John Boland, Patrick Cooney and Gemma Hussey to provide an account of policy making in the Department of Education. Dr Harris writes about decision making, relations with external agencies, the inspectorates, and the evolution and formulation of policy from the vantage point of one who has been deeply involved in these issues in the Department, thus providing insights normally not within the experience of the researcher.

In chapter 2, Educational Policy for National Schools, 1960–1985, Professor John Coolahan disentangles five issues affecting primary education over the past twenty-five years; supply and training of teachers, the provision of school buildings, pupil progress, the curriculum and school management; and follows through on them in a longitudinal manner. He concludes by drawing together and interpreting some of the significant patterns and issues that have emerged as well as isolating some dimensions of the style of policy making directing primary education.

The focus in chapter 3, Official Perceptions of Curriculum in Irish Second-Level Education by Professor D.G. Mulcahy, is on the idea or concept of curriculum, which has been employed by policy makers, curriculum developers and other officials with particular reference to official publications and reports including, for example, *The rules and programme for secondary schools*. In focusing upon the concept of curriculum which has been employed, particular attention is devoted to a critical appraisal of the extent to which the concept relates to how curriculum is understood in other educational systems. This chapter concludes with a consideration of the appropriateness and suitability of the concept of curriculum employed in Ireland for dealing with the likely demands to be made on post-primary education in Ireland in the future.

In chapter 4, The Evolution of Policy in Third-Level Education, Dr Patrick Clancy begins with a brief review of the main developments in higher education since the mid-1960s exploring the growth, diversification and structural changes in the system. In scrutinising decision-making structures and processes, he focuses in the main on the interplay between the state and other agencies. The role of various commissions of enquiry (for example, Commission on Higher Education, 1967 and Steering Committee on Technical Education, 1969) is examined as is the changing role of the Higher Education Authority as a buffer agency between the state and third-level institutions. The failure to designate technical colleges and colleges of education, the effect of which has been to reserve additional power for the state while also incorporating a more direct role for local authorities and the Churches, is discussed. In considering the main trends in higher education policy it is suggested that the dominant trend is a shift towards vocationalism, a trend orchestrated principally by the state and underpinning many other aspects of policy including the endorsement of the binary structure and the widespread provision of short-cycle higher education. Efforts to provide equality of opportunity as reflected in student support schemes and in the changing fees policy are also examined as is the impact of the regional provision of higher education. Policy developments in Ireland are related to broader trends evident in other Western countries and it is suggested that international trends had a significant influence on Irish policy in higher education.

The focus of attention in chapter 5, The Involvement and Impact of a Professional Interest Group by David Barry, shifts from a consideration of policy making at national level to a consideration of the impact on both the process of policy making and the content of policy by a teachers' union, The Association of Secondary Teachers of Ireland. The chapter highlights the manner in which, since the mid-1960s, the ASTI insisted on becoming involved in the policy-making process, and it considers the extent to which the ASTI determined, shaped and re-shaped policy with particular reference to second-level education including such issues as the deeds of trust for comprehensive and community schools and the recommendations of the ICE Report.

In chapter 6, Central Initiatives and Local Realities, Ted Owens examines the fate and the impact in the schools of the Cork County Vocational Education Committee of central policies introduced in the mid-1960s regarding school rationalisation, curriculum and examinations. As such it throws important light on the interplay between national policy and its implementation at local level. Attention is also given to a consideration of the extent to which the tradition of vocational education in a particular area came under pressure to adapt itself increasingly to the secondary model of post-primary education and the economy. It serves to highlight the need for central policy making to take cognisance of interests and expectations which are likely to arise at the school implementation stage.

Chapter 7, The Interface of Research, Evaluation, and Policy in Irish Education by Dr Thomas Kellaghan, distinguishes between six types of research in Ireland — the analysis or review of policy and/or practice, research and development, parameter estimation, monitoring, modelling social phenomena, and experimentation and quasi experimentation. He considers the response of research to policy as well as the response of policy to research and suggests for consideration the establishment of a body which would perform a coordinating, liaising, problem-defining and disseminating function for all government departments involved in the formation and execution of social policy.

In chapter 8, The Ideational Base of Irish Educational Policy, Dr Denis O'Sullivan focuses on the character of Irish educational ideas as they are manifested in official reports, policy statements, professional deliberations, public debate and controversy, research studies, and educational practice or proposals for practice. The validity of the substantive conclusions or contentions arising from such diverse sources is not the immediate concern of the analysis. Rather the concern is with the cognitive and ideological repertoire of concepts, ideas, propositions, issues, and forms of discourse employed to mentally engage the phenomenon of Irish education and to inform the process and content of policy making. The adequacy of this repertoire, its establishment and legitimation, content and exclusions, maintenance and modification as well as its social and ideological base is considered. Three broad propositions relating to Irish educational thought are advanced: that it is conceptually and analytically weak, paradigmatically insulated and ideologically domesticated. Possible reasons for these features are outlined and a number of suggestions for providing Irish educational policy with a more elaborate, diverse and cosmopolitan ideational base are proposed.

The editors are mindful that this consideration of both the content and process of policy making represents a departure in Irish educational studies. As well as highlighting and coordinating relevant knowledge and insights, it suggests many issues for research and considerations for practice. It is the editors' aspiration that this book will nurture a tradition of policy studies in Irish educational enquiry.

1

The Policy-making Role of the Department of Education

JOHN HARRIS

The policy-making role played by the Department of Education varies considerably from time to time and can be greatly affected by the influence of certain key individuals as well as by the particular style and *modus operandi* of the Minister of the day.

Educational policy making is ultimately the prerogative of the government; specifically of that cabinet member designated as having particular responsibility for education. Under the Ministers and Secretaries Act 1924, the significant concept is of the Minister as 'corporation sole', a factor which influences greatly the manner in which the Department of Education functions. The principle of corporation sole means, in effect, that the Minister is responsible to Dáil Éireann for all the administration of the Department, and thereby for all aspects of policy and administration of the educational system. He or she is deemed responsible for all acts and actions of the civil servants working within the Department of Education: a factor which inhibits civil servants when making their own decisions, particularly when it comes to taking risks or introducing change. The fact that a Minister may be called to answer to Dáil Éireann for the actions of any civil servant necessarily imposes a considerable degree of caution on the officials of the Department and is perhaps one of the principal factors that makes the Department of Education fundamentally conservative.

It could be argued that this is not necessarily a bad thing. Ireland is, in many ways, a highly conservative nation and it is not unnatural that that conservatism will be reflected in the expectations which its people have of their educational system. It takes strong-minded and determined leadership from the top to bring about change. The very complexities of the educational system, not to mention the vast array of vested interests operating within it, make implementing change a very slow process. Proposals to innovate tend to be viewed with suspicion. Long-standing influences, particularly those associated with the relationship between the Catholic Church and the state in the control of education, are hard to change. Experience shows a consistency of reluctance within the country at large to consider any policy measure which might be seen to challenge the influence of religious bodies, institutions or even individuals. This is a factor of which Ministers and the Department of Education have had to be constantly aware. This factor remains significant, even though the number of members of religious orders involved in education has suffered a major decline in recent years. The relationship between religious leaders and Ministers and civil servants is at times an uneasy one.[1] Yet it can be argued that the resulting tension has, overall, worked in a positive way towards building up and maintaining an educational service of high quality. It can never be overlooked that the 'Church' (in the broad interpretation of that term) for many years played a role in providing post-primary education far in advance of that which the state itself played.

It may seem strange, in a chapter dealing with the policy-making role of the Department of Education, to start out with reference to the influence of another interest group altogether. However, it is important to recognise, as background knowledge, this particular influence which has had much bearing on the way in which both Ministers and Department of Education officials have approached many policy issues.

Decision Making

Despite the extensive role which the Department of Education plays in relation to the overall management of education, and despite the awareness of that fact by the individuals who work within the system, it is quite surprising to discover just how much confusion and ambiguity there is concerning how decisions are taken and who actually takes them. The Department is often criticised (or indeed praised) for decisions which it itself has not taken. This occurs particularly in relation to those decisions that are the prerogative of government, that is of politicians rather than civil servants. Many issues of policy, particularly those with financial implications, cannot be taken by the Department alone, or even by the Minister for Education in consultation with officials. Many matters must be placed on the agenda for a cabinet meeting. This process can be complex, lengthy and tortuous, involving consultations in advance with other government departments which might be expected to have an interest in the question under consideration. The cabinet, in reaching a decision about education, may be more influenced by the views of the Department of Finance than by those of the Department of Education.

Once a government decision is taken, recorded and transmitted to a department, the department is bound to operate strictly in accordance with the terms of that decision, whether they agree with it or not. A government minister, bound by the principle of collective responsibility, may find him or herself having to go from the cabinet room and announce and defend a decision which he or she had unsuccessfully opposed in discussion with government colleagues. Likewise, department officials may have to give effect to and defend government decisions which were made contrary to their advice. This particular hazard of the job of a civil servant often goes unappreciated by those who seek to vent their frustration against those whom they may erroneously believe to be responsible for some unpopular decision.

As the minister of the day acts as the political head of a particular department, he or she has to establish a working relationship with the permanent secretary and with other senior officers. Once again, it is important to realise that the kind of relationship established can vary greatly from minister to minister. It will also be significantly affected by the way in which ministers perceive their role, or order priorities between their different areas of responsibility.

One major difficulty arises from the fact that ministers have in effect three different jobs to perform:

1. the role of a constituency TD serving those who elected them;
2. specific departmental responsibility;
3. general responsibility as cabinet members for the range of decisions to be taken by government.

One may add a fourth role, that of being a member of Dáil Éireann with the obligation to attend and speak in the house and to be available for votes as required by the whip of their party.

In practice, ministers have to live with the constant dilemma of achieving a pragmatic balance between all these roles, each one of which could make up a full-time job in its own right. There have been ministers who have paid a bitter price at election time for having devoted their energies primarily to their departmental role rather than attending constantly to the myriad demands of their constituents and to being seen frequently around their constituency. The fact that they may have achieved considerable success as a minister, and may have earned a high national profile, may not impress a critical electorate which tends to judge their TDs' performance on the basis of how they attend to their constituents' needs and demands.

In addition there may be the problem of giving a large amount of time to departmental issues and insufficient time to preparing for cabinet discussions on issues that are due to arise from other departments. Sometimes Taoisigh or prime ministers may use cabinet reshuffles for the purpose of ensuring that ministers do not become unduly obsessed or absorbed by just one aspect of a government's responsibilities, losing thereby a balanced overview of the whole.

Given that Ministers for Education will, perforce, be available to their Department only on what may be regarded as a 'part-time' basis, the extent to which they will be involved in policy decisions at the level of detail will be limited. They can, of course, set the agenda, identify the priorities and leave the detail to be worked out by permanent officials. In such a situation, unless specific dates are set for action, and unless progress in priority areas is closely and regularly monitored, the real power to make decisions (or delay decisions) may pass to the civil service. Likewise if ministers' priorities rest principally with nurturing their constituents, with concern for cabinet business, or indeed with more 'ceremonial' aspects of their role, civil servants will tend to become the real decision makers. This may of course prove very satisfactory from the civil service point of view. The BBC television series 'Yes Minister' has helped to explode myths about the relationship between ministers and their officials, and to expose the kinds of ploys which some may be tempted to use from time to time.

O'Connor has pointed out[2] that when ministers spend only a brief period in charge of a particular department the ability to effect changes is severely restricted; at such times the pendulum of influence swings towards the permanent civil servants. During the years 1981 and 1982 no less than six persons served as Minister for Education. Inevitably in such a situation no one Minister could possibly see a complex issue through from conception to completion.

Thus, at different times, as ministers come and go, the policy decision-making locus may shift from politicians to civil servants and back again. Generally, during those periods when the power rests predominantly with civil servants, less change tends to take place. This comment is not intended as a criticism of individual civil servants, many of whom are imaginative and creative, with many ideas to offer for change. It is rather a comment on a Department which tends to be both bureaucratic and hierarchical and where there can be a reluctance to take risks for fear of upsetting the system. Nevertheless, certain individuals, holding senior office in the Department, have been influential in guiding ministers and in policy making generally.

It can often happen that a complex and problematic issue may emerge at a relatively low level in the chain of command. The normal procedure is to refer that issue to a higher level for decision. In fact, if the issue is particularly sensitive or difficult, or has political implications, it is likely to pass up the hierarchical ladder, perhaps as far as the Minister's desk. There is a danger that, somewhere along the line, creative thinking about the issue may become stifled, fears may be voiced about creating a precedent, or anxiety expressed about being accused of taking risks or making mistakes. This may result in the soft or safe option being taken, regardless of the merits of the case for the alternative. One hopes that, when files come finally to rest on desks where decisions are actually taken, the decision makers will not be unduly confused by the fog which may have been created around the issue on the way up.

Reference was made earlier to the difficulties a minister may have in monitoring the implementation of policy, given the limitations on time available. In recent years a practice has developed whereby ministers bring with them, or appoint to their departments, 'special advisers' or 'personal assistants'. As yet no clear pattern has emerged about the role of such personnel. Although appointed with the status of non-established civil servants whose terms of office expire no later than the date of any subsequent change of government, there is clearly a political dimension to their role. Personal assistants tend to act primarily as aids in handling the minister's constituency business. Special advisers tend to have a brief largely in the area of policy. The present writer has had the experience of acting as special adviser to three different Ministers for Education, John Boland, Gemma Hussey and Patrick Cooney. In each case the brief was to work in the general area of educational policy making, although other tasks included speech writing or editing, and monitoring the handling of day-to-day enquiries that came to the Minister's office about issues on which the Minister would have a view.

It was the writer's perception of the role that a special adviser should seek to form a link or bridge between the Department of Education on the one hand and the Minister and government on the other. It seemed important from the Minister's point of view that someone would be readily available within the Department, seeking to ensure that the Minister's policies were being progressed. It also seemed important from the Department's point of view to have someone who could explore the implications of policy implementation and convey departmental views about it directly to the Minister. When departmental committees were set up to carry through certain policy measures, for example the setting up of the Curriculum and Examinations Board, or the drawing up of the *Programme for action in education 1984 — 1987,*[3] the presence of the Minister's special adviser as a member of the working groups concerned ensured that this two-way communication could take place. In order for this to work effectively, it is important that the special adviser should earn the confidence of the permanent civil servants. It is a matter for others to judge as regards whether or not the writer was successful in this. Certainly he can vouch for the kindly, courteous and professional way in which he was received. He also valued greatly the advice of officials regarding the feasibility and practicalities of many policy ideas which came under examination.

Relations with External Agencies

In this chapter so far, the term 'policy' has been given a broad interpretation, applied to the issues that are of direct relevance to ministers and government. There is another level of interpretation, relating to the kinds of issues which the Department itself decides, generally without recourse to the Minister at all[4] (unless problems arise, where the Minister may be brought into the issue, perhaps through the actions or representations of some third party). Issues that arise under this heading include those concerning the direct relationship between the Department and schools or the various educational associations such as the teachers' unions or managerial organisations. A new dimension has also been added in recent years with the establishment of the National Parents Council. The kinds of issues in question here are those falling within the ambit of government policy and concerning the practical applications of such policy. In such cases, although it is often the Department which makes the decision, the normal practice would be for Department officials to consult with the relevant interest groups before decisions are taken. The attitudes of many of the interest groups concerned may themselves impose limitations on the freedom for departmental action, particularly if the aim is to avoid conflict and dispute. At times of major unrest, such as when teacher strikes arise, or when protest groups seek to mount a campaign of opposition to a particular policy, the process of meetings and consultations assumes a high profile, often featuring extensively in media coverage. On the other hand, seldom reported, is the continuous flow of communication and dialogue which takes place all the time between the representatives of the various organisations and officials of the Department. In the vast majority of cases there is a mutual respect and understanding built up between both sides, practical difficulties are sorted out, and many policy issues are decided quietly in this context.

Of course not all outside bodies stand in equal relationship with the Department of Education. Some, for instance, have statutory authority to take autonomous action in specified areas, such as the Higher Education Authority, the National Council for Educational Awards, or vocational education committees. This can on occasion give rise to disagreements about the limits of the Department's responsibilities vis-a-vis those of the statutory body.

One advantage which lies with the central authority is that considerable influence can always be exerted by those who control financial allocations to such bodies. Furthermore, the Vocational Education Act 1930 allows for procedures whereby the Minister may dissolve a vocational education committee and appoint an official to act in its place. Such a course has been followed, admittedly on relatively rare occasions.[5]

Even in its dealings with the different categories of school, differences exist in the way in which the Department may take decisions and institute policy. For instance, in the post-primary sector, there are different categories of schools: secondary schools, vocational schools, comprehensive and community schools and community colleges. The Department has more direct control and influence over policy in community and comprehensive schools than in any of the other categories. In the case of vocational schools, the Department is constrained by the powers given to vocational education committees under the 1930 Act. Secondary schools are private institutions, financed by direct grants. In many respects the Department's direct responsibilities for such schools end once the level of grant has been determined and the grant paid over. Curriculum issues are laid down in the *Rules and programme for secondary schools*.[6]

At third level and universities, the National Institutes for Higher Education and the National College of Art and Design are all funded through the Higher Education Authority. Regional technical colleges, however, are funded through vocational education committees. This kind of difference has implications for the extent of influence which the Department may exert over policy matters affecting these institutions.

The Inspectorates

Nothing has as yet been said in relation to the role of the inspectorates. In many ways inspectors are the front line in communicating with schools, although at post-primary level an inspector's visit to a school is a somewhat rare event, owing largely to the commitments of post-primary inspectors in relation to the public examinations. There is often misunderstanding at the level of the individual school and teacher about the role of inspectors within the Department. They may often be judged as being to blame for some departmental or government decision that has found disfavour. Yet their influence on decision making in many areas of educational administration is relatively small — regrettably too small. There is an unfortunate gulf at times between inspectors as professional educators on the one hand and administrators as professional civil servants on the other. On many issues of policy, including those in which the Minister takes a direct interest, the views of inspectors may or may not be sought, and even if they are they may be edited or amended by administrative officials. Generally speaking the inspectorates' views are channelled to the Minister through the administrative side of the Department, unless the Minister specifically arranges otherwise. Yet some of the most effective committees (of which the writer has had direct experience) were those on which both administrators and inspectors participated. Very often the omission of inspectors, in the past, resulted more from oversight than a conscious desire to exclude. It is nonetheless regrettable that an important source of expertise may be under-utilised if the inspectorate voice is not heard more loudly.

The one major area where the inspectorates have always been involved is in the area of curriculum and, in the case of those at post-primary level, in examinations. The establishment of the Curriculum and Examinations Board (later recast as the National Council for Curriculum and Assessment) introduced a change in the role of the inspectorates. It is a matter of argument as to whether the role has been diminished or enhanced as a result. Had the Curriculum and Examinations Board been established by statute and given responsibility for running the state examinations the change would have been far greater, the intention having originally been to free the inspectorate from the weight of administrative work associated with examinations and to give them more time to visit schools.

Until 1986 inspectors had acted as chairpersons of post-primary syllabus committees. This changed on the handing over of syllabus committees to the board/council. However, inspectors will, presumably, still have a key role to play in advising the Minister about recommendations that come from the National Council for Curriculum and Assessment.

The Evolution of Policy

It has been argued that the role of the Department in policy making is not fixed or immutable; it is affected by the style and perceptions of ministers. It may also be affected by whether or not a government sees education as a priority area and as one in which it wishes to take certain initiatives. This may indeed reflect a particular Taoiseach's scale of priorities.[7]

A certain mystique surrounds the Department of Education, probably in large part as a result of the factors outlined here. Occasionally one gets glimpses of how the Department operates. The Department publishes a journal, *Oideas*, but this includes articles from many contributors who do not come from within the Department. Those that do, however, can help to cast some light. In *A troubled sky: reflections on the Irish educational scene 1957−1968*, the late Seán O'Connor, former secretary of the Department of Education, has opened a window on many aspects of how policy is made. He comments in some detail, for instance, about the style and influence of several Ministers for Education: Jack Lynch, Patrick Hillery, George Colley and Donogh O'Malley. The last-named is of course one of the legendary names in Irish education and O'Connor's account of how the policy of free post-primary education was introduced makes instructive reading.[8]

It is not surprising that few books or articles have been written giving the 'inside story' of the Department of Education. Having to avoid taking the risk of exposing anything that might be deemed an official secret imposes obvious constraints on any who have been involved. For those seeking to report on or trace the evolution of policy with the Department, the principal sources of information are ministerial speeches, published statements, or records of interviews given.[9] In the case of speeches, the most obvious source to look to is the Dáil record, although ministers often prefer to make important policy statements outside the house, on public platforms where media coverage is likely to be given. The speeches and statements alone, of course, do not necessarily reveal much about how policy is made. It is necessary to analyse closely, in order to infer what the background is behind the words which are often couched with maximum political impact in mind.

The present writer can record his own experiences with regard to key areas of policy development during the 1983−87 period.

Without being specific as to detail, which it would not be appropriate to give, it is possible to identify a certain pattern of approach which was adopted. This applied in the case of drafting the *Programme for action in education 1984 – 1987*, preparing for the establishment of the interim Curriculum and Examinations Board, drafting the discussion paper for and processing the *Ages for learning* debate[10] and drawing up the Green Paper *Partners in education*.[11]

A departmental working group was set up in each of the above examples, at the instigation of the then Minister, Gemma Hussey. These groups were representative of key officials with responsibility in the areas in question. Both administrators and inspectors were involved in most cases, as a matter of deliberate policy. In all instances the Minister took specific interest in the composition of the working groups. It was deemed that the Minister's adviser should be involved in order to keep the group on target with regard to the Minister's intentions and also to clarify with the Minister any points which might arise in the course of the work.

When working groups had been set up, and when they had received their terms of reference from the Minister and secretary, they would examine the issues under debate and draw up drafts for proposals to go to government. As appropriate, the groups consulted with outside bodies. The Minister had indicated a general commitment to consultation with a wide range of interests; and this resulted in each group spending many hours in meeting with interest groups, and in reading and analysing written submissions received. Views brought forward through these consultations were taken seriously and a genuine attempt was made to respond positively to ideas. This was not always possible, given the range of such views, often conflicting, and given the feasibility of what was proposed. As this approach to policy formulation was relatively novel, in some of the consultations the working groups met with scepticism or suspicion from the parties consulted.

When the work of each group was at an advanced stage, proposals were submitted to the Minister, who usually arranged to meet with the members of the working group to clarify any points or to ask for revisions as necessary. Where government decisions were needed, the appropriate documentation was prepared, circulated to other relevant departments, and memoranda were prepared for cabinet. This process was often quite protracted, and required detailed discussions with other departments, particularly with the Department of Finance whenever financial considerations were involved.

Once decisions were reached at government level, it fell again to the working groups concerned to carry through on those decisions. This usually involved arranging for the launch of a policy statement or discussion paper, generally by means of a press conference. It was also important to inform the major organisations consulted of the outcome of the deliberations on the subject in question.

In the case of the working group concerned with the *Programme for action*, the group stayed in existence over the whole four-year period, holding regular meetings to monitor the implementation of the programme and preparing an annual progress report for the Minister, which was published early each year. The same working group also took overseeing responsibility for the *Ages for learning* debate, although aspects of the work were delegated to sub-groups or working parties.

The evolution of the Curriculum and Examinations Board (now replaced by the National Council for Curriculum and Assessment) makes a useful case study of how policy is formulated.

The Council of Education had reported in 1960 on the curriculum of the secondary school,[12] concluding that the curriculum was more or less all right and not proposing major changes other than syllabus revision. Not long afterwards, however, the Minister of the day, Patrick Hillery, was announcing plans for comprehensive schools, with implications for changing curricula, and shortly after that plans were announced for the standardisation of courses and examinations within all categories of post-primary school.

Towards the end of the 1960s, talk was being heard about plans for an independent examinations board. The fourteen-point programme agreed for the 1973 – 77 coalition government included a commitment to establish such a board. Although work reached an advanced stage with regard to drafting legislation to give effect to this commitment, no Bill was ever published, or clear statement of intent issued by the government. In any event the board under consideration had been one whose sole responsibility would have been to organise the leaving and intermediate certificate examinations.

In December 1980 the Fianna Fáil government *White Paper on educational development* proposed the establishment of an advisory curriculum council; no mention was made of assessment or examinations.[13] No council was in fact set up before the government left office in June 1981. The coalition government, which assumed office at that time, included in its programme a commitment to set up an independent board to deal with both curriculum and examinations. The Minister for Education, John Boland, made a speech to Seanad Éireann on 29 October 1981 outlining his plans for this board.[14] Copies of this speech were circulated to all schools. The government changed again in March 1982 but during the next government's nine-month term of office the idea of a board was not acted on. The coalition government, which came to office in December 1982, once again picked up the plans to set up a board and established the 'Interim' Curriculum and Examinations Board in January 1984, pending the preparation of the necessary statute to establish the Board on a permanent basis. The preparation of the Bill took longer than expected and the process suffered delays, caused by a cabinet reshuffle in early 1986, resulting in a new Minister for Education, and by a teachers' dispute and strike later the same year. Although the Bill was published in late 1986, it was not debated in the Oireachtas prior to the change of government in March 1987.

On assuming office the new Fianna Fáil government decided not to proceed with the establishment of a board by statute and instead replaced the interim Board in the autumn of 1987 by the National Council for Curriculum and Assessment, a format more in line with the 1980 White Paper proposal. The major difference between the Board and Council was that the former had been intended to have executive responsibility for the running of the state examinations whereas the latter has only a general advisory function about matters of assessment.

It will be clear from the above summary of events that the issue at all stages was largely political, with different approaches being adopted as different governments came to power and reflecting the different priorities of the respective political parties in office. During this period, the Department must have suffered from considerable confusion, not knowing for very long at any one time, which format of board/council it was supposed to be processing. It is an open secret that there were widely differing views within the Department on whether or not such a board should be established and, if it should, what form it should take.

During the period just prior to the setting up of the Interim
Curriculum and Examinations Board, however, a large amount
of work was undertaken by an internal departmental working party
which drew up a detailed report for the Minister with
recommendations about structures for the Board. In compiling this
report, extensive consultations were held with interested parties
throughout the summer of 1983.

This case study may not be typical in demonstrating how
educational policies evolve within the field of Department/
government but it is not without parallels (for example the question
of the regionalisation of post-primary education has been another
issue to surface or submerge as governments changed). It does,
however, give some insight into the complexity that lies behind
making policy.

Principles of Policy Making

It is difficult to give any comprehensive overview of the role of
the Department of Education in policy making. Things do not
remain constant for long, and patterns do not necessarily repeat
themselves. The influence of particular individuals, either
politicians or civil servants, may prove crucial at any time.
Pressures from outside groups − if well orchestrated politically
− may also force change.

It will be interesting to see in future how the idea may develop
of ministers appointing special advisers. The role definition for
such persons is still far from clear. Suggestions have been mooted
for the introduction of 'cabinets' within departments to serve
individual ministers. A cabinet could be formed of, say, four or
five members, each specialising in different aspects of policy, or
alternatively with some members dealing with areas of a minister's
direct responsibility and others concentrating on the broader issues
which the minister must address at cabinet. The concept of the
special adviser, already in place, may be a first step towards such
a system. To develop in this way would be to come into line with
the practice widely used in Europe.

Another aspect to consider, too, is the possible development of
the 'Devlin' proposals[15] to separate policy making and executive
functions within departments and to form an 'Aireacht' of senior

civil servants to advise ministers. If structures along these lines were introduced, considerable change might be brought about in the way a department influences policy decisions. However, to date, little if any movement has occurred towards this end.

Then there is the question of whether the inspectorates should be given a more prominent role. Inspectors working in the Department of Education may envy the greater degree of autonomy afforded to their British counterparts. HMIs (Her Majesty's Inspectors) have an independent standing and are free to publish their views on aspects of educational policy, whether or not these views will be welcome to either the British Department of Education or to the Minister. The present structures in Ireland do not allow for this but it is certainly a possibility to be considered that the system might benefit from such openness, if the reluctance of causing public embarrassment to governments can be overcome.

While recognising the diversity of practice in the policy-making area of education, one may consider whether or not certain principles should or already do apply.

The overall principle is that the Minister is in fact, *the* policy maker, with the Department of Education acting as servant and guide to the Minister, as well as liaising on ministerial decisions with educational agencies. This principle of the authority and responsibility of the Minister applies, no matter how the Minister chooses to operate, whether or not he or she chooses to make his or her own decisions or to delegate these functions, either deliberately or by default, to subordinates. This principle is guaranteed by the Ministers and Secretaries Act and could be said to be an essential function of a democratic state.

Following from this is the answerability of the Minister to the Oireachtas and ultimately to the electorate. The working out of this principle influences the way the Minister and Department operate on a day-to-day basis. The Minister has to have regard to the need to maintain Oireachtas support for the determining and delivery of policy. The Department must ensure that that answerability of the Minister is not subverted in any way by its own actions; thus its concern that its Minister should not at all costs be caused public embarrassment.

It is a matter of good sense, as well as being an important principle in its own right, that the central authority, both Minister and Department, should seek to establish good working relations with its subordinate agencies (subordinate in the sense of their responsibilities in macro-policy making). These agencies should include all interest groups. With a greater awareness of the importance of communication in all aspects of public life, it is hardly surprising that, in a high-profile area such as education, this will need to feature prominently. The vulnerability of the central authority has become evident in recent years in the implementation of measures to cut spending on education. More than one Minister for Education has learned bitter lessons with regard to the acceptability of such measures and has found that some have proved quite unworkable while others could be implemented only in a manner which left a trail of bitterness and resentment behind them.

The central authority's responsibilities for overall policy making must include concern for quality control. This is exercised through:

1. its role in determining curricula and national assessment systems;
2. its professional officers (the inspectorates), who visit schools and other institutions and report back on them.

It can be argued that it has been more successful in the former than in the latter. It could be said that its influence on curricula and examinations has in the past been excessively authoritarian; this may now be redressed to some extent by the establishment of a national representative agency to advise in this area. The main reason why school inspection has failed to be as effective a quality control system as it might have been is largely due to the inadequate staffing of the inspectorates in terms of the numbers employed and also because of the lack of procedures and structures for inspection, particularly at secondary-school level.

Another important principle which should affect the role of the central authority in policy making is the limiting of that role with regard to what may be termed macro-policy issues. Within broad parameters laid down centrally it is highly desirable that the individual units such as schools and colleges be free to make the decisions necessary to meet local needs. It may be suggested that the central authority can be faulted for a failure to honour the proper spirit of this principle.

If, for instance, the local or regional councils which were proposed in the Green Paper *Partners in education* were to be established in some form, these could shift the relative influences of groups in the policy-making area. On the one hand, they might result in even greater power being concentrated on the central authority. Alternatively, the situation might develop whereby micro controls and policy decisions would be delegated to subordinate agencies, such as local education councils or even to individual school management boards. In such a situation the Department could concentrate its interests on macro issues and global budgeting. Many would argue that this should be done as a matter of urgency within existing structures. It can be suggested that through excessive preoccupation with micro controls the central Department may be dealing inadequately and superficially with macro issues. In recent years, the Department of Finance has demanded that Department of Education officers exercise ever-increasingly detailed control of the minutiae of expenditure within all areas of the education budget − and this at a time when the same Finance Department is pressing for a reduction in the number of civil servants employed to do such work. There is a case for the central Department of Education delegating, as far as is prudent and manageable, to subordinate agencies, the power to decide on the detail of how financial allocations will be spent; it would still retain overall control by determining the size of those allocations and holding those with executive power for spending more personally accountable than at present for any overrun in spending.

Policy making remains a most complex activity, fraught with the uncertainties and vagaries which the political system tends to generate. There is reason for thinking that the political system itself is undergoing a period of considerable change, not least as a result of Ireland's developing relationships within the European Economic Community. It appears that general elections may in future be less likely to produce majority governments drawn from a single political party. As the system adjusts to cope with this and with new forms of inter-party arrangements in the formation of governments likely to emerge, changes may be forced on the whole area of policy formulation and implementation.

Yet the nature of education is such that too much change and uncertainty could work to destabilise some of the basic structures underpinning the delivery of education in a way which would not be beneficial to the 'consumers' of the system − to pupils and their parents in particular. To compensate for this, it is most desirable that those working within the political system, together with the permanent officials in the civil service, work out strategies for medium- and long-term planning. Too much of the policy making is short-term, based on *ad hoc* decision making on a year-to-year basis. One of the factors which has worked against long-term planning in education has been the paucity of legislation. It might prove beneficial to enact comprehensive legislation in the form of an education Act, despite the enormous political difficulties that this would undoubtedly create and the many public controversies that would inevitably arise. The drafting of an education Act would force the political system to define its objectives for education, and even to establish a philosophy of education, which is sadly lacking at present.

Educational policy making is surely too important to be left in its current state of hit-and-miss uncertainty, subject to whim or fashion and often depending too much on the excessive influence of particular individuals. It is important that individuals or minority groups neither block change nor impose it by exerting pressure against a popular consensus. Formal structures are needed to ensure adequate consultation with the many interests which have a legitimate concern about what happens in the complex world of education. No matter how things develop, it is necessary that both the Minister for Education and the Department continue to play the central co-ordinating and leadership role in formulating national education policy.

Notes to Chapter 1

1. See Seán O'Connor, *A troubled sky: reflections on the Irish educational scene 1957–1968* Dublin: Educational Research Centre, St Patrick's College, 1986, pp. 2-3.
2. O'Connor, *A troubled sky* pp. 107-108.
3. *Programme for action in education 1984–1987* Dublin: Stationery Office, January 1984.
4. For an overview of this role of the Department see John Coolahan, *Irish education: history and structure* Dublin: Institute of Public Administration, 1981, chapter 8, pp. 160-64.
5. See O'Connor, *A troubled sky* pp. 163-64.
6. *Rules and programme for secondary schools* Dublin: Stationery Office, annual.
7. O'Connor has suggested that education assumed a particular importance on the government agenda during the period when Sean Lemass was Taoiseach because of Lemass's personal interest in this area — see O'Connor, *A troubled sky* p. 162.
8. O'Connor, *A troubled sky* pp. 141-46, 151-55.
9. See Eileen Randles, *Post-primary education in Ireland 1957–1970* Dublin: Veritas, 1975 where extensive reference is made to such sources.
10. *The ages for learning: discussion paper on the age of entry into the educational system, the age of transfer at subsequent levels and the restructuring of the post-primary sector* Dublin: Stationery Office, June 1984. *Ages for learning: decisions of government* Dublin: Stationery Office, May 1985.
11. *Partners in education: serving community needs* (Green Paper) Dublin: Stationery Office, 1985.
12. Council of Education, *The curriculum of the secondary school* Dublin: Stationery Office, submitted in 1960 and published in 1962.
13. *White Paper on educational development* Dublin: Stationery Office, 1980, p. 48.
14. Speech by John Boland, Minister for Education in Seanad Éireann to the motion 'That Seanad Éireann welcomes the Government's intention to establish an Independent Curriculum and Examinations Board', Thursday, 29 October 1981.
15. *Report of Public Services Organisation Review Group 1966–1969* Dublin: Institute of Public Administration, 1970 (Chairman, Liam St John Devlin, after whom the report is popularly named), see particularly chapter 13. See also *Serving the country better: a White Paper on the public service* Dublin: Stationery Office, 1985.

2

Educational Policy for National Schools, 1960–1985

JOHN COOLAHAN

> Ireland has operated the schools in a spartan and frugal manner especially at primary level, in the National Schools, with historically extremely large classes, taught by poorly paid teachers, in ill-equipped and poorly maintained schools.[1]

This rather stark description by Dale Tussing reflected the disappointing reality of Irish national schools for many decades of the twentieth century. If the feature of a rigid and narrow curriculum were added then the national schools system after almost forty years of independence did not present an impressive image. When the curricular and organisational matters of the 1920s had been achieved, there was a striking lack of policy or public concern for the national school system. Control of most features of the system had become highly centralised within the Department of Education; it adopted the approach of keeping the system ticking over with little or no serious re-appraisal of policy or of the direction in which the system was going.

In the years after the second world war, some agencies called for changes in policy. A notable instance of this was the Irish National Teachers' Organisation (INTO) which in 1947 issued its *Plan for education* which sought a re-structuring of the system.[2] Its proposals were not taken up, and a similar fate befell more modest proposals for reform issued by the Council of Education in its report on the primary school in 1954 — it called for a widening of the national school curriculum by the inclusion of drawing, nature study and physical education as obligatory subjects.[3] No action was taken on these proposals although a major curricular reform was implemented in 1956 in the elementary schools of Northern Ireland. In the South there was no tradition of issuing Green or White Papers on education. Very little educational legislation was enacted. In relation to national education it was the Minister for Education, with, where appropriate, the agreement of the Minister for Finance, who made new regulations or changed existing rules. The Department of Education did not have a distinguished record in taking initiatives. The key concern was to keep the system operating with minimum upheaval. Indeed, a Minister for Education described his view of the Minister's role in Dáil Éireann in 1956:

> I regard the position of the Minister in the Department as that of a kind of dungaree man, the plumber who will make the satisfactory communications and streamline the forces and potentialities of the educational workers and educational management in this country. He will take the knock out of the pipes and will link up everything.[4]

This coincided with public perception: innovation and leadership were not associated with the office of Minister for Education. By the 1960s Ireland faced a wide range of fundamental problems in its education system. In the Dáil Dr Garret FitzGerald remarked that some of these problems 'are the consequence of the accumulation of neglect, lack of action, lack of policy by the Government over a long period of time.... Over the last fifty years all Governments have given inadequate attention to education, have tended to let education drift'.[5]

By 1960 the primary school education system was faced with a number of key problems. Many of the national school buildings were small, frequently very old, in a bad state of repair, and with the minimum of pedagogic and hygienic facilities. By 1957/58 the number of teachers in national school was 13,554, actually less than the total of thirty years earlier (in 1927/28) when the number of teachers was 13,577. About 22 per cent of the teachers in 1957/58 were untrained. About one-third of the children terminated their formal education at primary level; many of the others did not complete the second level. All schools implemented a common curriculum that was narrow, unbalanced and out of date. The school management system had not been altered for almost one hundred and fifty years, and in the vast majority of cases, was under the control of local clergymen who varied in their degree of interest in the educational work of the school.

Educational policy for national school education over the period 1960 to 1985 is largely focussed on efforts to redress the problems that existed by 1960. Overall, from the perspective of today many creditable reforms have been effected. In retrospect these reveal more of a pattern than was clear to contemporaries. This was partly due to the lack of long-term planning and also to the continuation of the old tradition of not issuing policy statements or planning documents. Despite the considerable change undertaken, no White or Green Paper was issued, although they were promised by a number of Ministers in 1967, 1969, 1973 and 1977. The attitude of a Minister for Education in 1972, 'There is nothing of such a complicated nature in our policy that would demand an elaborate White Paper to explain it'[6] could be read in a number of ways, none of which reflect creditably on him.

Eventually a long-awaited *White Paper on educational development* was issued in December 1980. It proved to be a great disappointment to those who wished to see clear decisions and a rationale for them. Even the annual reports of the Department of Education ceased to be issued in 1964 and, despite ministerial promises to issue more comprehensive triennial reports on the system to accompany the statistical tables, these reports have never been issued. The rules for national schools ceased to be published in 1965 and changes have to be gleaned from ministerial or departmental letters and circulars. An advisory council on education promised in 1967 did not materialise. The Investment in Education Team in 1965 issued stringent criticism of the lack of necessary statistical data to help educational planning and debate, and urged the publication of expanded and more punctual educational statistics. The punctuality is still a problem.

The key recommendation of the Investment Team on the establishment of a development unit within the Department of Education was adopted but in an altered form, and it was given a short life-span before it was abolished. It did not publish any reports. Some political parties issued educational policies when in opposition but, while useful, there often looms a chasm between the promises and the realisation when oppositions became governments. The main formal occasion for educational debate was during the presentation in the Dáil of the annual departmental estimates. But, even here, the review of the year's activities tended to be bland and little precise information was included on future plans. However, there were also a number of years, particularly in the 1970s, when no debate took place on the education estimates.

Thus, one could conclude that the Irish experience has been to shy away from policy statements or the issuing of public discussion documents on education. For much of the period under review one has to glean lines of policy from occasional speeches and circulars. The lack of educational policy statements, annual reports, up-to-date detailed statistical data and planning generally has been criticised by a variety of bodies including the Investment in Education Team, the National Industrial and Economic Council (NIEC), the National Economic and Social Council (NESC) and the Economic and Social Research Institute (ESRI), as well as by individual commentators but the performance by the Department in this regard has been unsatisfactory to date.

In tracing the lines of development affecting national education over the last twenty-five years or so, it seems helpful to disentangle a number of issues and follow through on them in a longitudinal manner. While facilitating clarity of treatment, it must be borne in mind that this is an artificial mode of approach since many of the elements interact and overlap. For instance, the supply of teachers is closely linked to teacher – pupil ratios, which is linked to the rationalisation of school building policy and this in turn relates closely with curricular reform. Nevertheless, it seems best to focus on a sequence of themes which reflected changes in educational policy while making some cross references in the process. The chapter, which is divided into sections, examines the following:

1. issues affecting teacher supply and training;
2. the provision of school buildings;
3. pupils and their progress;
4. curriculum;
5. school management.

The concluding section attempts to draw together and interpret some of the significant patterns and issues that have emerged.

1. The Teaching Force

Since 1960, the teacher–pupil ratio was the topic most consistently discussed in relation to national schooling. Historically, Irish national schools had very high teacher–pupil ratios. The Council of Education, in its report on the primary school in 1954, put forward proposals to improve the situation and urged that 'a plan to ensure the satisfactory staffing of schools, on the basis proposed, should be undertaken immediately'. It also urged that untrained teachers should no longer be employed and those currently employed, amounting to 23 per cent of the teaching force, should undergo teacher training.[7]

From 1958 it became government policy to improve the teacher–pupil ratio and, from that time, a feature of the speeches of Ministers for Education when presenting their estimates to the Dáil was their concern on this issue. While varied strategies were adopted to achieve this policy, it was to be a long and tortuous process before significant reductions in teacher–pupil ratios were realised. In 1953 a scheme had been introduced, which allowed teachers deemed satisfactory by inspectors to continue teaching for up to three years following the normal retirement age of sixty-five. This scheme was continued until the 1970s. In 1958, the marriage ban was lifted, which allowed women teachers to continue teaching following marriage. Also, in 1958, the decision was taken not to employ any more junior assistant mistresses (untrained teachers), although schemes for training many of those already employed were not introduced until 1966. Reductions began in 1959 in the unit figures which regulated the employment of assistant teachers in the larger schools.

TABLE 1
Students in Training Colleges

Year	Total number of students
1957/58	973
1967/68	1,242
1977/78	2,867

Source: Dáil Debates Vol 308, Col 1357

A key problem in teacher supply related to the small number of newly trained teachers emerging from the training colleges. Decisions were taken to expand and modernise the various colleges. An expanded scheme for graduate trainee teachers was introduced in 1965 while, in 1972, approval was given for the recruitment of 'mature' students up to the age of twenty-eight. These various initiatives led to increasing the number of students enrolled in the training college (see Table 1).[8]

Between June 1958 and June 1963, the teaching force had been increased by 664, or about 5 per cent.[9] The *Second programme for economic expansion* was laid before the Oireachtas in July 1964 and included a specific section on education. As such, it was an important benchmark on government educational planning. It stated, 'The improvement of the education services must begin with the primary section which is the foundation of the entire structure'.[10] The *Programme* referred to changes in pre-service teacher preparation and the provision of summer 'refresher' courses for serving teachers. The establishment of an educational research centre on the campus at St Patrick's College, Drumcondra, as well as a psychological service within the Department of Education, betokened a new approach towards education, which hitherto had strongly relied on practical and impressionistic experience as a guide to action. The *Programme* signalled that the 'Government plans to extend the range of the primary curriculum'. It indicated that the school day would be lengthened to provide time for instruction in drawing, nature study and physical education. It was also promised to raise the school leaving age from fourteen to fifteen years by 1970. It was highly significant that education featured in the *Second programme for economic expansion*. It was being recognised that education and economic development were closely linked. The specific statements of government educational policy signalled the direction in which it wished the system to develop.

In December 1965 the landmark report, *Investment in education*, was published. This statistical and analytical appraisal of the Irish education system had been undertaken under the joint auspices of the OECD and the Irish government. Its disturbing findings on many features of the system destroyed any remaining complacency which might have still existed about the suitability of the education system for the conditions and needs of modern Irish society.[12]

As regards the use of teaching resources in national schools the *Investment in education* report pointed to the gross disparities between the teacher–pupil ratios in the small one- and two-teacher schools which amounted to two-thirds of the total schools and the teacher–pupil ratios in the large urban schools. The government did not have to wait for the publication of the report to be alerted to its findings. Neither did the Irish National Teachers' Organisation (INTO) which, in 1964, had carried out its own surveys in urban schools and maintained strong pressure on the Department for a significant reduction in the teacher–pupil ratio in these schools. The Department of Education responded and made a special effort, first in the Dublin region and then in some other cities, to alleviate the problem by providing additional teachers, the re-organisation of classes and providing temporary pre-fabricated classrooms.[13]

The problem of teacher–pupil ratios now became part of the large policy issue of the closure of small schools and the redistribution of the teaching force. By the mid-1960s education had become a major issue of public debate in Ireland and the Department of Education had assumed a higher profile within the government. While Fianna Fáil formed the government, the Labour Party and Fine Gael were also taking a keen interest in educational policy issues. The Labour Party had isssued its policy document in 1963, and Fine Gael published its education policy in 1966 as part of its *Just society* programme. Among many radical proposals in both documents was an improvement in the teacher–pupil ratios in national schools. As will be discussed later, the government policy on the closure of small schools aroused a great deal of public controversy.

Meanwhile, in July 1966, the first course for existing untrained teachers in national schools got under way and continued for about six years until they were absorbed into the trained teaching force. In October 1967, schools were issued with a circular aimed at breaking an old tradition of 'holding back' children for one or more extra years during their school careers.[14] It was now stated that children should be promoted to a higher standard at the end of each school year. Henceforth, children would be promoted more quickly through the school. This was a Department of Education decision, involving no consultation with the teaching force. Research, however, had indicated that when non-promotion was carried out on a large scale, as in Irish schools, 'it had educationally undesirable effects'.[15] This measure, coupled with the introduction of the 'free' post-primary education scheme of 1967, had a significant effect on establishing twelve plus as the normal age for completing the national school course. In February 1968, Minister for Education, Donogh O'Malley stated in the Dáil:

> The intention is to continue improving the pupil—teacher ratio until the position will be reached when no teacher will have more than thirty-five pupils in his class. To achieve this two things in the main will be necessary: more effective use of teaching personnel and an increase in the number of trained teachers coming into the service.[16]

This figure of thirty-five pupils became the one adopted by the *Third programme of economic expansion* issued in March 1969. This *Third programme* also indicated that the curriculum was being broadened and modernised. The 'new' curriculum would further emphasise the need for smaller classes to allow for more individual, child-centred attention. The *Third programme* also announced that special assistance would be provided for retarded or slow-learning children, as distinct from handicapped.[17] This was the beginning of a special category of teacher which was to become an important resource to national schools from this time, the remedial teacher. The number of remedial teachers grew from 230 in 1973 to 342 in 1977 and research emphasised the value of remedial teaching.[18] Recognition was also extended in 1969, subject to certain conditions, to teachers trained in Northern Ireland and Great Britain.

While the national average teacher—pupil ratio had decreased as follows: 34:3 in 1961, to 32:9 in 1967, to 32:8 in 1972, to 31:6 in 1976, to 30:7 in 1977, this masked very high ratios which still persisted in some districts.[19] For instance, in 1971, 35 per cent of pupils were still in classes of more than forty, while 6 per cent were in classes of more than fifty.[20] In Dublin, 77 per cent of pupils were in classes of more than forty. In 1973, a departmental circular was issued indicating that enrolment in any class should not exceed forty-five pupils.

While the policy of increasing the number of trainee teachers was directly aimed at increasing teacher supply, the question of the nature of the training courses also caused a great deal of debate in the 1960s and early 1970s. The two-year course had become the established pattern since the early years of the century. The INTO had continually pressed the case for extending the training course and associating it with university studies. There was a concern to improve the quality and to raise the status of the training courses which, in turn, would help promote the INTO's case for parity of salary for all teachers.[21]

The Commission on Higher Education, in 1967 and the Higher Education Authority, in 1970, had both recommended non-university degrees for national teacher trainees.[22] These proposals were rejected by the INTO and teacher education interests. Eventually, in 1973, the Minister for Education, Richard Burke, requested the National University of Ireland to investigate the possibility of awarding a degree course to national teachers. Negotiations took place between the university authorities and the college of education authorities which resulted in the establishment of a professional degree, the BEd, which would be validated by the university. Negotiations proceeded smoothly, the main problem being the question of awarding an honours degree within the framework of a three-year course, which was all that the Department would allow. It was eventually agreed that the three-year BEd degree could be conferred with honours. Arrangements were also agreed with the University of Dublin whereby BEd degrees were made available to student teachers in the Church of Ireland College in Rathmines, Dublin, the Christian Brothers' College in Marino, Dublin, and the Froebel College in Sion Hill, Dublin, though a fourth year of study was required for an honours award, in line with the tradition of the university. Thus, this long-standing concern of the national teaching force was resolved and future successful trainees would graduate as university degree holders.

The HEA Report in 1970 also made important suggestions about expanding teacher supply, reckoning that 950 a year would be required from 1970 to 1980. It furthermore urged that in-service education should be provided on a more extended basis and it recommended the establishment of a professional body, An Foras Oideachais, with many responsibilities over teaching affairs. In October 1973, the Minister, Richard Burke appointed a committee to make proposals for such a framework. Its report in April 1974 recommended that a teaching council be established which would act as a teacher registration body for all teachers, a validating authority on teacher pre-service and in-service courses, an advisory agency on teacher supply and a disciplinary agency for breaches of professional ethics among teachers.[23] The establishment of the council with such wide-ranging powers would have been of singular importance in the history of the teaching profession. As was the case with a number of departmental proposals at this time, such as regionalisation of education structures and the setting up of a public examination council, the proposed teaching council did not come into being. This was probably owing to a variety of causes. The economic recession, induced by the oil crises of 1973 and 1975, was biting into educational expenditure. There was dissatisfaction within the Teachers' Union of Ireland about the proposed composition and disciplinary powers of the council. The Department of Education was not enthusiastic about giving such wide-ranging powers to the teachers, and the climate of opinion generally moved against such an initiative. Subsequent to 1974 the teachers' unions successfully negotiated that their representatives would form a majority on the proposed council.[24] However, the council has not featured in ministerial pronouncements since 1977, although teacher representatives have periodically called for the establishment of the teaching council.

The target of reducing the teacher–pupil ratio so that no teacher would have more than thirty-five pupils in a class, announced in the *Third programme* of 1969, proved exasperatingly elusive through the 1970s, as the figures in Table 2 indicate.[25]

TABLE 2
Class Sizes in the 1970s

	1972/73	1973/74	1974/75[a]	1975/76	1976/77	1977/78	1978/79
Classes of 40-44	2,389	3,044	2,671	3,084	3,109	2,866	1,915
No of pupils	100,224	127,794	111,959	132,729	133,213	122,603	73,965
Classes of 45+	2,596	1,492	999	504	448	394	229
No of pupils	124,256	69,409	46,266	23,415	21,415	18,782	19,693

Note: [a] The returns were not complete for 1974/75.
Source: Dáil Debates Vol 283, Col 1671 and Vol 313, Col 149.

As can be noted, the number of classes in both categories declined over the years with the more significant drop in the amount of classes with more than forty-five pupils. Yet, in 1978/79, twenty years following the initiation of the policy on improved teacher–pupil ratios, the fact remained that there were still 2,144 classes with forty or more pupils and 93,658 pupils in them, or about 18 per cent of the total pupil enrolment. This was a far cry from a maximum of thirty-five pupils per class, the objective set by the *Third programme* in 1969. By 1983 the number of pupils in classes of forty-five or more had declined to 2,482 and the number of classes with forty or more had declined to 1,129.[26] A pronounced feature of the large classes was the big numbers enrolled in infants' classes and first class. For instance, in 1978, pupils in infants and first class comprised 47,603 of the 73,965 pupils in classes of forty to forty-four and made up 9,341 of the 19,693 in classes of forty-five or more pupils.[27] It is arguable that this was a serious imbalance in that children in these early classes might require the greatest amount of individual attention to master the basics and overcome learning difficulties. The number of teachers employed to cater for the needs of pupils with learning difficulties remained small through the 1970s, numbering 342 in 1977/78. This figure improved subsequently, so that by 1985 there were approximately 850 remedial teachers serving the needs of about 3,270 national schools.

In an effort to make a significant impact on the teacher–pupil ratio, the Minister for Education, John Wilson proposed a novel scheme of 'special trainee teachers' in 1977. This was a scheme to employ a large number of graduates in national schools; these graduates would have passed an interview and been given a short crash course in teacher training. The scheme proved controversial and was rejected by the INTO membership as well as by teacher training personnel. Only 218 special trainee teachers completed the once-off one-year course.[28]

Overall government policies had resulted in the reduction of large classes during the 1970s. In the decade between 1970/71 and 1980/81 the percentage number of pupils in classes of forty or more had fallen from 44 per cent to 13 per cent, and these pupils occupied 10 per cent of the total number of classes in national schools. The average teacher–pupil ratio had been reduced from 34.5 to 30.4. During these years the number of pupils in national

schools had increased by 9 per cent but the number of teachers
had increased by 28 per cent.[29]

The Fianna Fáil election manifesto of 1977 had also promised
a White Paper on education, which was eventually published in
December 1980. In its statistics section it demonstrated the growth
in pupil numbers in national schools from 488.2 thousand in
1965/66 to 529.6 thousand in 1975/76. It projected that for the
period from 1980/81 through to 1990/91 the increase would
continue, and there would be 588.6 thousand pupils by 1990/91.
It expected an annual increase of about 38,100, or 7 per cent in
the national school population through the 1980s. It projected that
the training colleges would be able to supply the extra teachers
that would be required.[30] However, these projections have not
proved accurate; the 1980s are witnessing a significant change in
demographic trends. The annual number of births has declined
from a peak of 74,388 in 1980 to 64,737 in 1984 and the decline
has continued so that only 58,864 births were recorded in 1987.
National school pupils in 1984 numbered 563,000 but it is estimated
that these numbers may be down to about 522,700 by 1994.[31]
The drop of about 43,000 will have serious repercussions on teacher
supply. The national average teacher – pupil ratio had been reduced
to 1:27.6 in 1984. The *Programme for action in education
1984 – 87* issued by the Minister for Education, Gemma Hussey
in January 1984 stated:

> It is recognised that the pupil – teacher ratio in National Schools
> compares unfavourably with that obtaining in other developed
> countries and the Government remains committed to an
> improvement in the position as soon as financial resources
> permit.[32]

It appears that there are no plans to work towards further significant
reductions in the ratio. Rather, a stage has been reached where
the majority of the new teacher graduates are finding it difficult
to secure permanent employment. In spring 1986 a decision was
taken to cease the pre-service teacher training activity of a major
college, Carysfort College, Blackrock. This has registered as a
striking indication of the changed situation after about twenty-five
years of effort to increase teacher supply and to reduce the
teacher – pupil ratio in Irish national schools.

The total number of national teachers increased from 13,866

in 1960 to 20,622 in 1984, an increase of 50 per cent. The teaching force is now a fully trained one, many of whom are university graduates, all of whom participate in a salary scale common to the whole teaching profession. Although not directly linked to government policy, it is worth noting that the composition of the national school teaching force has changed greatly between 1960 and 1980. The percentage of women has increased from about 68 per cent in 1960 to 75 per cent in 1984. In 1960 male and female clergy amounted to about 23 per cent of all national teachers, but by 1984 this percentage had decreased to about 7 per cent of those teaching in national schools.[33]

2. School Buildings

In the early 1960s Ireland faced significant problems in relation to its stock of national school buildings. As the Investment in Education team reported, the size, pattern and distribution of national schools were the results of political, social and demographic circumstances in nineteenth-century Ireland. The following statistics illustrate the situation clearly. In 1964 almost half the national schools, 45 per cent, dated from the nineteenth century. The vast majority were very small; 66 per cent were one- or two-teacher schools. The average enrolment was less than a hundred pupils in 76 per cent of the schools. Over 2,000 of the small schools did not have drinking water, flush toilets or chemical closets. Over 22 per cent of all school buildings had been declared obsolete by the Board of Works. The general maintenance and provision of facilities within many of the schools were highly unsatisfactory, while teaching equipment in national schools was minimal.[34]

The state was paying about 86 per cent of the cost of new school buildings and major improvement schemes, with local management providing the remaining cost.[35] The maintenance of the school building was a responsibility of the local manager. However, the inter-departmental committee on school building reported to the Ministers for Education and Finance in 1961 that the state's investment in school buildings had been allowed to deteriorate very rapidly through lack of adequate maintenance.[36] Arising from this, the Minister for Education announced a new scheme, operative from April 1962, whereby the state would pay two-thirds of the cost of painting schools.[37] Grants for heating and cleaning were improved in 1964. Interesting changes in the design of new school buildings were also brought into effect at this time. Circulation space began to be incorporated into the classrooms and in 1962 the space per pupil in classrooms was increased from eleven to fifteen square feet. The new classrooms became largely self-contained, each with its own toilet and cloakroom facilities.[38] The Department kept in touch with international thinking on school design and more exciting changes were to occur in association with the 'new' curriculum in the 1970s. In the meantime, it was government policy on the closure of small schools that became the focus of public controversy.

The statistical data on national school buildings, as presented by the *Investment in education* report, emphasised the position forcefully. The report raised the question 'whether the present distribution of schools is the most suitable, satisfactory or economical method of providing primary education'.[39] A radical change took place in departmental policy on small schools. The Minister for Education, George Colley told the Dáil in July 1965, 'It seems to me quite clear that we have to take a very firm decision on this matter of the small schools.'[40] He went on to assert:

> we in the Department of Education have good reason to believe that in the case of small one-teacher and two-teacher schools, in general the educational attainment of the children is, on average two years behind that of children in larger schools. This is a very serious matter. I have made up my mind that it is a matter I will do something about. I know that we are going to run into considerable opposition, most of which will be based on misguided sentiment.[41]

For many communities the school had come to symbolise their continued well-being. The daily routines of children going to and coming from school, the noise of children at play in the playgrounds, the sentimental attachments of some parents to the school of their own schooldays, the use of the school for aspects of adult education or community occasions, all tended to emphasise the close ties of the school with the daily life of a district. As well as inconveniences arising from closure, the very fact of closure could be seen by communities as a vote of no confidence in their future, and this tended to hurt deeply. On the other hand, it was estimated that 40 per cent of the total number of national schools would need to be replaced within a sixteen-year period, with the percentage far greater in rural areas.[42] It was thus a key issue for decision: to continue the older policy of supplying each townland with its own school or to try to centralise school provision within parish units. The small schools were regarded as the most expensive to build and maintain; the curriculum tended to be limited; the use of teaching resources was imbalanced; and the children in them did not seem to be benefiting educationally.

Several factors pointed the policy makers in a new direction: the government had a policy of reducing teacher−pupil ratios; plans for curriculum reform were gestating; new standards were being set for school buildings and facilities; and the introduction of 'free' transport schemes would alleviate the problem of young children having to walk over three miles to school.

The policy of closure was first applied to cases where small townland schools were due either for replacement or large-scale renovation. The words 'amalgamation' and 'rationalisation' became current in political debates. The Fianna Fáil government's policy drew a wide measure of support from the opposition parties. The Labour Party and many in the Fine Gael party supported the policy. Of course, in cases of individual closures various deputies got involved in the issue in response to local pressures. Few went so far as a Fine Gael deputy who stated:

> the fact that schools are to be closed down, the fact that schools are to be centralised is, in my opinion, the first step towards state control of education.[43]

The Catholic hierarchy wrote to the Minister and sent a deputation to him with regard to the policy, but did not oppose it. The INTO executive committee also indicated to the Minister that it had no objection to the principle of the policy.[44]

One of the main criticisms of the policy was that the Department did not consult local communities in a satisfactory way about planned closures and that the rationale of closures and the advantages of the new policy were not always explained to parents. The procedure adopted by the Department was that when a school was being considered for repair or replacement, the inspector examined the situation, took note of the probable supply of pupils

and the local transport arrangements, consulted with the manager
and then informed the Department, after which decisions were
made. The manager was then taken as the representative of local
interests, but in some cases parents and groups in the local
community considered that they should have been directly
consulted.

The public relations side of the Department's role was criticised.
It was natural that some local communities would resent losing
their school and feel upset about the obvious wrench involved.
In defence of his policy the Minister for Education, George Colley
stated in the Dáil that he was well aware of the social implications
of the measure but he argued that far from weakening community
life in rural Ireland, it would in fact strengthen it. He believed
that the improved educational facilities of the centralised parish
schools would be a significant advantage to rural parents, and would
help to keep young families in the locality.[45] While this was the
case in the long run, the handling of some school closures at local
level was less than satisfactory; a more careful and consultative
procedure would have reduced some of the sense of frustration
which occurred locally. The closures went ahead so that between
1966 and 1973 the number of one- and two-teacher schools had
been reduced by about 1,100. Overall the number of one- and two-
teacher schools was reduced from 3,194 in 1962 to 900 in 1984.
The number of national schools was reduced from 4,882 in 1960
to 3,270 in 1984, a reduction of 33 per cent in the total stock.

Apart from the closure policy some schools were in a deplorably
bad condition because of lack of maintenance. In 1967 the INTO
adopted a harder line in relation to schools 'where the conditions
are sub-standard, and, in some cases, uncivilised', declaring that,
on the substantiated complaints of teachers, members would be
withdrawn from schools.[46] This attitude resulted in the issuing of
a departmental circular to managers in September 1967 speeding
up the provision of proper heating and sanitary arrangements in
schools where these were defective. Despite this, instances of
neglect continued. A notable instance of teacher protest took place
in Ardfert, County Kerry in 1968. Teachers withdrew their labour
for a three-week period until repairs were satisfactorily carried
out. The bad publicity attending this event had the effect of
expediting maintenance work in other schools throughout the
country. A departmental survey conducted in 1972 showed that

85 per cent of national schools now had flush toilets while 70 per cent benefited from piped drinking water.[47]

In line with efforts to reduce the teacher–pupil ratio, the Department resorted to the use of pre-fabricated buildings, which, while housing pupils and teachers, imposed severe restrictions on teacher and pupil activity. Following the introduction of the new curriculum, the early 1970s ushered in a period of great improvement in the design of more permanent school buildings. The square foot allocation for pupils in each classroom was raised to 19 square feet, while the gross floor area of a large school allowed 32 square feet per pupil.[48] The Department also planned the design of some schools so as to allow for a more flexible use of teaching space, breaking from the monopoly of the individual discrete classroom format to encourage shared-area, co-operative teaching in large schools. The implementation of shared-area teaching has by no means been given an unqualified welcome and this plan is likely to be operative in only a low percentage of schools. Some teachers were annoyed at the manner of its introduction – they felt there was insufficient discussion, preparation or experimentation.[49] However, it is but part of an innovatory approach to school design, incorporating improvements in the type of furnishings, range of facilities, decorative standards and quality of maintenance. This policy has transformed the physical appearance of a great many schools on the Irish landscape.

3. Pupils

The pupil population of the national schools has also experienced great changes since the early 1960s. The number of pupils enrolled in ordinary national schools increased from 472,124 in 1964 to 490,039 in 1970, to 540,815 in 1980 and to 552,478 in 1984. Significant changes have taken place in the composition of the pupil population. In 1964, 37,173 pupils were aged thirteen years or over. By 1980, there were only 6,091 such pupils, a level which has remained much the same since then. Thus, while the total number of pupils increased, there was a significant change in the age range within the national schools. Without issuing a formal declaration on the matter, the general termination of the national school course became set at twelve plus. As early as 1966 George

Colley had declared, 'What is contemplated in conjunction with the raising of the school leaving age is the provision of a post-primary course of three years which we hope in the normal case would run from 12+ to 15+'.[50] In the event, the school-leaving age was not raised to fifteen until 1972. By this time, however, the free post-primary education scheme had been in operation since 1967 and the tradition of transfer to post-primary at age twelve had set in.

The *Investment in education* report had also drawn attention to the delays which occurred in the progression of pupils through the national school. It pointed out that by fifth standard 30 per cent of pupils were delayed one year and 13 per cent were delayed two or more years in 1963. The statistics for 1965 showed that corresponding figures were 26 per cent delayed for one year and 10 per cent delayed two or more years.[51] The Department was anxious to break this pattern and it issued a circular to national schools in March 1967 stating that 'The normal procedure should be that a pupil is promoted to a higher standard at the end of each school year'.[52] If, in a special case, a child was to be held back it should only be for one extra year through his (or her) school career. This was a significant intervention by the Department in what hitherto had been a matter for the discretion of school staffs.

Further concern was expressed at the number of pupils who dropped out of education before completing the primary school course or attaining the primary certificate examination. This question formed part of the re-think which was then taking place on the suitability of the school curriculum. The year 1967 was the last one on which the primary certificate examination was held. In 1968 it was replaced by a pupil report card which was planned as a more satisfactory and comprehensive profile of the pupil at the end of the senior standards of the national school. There was also more concern for children in disadvantaged areas. To help provide guidance for the early education of children in deprived inner city areas the Rutland Street School Project was planned in 1968; the school received its first pupils in June 1969.[53] The report of a committee on educational facilities for the children of itinerants was issued in 1970, and it adopted an integration guideline as the basis of policy.[54]

The introduction of the new curriculum nationwide in 1971 heralded a significant change in the life experiences of both pupils and teachers within the schools. The main intention was to place the child and his interests at the centre of a varied and flexible school programme. Schools became more pleasant, interesting and humane places. Corporal punishment which had been a strong and controversial tradition in Irish national schools became a less prominent feature of school life. Corporal punishment was formally abolished by order of the Minister for Education with effect from 1 February 1982. Teacher union interests were unhappy at the alleged abrupt and overbearing manner in which this was done. They would have preferred that a code of alternative sanctions was agreed by all parties in advance of the abolition order. Eventually the Minister for Education, John Boland agreed to set up a representative committee to examine corporal punishment and associated school discipline problems. Some teachers hold that disciplinary problems have become more acute owing to a deteriorating social and domestic environment which children are experiencing. The report of this committee was published in the autumn of 1985.

Another issue that caused considerable disagreement between the Minister and the INTO in the early 1980s was the decision to raise the age of entry to national schools. Since 1934 the minimum age at which children could be enrolled was on or after their fourth birthday. (Attendance was not compulsory until the age of six.) In August 1981 the Minister issued a circular changing the age of entry with intended effect from 1 October 1981. The effect of the new regulation would be that children could only be enrolled at four-and-a-half or at five years of age.

The INTO objected strongly to the new ruling and the manner in which it was introduced. The general opinion was that the decision was closely influenced by the Department of Finance's concern to cut back on educational expenditure. The Minister pointed to the unusual tradition in Ireland of enrolling children in formal schooling at a younger age than was the general pattern in many countries. The INTO argued strongly on educational, social and trade union grounds that the change was undesirable in Irish circumstances. A full-scale confrontation occurred between the INTO and the Minister. The media and various interest groups took up the issue. The opposition party, Fianna Fáil, supported the teachers. It was a time of great political instability and when the government fell in early 1982 the newly elected Fianna Fáil

government reversed the decision. It was a striking example of
an educational issue becoming highly politicised, a trend that has
become pronounced in the 1980s. The age of entry, the age of
transfer and the length of post-primary courses continued to be
subjects for debate. Eventually, in 1985, the government made
a decision on these matters. The Department sent a circular to
national schools in October 1985 stating that no child should be
retained in infants beyond the 30 June that followed his reaching
the age of six-and-a-half nor should he be admitted to first standard
unless he has reached the age of six years by the 1 September in
which he is enrolled in that standard.[55] Thus, the pattern is
established whereby most children will continue to enter school
at age four, transfer to first standard at age six and transfer to post-
primary school at age twelve.

It is appropriate to allude to special education here because
improvements in this area reflect the greater concern for the welfare
of the individual pupil that has become evident in recent decades.
While only about 2 per cent of school children are involved in
special education, this aspect of educational provision has received
greatly increased attention and is one of the success stories of
educational policy. Since the mid-1950s, the state has assumed
much greater responsibility for meeting the educational needs of
children who, because of mental, physical, sensory or emotional
differences, are unable, or find it difficult, to participate in ordinary
schooling. In 1960 a one-year full-time diploma course was
inaugurated for in-service teachers in special schools. The *Report
of the Commission of Inquiry on Mental Handicap* in 1965, as well
as reports of many special committees since then, have helped to
provide guidance for policy in this field of special education. There
is now a wide network of well devised educational provision for
handicapped and deprived children in special schools, in special
classes incorporated in ordinary national schools, and in certain
voluntary centres where appropriate educational services are
provided. Very interesting work has been undertaken in devising
suitable curricula for the needs of particular groups. The policy
today, in line with international thinking, is to integrate handicapped
children as far as possible into the mainstream, but this is not easily
achieved in the conditions which exist in many schools.[56] The
number of national schools categorised for special education
increased from 13 in 1960 with 2,252 pupils to 120 in 1983 with
8,595 pupils.[57]

4. Curriculum

The move towards reforming the curriculum in national schools was the most welcomed change of policy in the period under review. The curriculum of the early 1960s had been devised in the first years of independence. In line with the ideology of cultural nationalism, the greatest concern was to promote the Irish language so that it would again become the vernacular. The curricular policy remained largely untouched over four decades by which time it had many critics. Both the INTO (1947) and the Council for Education (1954) criticised its narrowness and rigidity. By the early 1960s individuals, and groups such as Tuairim (1960), The Teachers' Study Group (1962), the Labour Party (1963), and Fine Gael (1966), had become strong critics of the curriculum.

During the early 1960s, it seemed that the process of curricular change was going to be piecemeal. New *Notes for teachers* for the Irish language were made available. Changes were made in the history programme in 1962 and also in needlework. For the first time the state in 1963 began issuing sets of reference books to schools on a gradual basis. This scheme was later to expand, in association with local authority library agencies, to provide a good network of school library provision. In these years the comments of the inspectors on the work in the schools referred to the need for more project work, research into local history, group work, use of assembly halls, activity methods, concrete teaching of mathematics, increased emphasis on nature study and so on, reflecting a concern about new approaches and emphases.[58] There was an effort to widen the horizons of children through promoting school educational tours. The number of school children who visited Irish colleges, many of them in the Gaeltacht, in the summer months increased. The publication of John Macnamara's *Bilingualism in Irish education* in 1966 caused considerable unease. He pointed to the large amount of time devoted to the teaching of languages, particularly the Irish language, and he indicated that Irish children were significantly behind their English counterparts in English and arithmetic.[59]

In 1964 the *Second programme for economic expansion* declared, 'The Government plans to extend the range of the primary school curriculum'.[60] In June 1965 the Minister for Education told the Dáil that the syllabuses in national school subjects were being reappraised and brought into line with the needs of contemporary living.[61] The piecemeal approach was still reflected in his remark that the new courses would be issued gradually as they were prepared. The thinking on curricular change now coincided with other changes affecting national school policy.

The move to improve the pupil–teacher ratio was gathering momentum. The findings of the *Investment in education report* encouraged the move towards the closure of small schools and a more efficient utilisation of teacher resources. New approaches to school buildings and equipment were adopted. In 1967 the decision, long sought by the INTO, was taken to abolish the primary certificate which had taken the form of written examinations in Irish, English and arithmetic. Many contemporaries had felt that this examination narrowed the work of the senior standards and as a common examination for all pupils had the effect of branding the label of failure on pupils who were not suitable candidates for the examination. The introduction of the 'free' post-primary education scheme removed the examinations for post-primary scholarships; some teachers felt that these examinations distorted the ordinary educational work of the national school in the senior standards. At the same time the policy of regular promotion of pupils through the classes was adopted. These various changes opened up new possibilities for teachers in the schools and many of them were not slow to use the opportunities. Indeed one of the key authors of the 'new' curriculum stated that it arose from the demand of teachers who had proved in the schools that the old programme was too narrow and who expanded its scope thereby creating a momentum for the new programme.[62] Some Irish teachers were also informed on developments in primary education in Northern Ireland, which re-structured its child-centred programme in 1956, and in England, where the Plowden Report of 1966 initiated a great period of curricular renewal on child-centred lines.

Meanwhile, within the Department of Education, the Minister for Education, Donogh O'Malley indicated in 1966 that he wished to have a White Paper on education prepared, for publication in 1967. In December 1966 a steering committee was set up within the Department of Education to advise on the primary education aspects of such a White Paper. The steering committee examined the issues in the spring of 1967 and concluded in relation to the school programme that it was better to start from first principles, rather than adapt the old programme.[63] Influenced by the thinking of Piaget and the Plowden Report, they considered that the existing programme:

tends to treat children as if they were identical, environment as if it were irrelevant, and subject content as if it were easily defined. Its greatest fault, perhaps, is that it fails to look on education as a trail of discovery, enrichment and understanding for the growing child, and sees it instead as a logical structure containing conveniently differentiated parts which may be imposed by adults on children.[64]

The proposed White Paper was not proceeded with but the momentum for radical curricular change in the national schools was sustained. The keynote of the new approach was: 'Purposeful activity, pupil mobility, flexibility of deployment, freedom, experimentation; these are the recurrent themes of the education process'.[65]

A subcommittee, composed of members of the national school inspectorate, was set up in December 1967 to prepare the detailed plans for a new curriculum based on the rationale which had been set out by March 1967. In spring 1968 about three hundred schools were chosen as pilot schools to experiment with different elements of a proposed curriculum. A draft of the proposed curriculum was prepared and discussed with senior personnel within the Department of Education in September 1968. Representatives of managerial bodies and colleges of education interests were invited to a meeting in the Department of Education on 11 October 1968 at which the rationale of the draft curriculum was presented to them and their responses were invited. These bodies gave a warm welcome to the programme. Teachers found it more difficult to get copies of the draft programme. Eventually it was published in the February 1969 issue of the INTO's *An Muinteoir Náisiúnta*. The Minister for Education, Brian Lenihan addressed the INTO congress in April 1969 on the draft programme. The INTO welcomed the programme in January 1970, seeing it as prefigured in its own *Plan* of 1947. The Teachers' Study Group gave the most detailed response in its booklet of April 1969.[66] As one of the groups which had been pressing for change since 1962, it welcomed the programme but its analysis pointed up certain problems about the programmes in individual subjects. It also highlighted a key defect in the general approach whereby there was inadequate alignment between the draft programme and the new programmes for junior cycle post-primary. It pin-pointed a weakness in the planning whereby there was no discussion or liaison with the post-primary inspectorate or post-primary school interests, although the post-primary courses had themselves only recently been changed.

Meanwhile pilot work continued in various subjects. Also in summer 1969 special in-service courses for principal teachers were organised which continued for a number of years, with over four thousand principal teachers benefiting. The Rutland Street Project for pre-school disadvantaged children also got under way in June 1969 for its five-year experimental period. During 1970 and early 1971 work went ahead on preparing two volumes of a *Teachers' handbook*, which contained the new curriculum as well as recommended modes of implementing it. Eventually the handbooks were issued to all national teachers in September 1971 and the primary school curriculum became the official curriculum of all national schools.

The introduction of the 'new' curriculum in 1971 was a landmark in the development of national school education. It involved a radical shift of ideological position and methodological approach to primary education. It was based on a child-centred ideology, allowed a wide degree of freedom to the teacher and set out a greatly expanded range of subjects which it suggested should be taught in an integrated fashion. It encouraged a heuristic teaching methodology with much small group and individual teaching. It encouraged close links between the school and the local environment. The 'new' curriculum caused a considerable buzz of excitement. Most teachers were delighted with the new developments, others were apprehensive and uneasy about the changes. Many parents were confused about the changes. The issuing of a booklet, *All our children*, by the Department of Education in May 1969, was a useful effort to inform parents about general educational changes. It was not, however, followed up. More regrettably, no use was made of television, the major new medium in almost all homes to explain and demonstrate to parents what the changes entailed. Insufficient care was taken to inform post-primary interests of the nature of the changes and the need to re-orient expectations as regards the curricular experience of primary pupils on transferring to secondary education. This continued to cause problems for both primary and post-primary sectors. Even the report of a special pupil transfer committee in 1982 has not alleviated all the problems which exist in the alignment of the two sectors.[67]

Although the new curriculum evolved at a period when a range of improvements was taking place in the national schools, the satisfactory implementation of the programme placed daunting challenges before teachers in the general circumstances still prevailing in many schools. The Minister for Education, Pádraig Faulkner recognised that its implementation would be gradual when he stated in the Dáil in November 1971:

> The degree of acceptance by the teaching profession of the new curriculum is such that it is hoped to have it in operation in the schools generally in about five or six years . . . this new curriculum is being implemented gradually.[68]

As has been noted, a large number of very small schools were still in existence and the efforts to reduce teacher—pupil ratios had not succeeded in bringing the ratio in many schools down to the limits where the teacher would have a good chance of employing small group and individual teaching techniques, and fostering discovery learning.

The questions of teacher in-service training and inadequate school equipment loomed large. The colleges of education had been altering their approaches during the 1960s and were to change further to degree courses in the early 1970s. However, the needs of the great mass of teachers in the field needed attention. The great majority of principal teachers benefited from short in-service courses between 1969 and 1972. The Department of Education and the INTO had been organising short summer refresher courses for teachers during the 1960s. These were now expanded and, for a few years, the level of activity was impressive. In 1972 some teachers were selected for a special three-week residential course. It was intended that these would act as catalysts in local regions later, but this did not take place as planned. Teachers were encouraged to visit schools in which pilot work on aspects of the new curriculum had taken place. A potentially very significant initiative was the establishment of teacher centres by the

Department of Education. These began in 1972 and gradually expanded to various regional centres. While originally seen by many as being particularly concerned with disseminating aspects of new curricular theory and methodology, they were open to all grades of teacher and were governed by committees of local teachers. In December 1971 the Minister announced that he had appointed a special committee of inspectors and various educational interests to plan long-term in-service education plans. His hope was that all teachers between twenty-five and sixty years would have formal entitlement to in-service education courses every fifth or seventh year. He held out high hopes for such developments, remarking that this was only the beginning.[69]

Regrettably, such was not to be the case. With the onset of the first oil-crisis in 1973-74, the outlook became bleak for comprehensive action on in-service courses. While the annual costs of 'special courses for teachers' grew from £30,000 in 1969 to over £80,000 in 1974, the figure for 1975 was reduced to £12,000 and in-service provision remained very inadequate over subsequent years.[70]

The failure of the Department of Education in this regard so annoyed the INTO that it took a decision not to hold any courses itself and prohibited its members from organising any courses for a number of years. Teacher dissatisfaction with in-service education provision led to the setting up of the Committee on In-service Education in June 1980. Its report, published in April 1984, called for the setting up of a national council, which would co-ordinate a comprehensive plan for the in-service education for teachers.[71] Its recommendations were not accepted by the Minister for Education, Gemma Hussey in her *Programme for action on education, 1984–87.*[72]

National schools have traditionally suffered greatly from inadequate teaching aids and equipment. The grant for such 'school requisites' was increased from £55,000 in 1969 to almost £425,000 in 1974. A new capitation payments scheme in 1975 improved things. However, subsequent cut-backs and very high inflation rates ensured that the real value of the grants did not keep pace with the needs of schools. It has been calculated that the combined additional expenditure on in-service education and equipment which was directly related to the introduction of the 'new' curriculum accounted for about one per cent of the annual budget for national education in 1974.[73]

It can be concluded that the national school inspectorate and the Department of Education did creditable work in devising the new curriculum in a short time-span and with limited resources. The pilot work and some of the consultations were well conducted. The handbooks of the primary curriculum were presented in an impressive format. The early initiatives on in-service education and improved equipment were on the right lines, as was the design plan for new national schools. The inadequate follow-through on in-service education, the cut-backs in educational resources as well as continuing difficult teaching conditions in many schools seriously impeded the full implementation of this radical programme.

The introducton to the *Teachers' handbook* stated that the curriculum should be subject to on-going review but no procedures for review were put in place. Replying to a question in the Dáil in March 1978, almost seven years following the initiation of the new programme, the Minister for Education, John Wilson stated, 'I have no immediate proposals for a major review of the primary school curriculum'.[74] Nevertheless, a number of appraisals have been undertaken by the Irish National Teachers' Organisation, the Conference of Convent Primary Schools, the Department of Education in association with the Educational Research Centre, and, more recently, by the Curriculum Development Unit within the Department of Education. The general thrust of these various studies indicated that many improvements had occurred in national schooling. For instance, the general learning environment had improved; progress was recorded in a number of subjects, or aspects of subjects; in-school curricular innovation had increased. However, it would appear that many of the features of the 1971 curriculum have not been satisfactorily implemented. These would include features such as heuristic pedagogy with group teaching, use of the local environment, the teaching of physical education, and the arts. The textbook is seen as still holding a dominant role while concern about aspects of Irish teaching, mathematics teaching and the infant school programme has also been expressed.

In three of its published documents the Curriculum and Examinations Board, established in January 1984, has called for a major review of the curriculum in national schools.[75] (In autumn 1987, the Minister for Education, Mary O'Rourke set up a review body for primary education, with special reference to curricular matters.) The Board seemed less concerned with the approach and content of the curriculum than it was with identifying and clarifying the obstacles which prevent more satisfactory implementation. A recent report by a sub-committee of the Board remarked, 'The implementation of many valuable features of a curriculum which had received a general endorsement is still a current and on-going problem'.[76] Among obstacles referred to by the Board are large classes, inadequate equipment in many schools, unsatisfactory provision of in-service education for teachers, the lack of an educational psychological service for national schools, insufficient supply of remedial teachers, an under-staffed and under-resourced inspectorate. Many of such problems existed to an even greater degree in 1971. Some national teachers also hold that the nature of the entrance examinations conducted by some secondary schools has injurious effects on the implementation of the curriculum in the senior standards. It appears clear that if the much-heralded curricular and pedagogic changes introduced in 1971 are to be realised more fully on the classroom floors, the whole question of financial resources has to be tackled more seriously. If such resources are not forthcoming, as seems likely in the current state of public finances, the reality within the classrooms will continue to differ from the *Teachers' handbook*, and camouflage by officialdom will not make it otherwise.

5. Management

The management of national schools, which had been a matter of continual dissension and controversy during the nineteenth century and the early years of the twentieth, became less contentious in the years following independence. The state accepted the situation whereby the vast majority of schools were managed by local clergymen of various denominations. The manager, and, through him, the local community was responsible for providing the site of the school, up to one-third of the building costs, and for the general maintenance and equipment of the school. The manager had the power of appointing teachers and the right of general supervision of the school's activities. On a number of occasions the INTO criticised the system because of the unsatisfactory standards of school maintenance and urged the state to assume full responsibility for it. The Catholic hierarchy strongly rebuffed such proposals seeing them as potentially harmful to managerial interests, 'it would circumscribe and endanger the rights of managers if the maintenance, heating and cleaning were taken completely out of their hands'.[77] Although the 1937 Constitution had emphasised the prior rights of parents in the education of their children, a notable feature of local school administration was the distancing of parental involvement.

It was only with the re-appraisal of Irish schooling in the 1960s that the managerial question began to re-emerge. In 1963 the Labour Party stated that it would encourage the formation of local advisory committees made up of parents and school managers to assist in the running of national schools, but only in a consultative capacity.[78] In 1966 Fine Gael also proposed school committees, 'to work with school managers in the management of the national schools'.[79] These were carefully modulated proposals about an area of which little was publicly said, but which all informed parties knew was potentially very controversial: the control of national schools at local level. In any event, Fianna Fáil held power from 1957 to 1973 and did not issue a policy statement on school management.

The pronouncements of the Second Vatican Council of 1962 on education reflected the more comprehensive view of that Council on the Catholic Church as comprising all members, lay and clerical, as distinct from the more traditional view which tended to see the 'Church' as represented by the clergy. In line with this, clergy were now encouraged to involve parents more closely as partners in the running of the schools. Gradually this type of thinking bore some fruit in Ireland and, in 1969, the Catholic hierarchy issued a pastoral letter.

> The bishops approve of some broad principles for the formation of management, teacher, parent associations for primary schools. The object of such associations is to help facilitate the involvement of parents in the work of the schools, particularly as regards the religious and moral formation of the children and to encourage communication and co-operation between parents and managers and teachers, without prejudice to their respective functions.[80]

While the last phrase indicated that no radical change in authority structures was intended, the statement did give official blessing to the parent–teacher associations (PTAs) which were emerging in various areas. A climate of support for parents' involvement was developing and parents themselves began to group under agencies such as the Parent School Movement. But, as Yvonne McGrath, the chairperson of this Movement, remarked in 1972, 'Although there now appears to be some positive recognition of the parental role by church and state in the changes that are taking place in education, there is still too little evidence to parents that this recognition is being translated into practical action.'[81] Teachers tended to be cautious and unenthusiastic about parent–teacher associations.[82] The Minister for Education, Pádraig Faulkner indicated to the Dáil in 1970 that he was content with the existing management system. 'The management system, by and large, has served the country well', he said, 'and the majority of our people have confidence in it . . . I have no intention of changing it.'[83] However, he did favour parent–teacher meetings 'on lines suggested by the Hierarchy'.[84]

The question of national school management was taken a stage further, however, following the election of a coalition government of the Fine Gael and Labour parties in 1973. In an address of June 1973 to the Clerical Managers' Association in Athlone the assistant secretary in the Department of Education, Sean O'Connor raised the issue of the involvement of parents in school management committees. Defending the new approach in the Dáil the Minister for Education, Richard Burke held that it was necessary to move forward from the position where there was only 'lip-service to the role of parents hitherto'.[85] Negotiations got under way with church interests, teacher union representatives, and some parents' groups, though in the latter case the lack of a tight or unified organisation made this less than satisfactory.

This was the first negotiation to re-structure national school management since the system had been established in 1831. The Department of Education held out a carrot of improved funding for the running of national schools which set up management boards. The initial arrangement was £6 per capita from central funds to be matched by £1.50 from local funds. As might be expected, the negotiations did not prove easy as various interests sought to protect or to secure power or influence. The Churches, who had held the reins of management hitherto, were in a strong position. It seemed for a while as if these local management changes would be part of a more major change in the administrative structure of Irish education in that Department issued proposals for a new structure of county and regional educational authorities in July 1973, but omitting national schools from the control of the proposed county committees. However, negotiations on these matters proved unsuccessful and ended in January 1974.

A structure for boards of management of national schools emerged in October 1975. As regards the composition of the boards two main models emerged. In schools of up to six teachers, the great majority, the patron usually the bishop, would appoint four members, parents would elect two members and the principal teacher would fill the other position. In schools of seven teachers or more the patron would appoint six members, the parents elect two members, the teaching staff would elect one member of the board, and the principal teacher would be an ex-officio member. The patron appointed the chairman, usually the local clergyman in charge, in all cases. A detailed schedule of regulations was devised for the functioning of the boards. Their duties were predominantly administrative and financial in character and did not impinge directly on curricular or formal educational policy.

The boards of management were agreed by the INTO for a three-year period, following which there was to be a review of their operation. When this did not take place in 1978, the INTO withdrew from participation pending a more satisfactory re-structuring from its point of view. It was difficult to secure agreement in re-negotiations which the Department initiated in November 1978. Eventually, by October 1980 agreement was reached. Under the new arrangements the churches agreed to reduce the patron's nominees from six to four in the larger schools and from four to three in the schools with six or less teachers. As part of the new agreement the place usually held by a parents' representative on the selection board for assistant teachers was now given to an independent assessor, nominated by the patron. The restructured management boards came into operation in October 1981.

An interesting development in the 1970s, in the context of the history of Irish national schools, was the emergence in some communities of the desire to establish multi-denominational schools with democratic management structures. The most notable group which led the way in demonstrating how such a school should be

established was the Dalkey School Project which now manages
a successful large, multi-denominational national school. Groups
of parents in other areas such as Bray, North Dublin and Sligo
have followed the lead given by Dalkey. Such groups face daunting
obstacles in raising funds for the site, part of the building costs
and maintenance costs. While the state responded to the
constitutional demand of these groups of parents, it did not seek
to promote these schools. The number of multi-denominational
schools is very small at the moment, but a new pattern has been
established which may prove attractive to parents in the years
ahead.[86]

Although the boards of management in national schools have
been a step towards more democratic participation by involved
parties in primary education, some aspects of their composition,
the limited range of their authority and their modes of procedure
have tended to lessen the impact of the boards. It is interesting
that the predominant patron's influence on the first boards has given
way to a more balanced representation whereby the patron's
representation is now 50 per cent while the teachers and parents
make up the other 50 per cent. The patron still, however, nominates
the chairman. The level of interest in the work of the boards varies
between districts, from the highly involved to the generally
apathetic. There is little public debate on the activities of the boards.
Some parents have expressed dissatisfaction at the restricted range
of responsibilities of the boards and have chafed at being cast
in the role of local fundraisers without real power to influence
the educational policy of the schools. Various parent groups formed
the Council for Parents' Elected Representatives for parents on
national school boards to help provide greater co-ordination. This
got a major fillip in 1985 when the Minister for Education provided
funds to facilitate the establishment of a national parents' council.
This has now come into existence and the Minister for Education
has designated a range of issues on which the Department of
Education will formally consult with the National Parents'
Council.[87] The involvement of parents on national school
management boards, the range of parent organisations which have
come into being, and the establishment of the National Parents'
Council with powers of consultation and of making submissions
to the Department of Education are important new developments
on the Irish educational scene and are likely to mean a much greater
parental voice on educational issues in the years ahead.

The structures are in place and are capable of further evolution. The lack of public debate on the management boards may be a reflection of apathy and of the limited powers they have, but it may also reflect the smooth running of the boards, and the build-up of trust between the involved parties, removing some of the apprehensions which existed around the time of their establishment. It is noteworthy that when the Minister for Education, Gemma Hussey issued her Green Paper on regionalisation of education in November 1985 the national schools were omitted from the responsibilities of the proposed new local education committees. The reason given was that the urgent need to establish such committees for the post-primary sector necessitated the omission of the national schools which would otherwise have held up the overall plan.[88] A more real reason may have been the fear of opening up a hornet's nest which at the moment was humming away quite satisfactorily under the management boards. In any case, the prospects of implementing the Green Paper's regionalisation plans seem remote at present.

6. Conclusion

Undoubtedly the years from 1960 to 1985 have seen striking improvement in national school education. There has been a great expansion in the number of teachers who benefit from more expanded pre-service education and from some in-service provision and facilities. The teacher–pupil ratio has been markedly improved. National teachers are seen as equal partners with post-primary teachers, within a united teaching profession. The role of principals in large schools has been altered while a significant proportion of the teaching force holds posts of responsibility within schools. There has been a dramatic improvement in the school buildings wherein teachers and pupils carry on the teaching–learning process. A great many of the small dilapidated schools have been closed and the quality of some of the new buildings in terms of design, furnishings and decor is impressive. The scope for the exercise of professionalism by national teachers has been significantly expanded.

The pupils now usually proceed through the national school over an eight-year progression, from age four to twelve. Many classes now benefit from the full attention of their own class-teacher. The smaller classes as well as the availability of specialised remedial teachers help pupils with particular learning difficulties. More enlightened provision is made for categories of children who have particular needs such as children in disadvantaged areas, the children of itinerants, and children in special education. For all pupils the removal of the primary certificate and scholarship examinations has lifted a pressure from life in the senior standards; and the stigma of failure is not placed on pupils at such a young age. The entrance examinations conducted by some post-primary schools still are a cause of dissatisfaction to national teachers and there is scope for further improvement in easing the problems associated with transfer from primary to post-primary schools.

The new curriculum of 1971 has been the single greatest factor in changing the life-experience of both teachers and pupils within the schools. Its philosophy, content and methodology have helped to make schools more interesting, varied and satisfying places for those who spend a significant portion of their lifetimes in school. Many children no longer 'creep like a snail unwillingly to school'. The more humane concern for the child's welfare which underpins the curricular approaches, as well as the abolition of corporal punishment, have made school attractive and pleasant to many children. There is also evidence from inspectors' reports, and studies of the INTO and the Teachers' Study Group and other agencies that the standard of children's education in many respects have improved. It is the case, however, for a variety of reasons already discussed, that the new curriculum is not being fully implemented and problems continue to exist in some subject areas. However, the pendulum has swung significantly in the direction the policy makers wish it to go.

One of the aims of the new curricular policy was to integrate the school more closely with its local environment. The hope was that much of the curricular content would focus on the life and heritage of the local region, facilitated by trips to explore the historical, geographical and botanical richnesses of the local hinterland. This has not happened yet to the extent desired, but another structure for encouraging local involvement between community and school has been the introduction of school management boards involving representatives of patrons, parents and teachers. This was a significant change in the long-established tradition of national school management. With the increased interest of parents in their children's education and the resources of the National Parents' Council, it is likely that the partnership of the key agencies involved will take on interesting forms in the years ahead.

In briefly outlining the areas of improvement in the national school system, one does not mean to imply that everything in the school garden is rosy and that many problems do not exist. Rather one is measuring them from the poor base that existed in 1960. This is vital to bear in mind. In the ordinary democratic process there is no magic wand which can be waved to change a neglected and out-of-date system easily or quickly into a modern, well structured and finely tuned system. Apart from many demands on the public purse other than from education, change within education itself is a complex process, both in terms of length of time, attitudinal changes and a variety of other factors which arise when significant changes are being introduced. For instance, improvements in teacher–pupil ratios cannot be satisfactorily achieved in the short term as the Irish experience demonstrates. It can involve increasing intake to training institutions, expanding these institutions, providing new school buildings, new organisation of the school stock, and so on. To bring all these things into line takes time as well as a significant increase in resources.

There is also the subtle but important aspect of public support for action on educational reform. While it is true that for much of the first four decades following independence the Irish economy was rarely in a strong position, and Irish political leaders did not give leadership on the development of the education system, yet there was also a lack of public concern about the defects of the national school system. This is all the more significant in that national schooling was the sole mode of formal education attained by a large proportion of the population. The educational changes initiated in the 1960s occurred in the context of a new economic buoyancy in the Irish and international economies. This provided the priming funds to boost the system which in turn helped provide the more educated workforce for an expanding economy. The economists at this time viewed education as an important investment area, not just for individual gain but also for the good of society. This gave a new confidence to educational policymakers to call on public funds with the assurance that it could be argued that such funds were not just a consumer service but were a central plank in the economic revolution which was being undertaken.

Rising living standards and greater social awareness encouraged the public to seek an improved educational system. This demand was fuelled by the findings of studies such as the *Investment in education* report. Politicians now both responded to the public mood and led it forward. It was no longer a question of the Minister as 'plumber knocking the pipes', rather it was the Minister as priming agent and innovator. Ministers such as Hillery, Colley and O'Malley adopted the new role with gusto and a certain flair. The public imagination was captured by some of the new moves, such as the free education and transport schemes. Politicians remarked in the Dáil on 'the far greater awareness of education in this country at the moment than ever before'.[89] The Department of Education assumed a new and higher profile within the government. The Minister for Education, Pádraig Faulkner stated in the Dáil in 1972, 'the Department of Education is recognised now as being one of the most important Departments of State. The interest shown by deputies during the debate is a reflection of the exceptional interest of the people in the subject of education'.[90] Some within the education system were uneasy at the state's new interest and the degree of driving force that it adopted.

As regards the specific policy measures undertaken, it did not require any deep analysis to identify what needed to be done. The necessity for action on a number of aspects of national schooling could no longer be denied. It was not so much a matter of what to do but of how to do it and at what pace. There was an impulsion forward from a position which had become intolerable. Yet there was no grand design at the outset, rather one thing tended to spark off another, as the interconnections became apparent. One of the reasons why no White Paper was published is that no overall plan existed though, at a certain period, a confluence of a series of initiatives was such that a White Paper, as planned by Donogh O'Malley for 1967, would have been appropriate and useful. The line adopted was not one of Green Papers encouraging discussion leading to White Papers on policy followed by action. The approach taken was one of pragmatic gradualism. There has been a great reluctance within the Department of Education to reveal more than it has to, or to go on public record on policy statements or analyses of the system. It can legitimately be argued that our political and educational system are the poorer as a result. An important advantage of the lack of published policy statements for the public service, however, is that it allows maximum scope for ad hoc planning and for changing directions easily without public controversy. In a conservative, traditional society whose institutions are undergoing significant, and, for some, worrying changes this can sometimes be an effective way of moving things forward on a gradual path, testing responses, slowing down or speeding up developments as circumstances permit. Up to recently, this has been the preferred mode of operation of the Department of Education.

Looking back we can see how various initiatives dovetailed and helped to consolidate a real shift in policy on national schooling. It was essential from the start that progress be made on the teacher–pupil ratio. A range of changes involving increased teacher training, expansion of graduate trainee numbers, re-deployment of the teaching force, acceptance of 'mature' students and of British-trained teachers, all helped to increase the teaching force. The cycle has now gone full circle and the policy of recent years has been to reduce the teacher trainee numbers; the closure of the pre-service teacher training activity of the largest teacher training institutions was part of this policy. The increased numbers of children in the four-to-fourteen age group were a strain on the effort to reduce the teacher–pupil ratio. To help reduce this strain, the policy was adopted of progessing pupils through the national schools with the minimum of delays, so that the age of twelve became the normal transfer age.

The closure of small schools only emerged as a serious policy in 1965. The policy became closely intertwined with the need for more efficient utilisation of the teaching force, the policy to improve the standard of school buildings and equipment, and the moves being initiated for a reformed curriculum. The greater number of pupils transferring to post-primary school and the introduction of free post-primary education in 1967 were factors in the abolition of the primary certificate examination in that year. These factors also favoured a more thorough review of the national school curriculum than was originally planned. The new curriculum came into operation in 1971, now aided by the improving teacher–pupil ratios, the changed building and equipment standards, and new

teacher education courses. The changes in school management were
not initiated until 1973 but by then a climate had evolved which
was favourable to the need for greater home–school links, closer
relationships between the school and its environment, and greater
parental support for equipping schools to facilitate the
implementation of the new curriculum. While some debate occurred
on Church-versus-lay control of the schools, pragmatic deals were
done and a modus vivendi was evolved over a short number of
years between the interested parties.

From the perspective of today, it would seem that there was
an inevitability about these developments because they seem to
interrelate so neatly. While there is some truth in this, it would
be simplistic to assume that the human actors involved in the
unfolding events did not have to wrestle hard to achieve much of
what was attained. For contemporaries the pattern of the future is
not easily discernible; it has to be forged in the present.
Nevertheless, most of the initiatives on national schooling over
recent decades were directed at improving the basics of the system.
The essential elements of a schooling system are the pupils going
through the system, the teachers, the curriculum, the buildings,
and management. Much has been achieved in the reforms affecting
each of these features, but much remains to be done.

It was important for planning purposes that education became
part of the more planned approach to the general economy in the
1960s, as reflected in the *Second economic programme* (1964) and
the *Third economic programme* (1969). It meant that goals were
being declared in advance and that a degree of approval from the
Department of Finance and the government was being secured.
Even if goals were not achieved, they were referral points for key
personnel within the Department of Education and for interested
educationalists in the wider community. This approach of publicly
putting forward goals was renewed in the 1980s with the publication
of *White Paper on educational development* (1980) and *Programme
for action in education, 1984–87*. It will be regrettable if Ministers
for Education yield to the temptation to abandon this approach
in the difficult economic circumstances prevailing, as a democracy
benefits from open discussion of policy proposals.

Policy making within the period under review presented a
fascinating patchwork of factors and influences which impinged
on, or shaped developments, as the earlier sections of this chapter

have indicated. While the lines of development are not always clear, the complex range of elements involved reflect the reality of Irish public life, and the ebb and flow of a system based on pragmatic improvement rather than radical changes in ideological position. The buoyancy of the general economy throughout the 1960s and early 1970s facilitated the innovative educational policy. Linked to this were the assurances of the economists that investment in education was a wise deployment of public resources. The greater participation of senior Irish civil servants in international conferences on education, and the availability of documentation on educational policy from international agencies, undoubtedly opened the eyes of Irish officials and helped to dispel complacency and misconceptions on educational provision. A number of dynamic and skilled officials attained senior status within the Department and felt a commitment to improving educational opportunity for the less well off. They supported Ministers who assumed a more direct role in educational policy making than had been traditional.

There was a reliance on common sense, practical experience and 'gut' feeling, but not to the exclusion of research findings from at home and abroad. For instance, the findings of the Investment in Education team on school staffing, resources and pupil participation had a direct and early impact on policy. Other research studies such as those on non-promotion of pupils in national schools, the provision of teaching equipment in schools, and so on, referred to earlier in this chapter, had an influence on decision making. More generally, a number of studies in the social sciences of psychology and sociology highlighted the learning problems encountered by some children and helped to develop the new-found interest in various aspects of the education of the handicapped, of itinerants, and of generally disadvantaged pupils. This resulted in significant and qualitative initiatives in these areas of primary education.

A study of a different character which caused a particular stir was Macnamara's study of bilingualism in Irish national schools. It raised serious questions about the wisdom of existing curricular policy and the time allocation of subjects. Even though its publication, in 1966, coincided with the fervour of the golden jubilee celebration of the Easter Rising, it also coincided with a deeper trend of decline in the influence of cultural nationalism, and a questioning of the curricular policies adopted in the post-independence period. This period also reflected new thinking on language teaching methods, and great expectations of what new audio-visual pedagogic techniques could achieve. These methods were adopted for national schools and, within the context of the new curriculum of 1971, both the time devoted to Irish teaching and the method of teaching the language altered significantly. Interestingly, while the overall number of Irish-language national schools continued to decline, a new development took place whereby groups of parents, particularly in urban areas, took the initiative of founding 'all-Irish' schools and pre-schools, called *naonraí*.

As has been pointed out, the influences shaping the policies on the new curriculum were varied. They included the concerns of teachers on the ground, such as the Teachers' Study Group and others, who were impatient with the rigidities of existing policies. The INTO (1947) and the Council of Education (1954) were more remote influences which had urged change. A sharper edge emerged in the 1960s; groups such as Tuairim sought reform and parties in political opposition issued policy documents on education. The approach within the Department up to the mid-1960s was to adopt a gradual and piecemeal attitude to curriculum reform. However, the opportunity of drafting a White Paper in 1966−67 was seized on by the inspectorate. They adopted a more fundamental approach, influenced no doubt by the Plowden Report thinking in England, at the time. The momentum behind the policy gathered slowly; but when the policy was adopted it was pursued with zeal by the inspectorate, and gave the professional side of the Department of Education one of its finest hours.

The range of educational initiatives within the different sectors, occurring more or less contemporaneously, caught the public imagination and propelled education to the forefront of public attention. The media stimulated the interest in educational reform and the response to reform measures. The vote-catching potential of educational reforms, which touched so closely on the daily lives of so many families, was not lost on the politicians. Equality of educational opportunity became a most attractive and much-used political slogan. Regrettably, less attention was paid to the complexities and problems of making such opportunity a reality. Nevertheless, in a way unprecedented in Irish public life, education became an issue of great interest and debate. By the end of the period under review, however, the public climate had changed significantly, causing deep apprehension among many educationalists that a slide back to poorer schooling conditions may be imminent. In any case, planning for the future will be very different from that of the 1960s and 1970s. An economy in recession and a declining population are two key factors that change the scene.

Since independence, the state had been extremely reluctant to encroach on the position of the Churches in education. The Catholic Church was by far the predominant one and had jealously guarded the prerogatives it had won in education. However, the Church too underwent significant change in the 1960s. The gradual leavening of Vatican II thinking changed attitudes and fostered a more open attitude as to the nature of the Church. In particular, the new emphasis on a partnership in education involving the Catholic Church, teachers and parents prepared the way for the first change in the management of national schools. From 1969 to 1974, members of the hierarchy indicated their support for PTAs and some pilot schemes were put in place. The state read the signs and decided, in 1973, to give a significant push towards the democratisation of school management. Even though occasional umbrage was taken by some clergy, in no sense did it become a Church – state clash, and tension was much less than it had been between religious authorities and the Department of Education on policy for secondary schools. What resulted was a cautious, and overdue, restructuring of national school management, which modified the control hitherto exercised by religious orders.

This was one of the areas of change in which the national teachers' union, the INTO, followed rather than led. Even though teachers, in the past, had expressed dissatisfaction with aspects of traditional school management, many teachers were reluctant to involve parents in the process. However, in time, the teachers agreed to participate, and furthermore, re-shaped the structures more to their liking. There were other areas where the INTO was particularly influential on policy. The organisation had opposed the primary certificate examination since its inception and, in 1967, a number of supporting factors helped it to have the examination abolished. The INTO was also persistent in its pressure on Ministers to improve the teacher – pupil ratio. As has been noted, this was government policy from 1958 but the regular demands of the INTO helped to give teeth to the policy which, over time, proved fairly successful. The INTO's strong insistence on parity of teachers' salary scales and on university degrees for trainee national teachers steeled successive Ministers to face difficulties in the path of these objectives. Apart from general salary matters, one of the issues on which a significant public show-down between the INTO and the government took place was on the age of entry dispute in 1982, when John Boland was Minister. The union's stance had a huge influence on the change of policy and restitution of the status quo by John Wilson in the succeeding government.

However, in bringing about many of the changes outlined in this chapter, very little lasting division of opinion occurred among the general public. There were no significant ideological disagreements. There was a large degree of all-party agreement and, as regards the national school system, considerable continuity of policy between changing governments. The closure of small schools was the policy which caused greatest unease. While that policy may have been necessary and beneficial, insufficient attention was paid to the wrench which the closure betokened for many communities. By relating with the manager the Department was formally keeping to the authority link of the system, but it ignored the reality that, for many members of the community, the decisions on closure were high-handed and based on bureaucratic *fiat*. It is significant that, in a survey of public opinion on educational innovation conducted in 1974, the changes, on the whole, won public approbation. The closing of small schools was the only item that did not attract a majority of supporters.[91] Eventually, with the provision of good schools, the more general availability of one teacher per class, and a good transport network, most communities came to realise the value of the policy. They could have been saved considerable distress in the process. It should be borne in mind that not all small schools were closed and, in 1982, one- and two-teacher schools still comprised almost 30 per cent of the national schools. In this context, the state showed particular care in the handling of small schools in the case of minority Churches.

The new curriculum met with approval. There was no question of leading far in advance of public opinion. The changes won a very wide welcome and endorsement. But here too inadequate attention was paid to communicating with parents and post-primary school interests about the nature and scale of the changes involved in introducing the new curriculum. Great scope existed for imaginative presentations of what the new curriculum involved and of its potential in local communities. The mode of implementation with the managements and professionals was on the right lines involving prior consultation, pilot studies, good handbooks, in-service provision, and improved resources in schools. The Department also took a gradual stance in relation to implementation, allowing schools and teachers time to adjust. The key problem was that the curriculum represented a radical shift in a range of directions from the experience of almost fifty years. Furthermore, while reforms in school conditions were afoot, the circumstances which still existed in many schools were such as to impose severe impediments in the way of full implementation. Then, the creditable start which had been made on in-service education and teaching resources petered out and fell into rapid decline after 1974.

There has been a strong tradition of individuality in national school teaching, whereby each individual is expected to offer the full spectrum of the curriculum, and teachers defend their autonomy in their own classrooms. The weakness of this tradition is that the balanced implementation of a wide-ranging curriculum may be unrealistic for all teachers. Recent years have seen efforts by the inspectorate to foster a whole-school approach to curriculum planning. With the development of 'school plans', to which various staff members contribute, there may be a greater fostering of some specialisation whereby teachers with special skills and interests in particular subjects (for example art and craft, music, physical education, local studies, computer studies) may undertake these areas for a number of class groups, with reciprocal work by other teachers, with their particular class group.

In relation to the policy measures on management boards, it could be said that the state was not premature or peremptory in its approach. Rather, it had demonstrated extraordinary caution in this potentially controversial area. It waited until, in the post-Vatican II climate, the Catholic hierarchy had signalled its welcome for more close involvement of parents and teachers in the running of the schools. In its management plans, the state laid down no specific structure for the boards; rather, it held out a carrot of improved funding for the schools which established the boards and negotiations were largely left to the key agents, though the Department assisted in the drawing up of regulatory procedures. The Department did not oppose the representative character of the boards as they emerged in 1975. It was the INTO which, after 1978, pressed the managers and the Department, through abstention policies and long negotiation, so that from 1981 the constitution of the boards reflected less of an imbalance in favour of the patron's nominees. It would seem that the Department was more interested in the principle of establishing the boards rather than in any real concern about the balance of the interests involved. The limitations on the powers of the board were such as not to impinge on the rights of the general policy for the schools hitherto exercised by the Department.

Management boards face different problems, depending on the area in which their school is located. Schools in socially deprived and disadvantaged areas have to cope with many difficult socio-educational situations, but with less financial resources than can be available to schools more favourably situated. While the state takes some note of these circumstances, the extra provision is very inadequate. In a period of cut-backs in public expenditure, there is a grave danger that the problems of the 'disadvantaged' schools become even more chronic, whereas schools in more affluent districts can benefit from voluntary contributions and better forms of private fund-raising.

While many of the dramatic changes affecting second- and third-level education attracted the limelight of public attention, nevertheless, there was a realisation that unless the foundation was soundly based, later attempts at promoting equality of educational opportunity would not prove fruitful for the children most at risk.[92] Pádraig Faulkner remarked in 1972:

> I should say that the equalisation of educational opportunity must commence at an early stage of the child's educational career. For this reason alone it is essential that we continue our efforts to bring about the most favourable conditions feasible in the primary schools.[93]

This theme was reiterated with an increasing sense of concern by groups such as the NESC, and the ESRI. The NESC in its report *Educational expenditure in Ireland* (1975) stated that 'Increased expenditure on the compulsory education age-group would do most to promote equality of opportunity in education'.[94] The report also pointed out the low level of expenditure from public funds per pupil in non-teacher items in the Republic's national schools, observing that the level was eighteen times higher per pupil in the primary schools of Northern Ireland.[95] The low level of expenditure on items other than teacher salaries and school buildings has continued to affect the national schools. Whereas in Ireland about 5 per cent of the current spending on primary education goes on non-pay items, this is very much out of line with international practice, where 15 to 25 per cent is the norm. In a report for the ESRI in 1978, Dale Tussing pointed to serious problems facing the Irish education system: a rising youth population, expanding enrolments, and rising costs. He argued for a redistribution of funding whereby more public funds would be allocated to the compulsory attendance groups six to fifteen; and there would be more reliance on private funding for senior cycle second-level and for third-level education. He held that within the education system 'the disproportionate importance of the national schools may sometimes be forgotten'.[96] In a later paper (1981) he stated, 'The most pressing single need in Irish education is for substantially increased resources for the national schools'.[97] No major shifts in the policy of public financing of education have taken place, but for what it is worth, the Minister for Education in her *Programme for action in education, 1984–1987* stated, 'The funding of national schools will be a major priority of the Minister and the Government in the allocation of the resources available for education. In addition special funding should be directed to disadvantaged areas'.[98]

To a large degree the approach to national school education policy in the mid-1980s is one of a holding operation. Any proposals involving a significant outlay of finance are being dismissed or deferred. A notable feature of general policy in recent years has been the establishment of a range of specialist committees on various facets of education. Indeed, the *White Paper on educational development* in 1980, made reference to eleven such committees. It is also obvious, however, that the recommendations of these committees are being ignored, if they entail increased public expenditure. Development, reform or expansion plans do not fit easily into the current climate of cut-backs on public expenditure. It is, however, a positive thing that a Minister for

Education would have the courage to issue a *Programme for action in education* in 1984. It is also praiseworthy that two annual *Progress reports* on that plan were issued. Even if educational progress is sluggish at the present time it is, nevertheless, a good thing, and a novel development in Irish education that people can more easily establish what is happening in educational policy.

Notes to Chapter 2

1. Dale Tussing, *Irish educational expenditures − past, present and future* Dublin: Economic and Social Research Institute, 1978, p. 12.
2. INTO, *A plan for education* Dublin: INTO, 1947.
3. Council of Education, *Report on the function and curriculum of the primary school* pr. 2583 Dublin: Stationery Office, 1954, p. 272.
4. *Dáil Debates* (Minister Mulcahy), Vol 159, c. 1494, 19/7/56.
5. *Dáil Debates* Vol 245, c 1407, 1408, 16/4/70.
6. *Dáil Debates* Vol 259, c 876, 2/3/72.
7. Council of Education, *Report on (1) function of the primary school; (2) curriculum of the primary school* Dublin: Stationery Office, 1954 pr. 2583, p. 288.
8. *Dáil Debates* Vol 308, c 1357, 15/6/78. These figures differ somewhat from those given in the Department of Education's Statistical Reports which read as follows: 989, 1331 and 2604 for the relevant years.
9. *Dáil Debates* Vol 208, c 1566, 15/5/64.

10. *Second programme for economic expansion, part II* (Pr. 7670). Dublin: Stationery Office, 1964, p. 194.
11. *Ibid.*
12. Seán O'Connor, *A troubled sky: reflections on the Irish educational scene, 1957—1968.* Dublin: Educational Research Centre, 1986, p. 120.
13. *Report of the Department of Education*, 1963-64, p. 46.
14. Department of Education, *Circular 10/67.*
15. Thomas Kellaghan, 'The organisation of classes in the primary school' in *Irish Journal of Education* Vol 1, No 1, 1967, pp. 15-36, p. 16.
16. *Dáil Debates* Vol 232, c 460, 6/2/68.
17. *Third programme for economic expansion* (Prl. 431). Dublin: Stationery Office, 1969, p. 193.
18. Thomas Kellaghan, 'The organisation of remedial instruction for slow-learning pupils' in *Irish Journal of Education* Vol 8, nos 1, 2, 1974, pp. 102-110.
19. *Dáil Debates* Vol 301, c 795, 926, 10/11/77 and 15/11/77.
20. *Dáil Debates* Vol 256, c 940, 3/11/71.
21. John Coolahan, *The ASTI and post-primary education in Ireland* Dublin: ASTI, 1984, pp. 267-308.
22. Commission on Higher Education, *Presentation and summary of the report* (Pr 9326), Dublin: Stationery Office, 1967, p. 37.
    Higher Education Authority, *Report on teacher education* Dublin: Stationery Office, 1970, E/67.
23. Report on An Chomhairle Mhúinteoireachta (Teaching Council), unpublished, 1974.
24. INTO, *Report of the Executive to annual congress*, 1977, p. 10.
25. Compiled from *Dáil Debates*, Vol 283, c 1671, 15/7/75 and Vol 313, c 149, 21/2/79.
26. *Statistical report of the Department of Education for 1982—83*, p. 19.
27. *Dáil Debates* Vol 315, c 1827, 10/7/79.
28. *Dáil Debates* Vol 311, c 1689, 21/2/79 and *INTO Congress report, 1977/78*, p. 37.
29. John Nolan, 'Government policies on national teacher demand supply in the 1980's', unpublished, p. 16.
30. *White Paper on educational development* (Prl 9373), Dublin: Stationery Office, 1980, pp. 3-5.
31. Dennis Murphy, 'How primary school numbers will slump', in *Sunday Tribune*, 15/12/85, p. 25, Department of Education estimates and Central Statistics Office projections.
32. *Programme for action in education, 1984—87* (Pr 2153) Dublin: Stationery Office, 1984, p. 16.
33. Figures supplied by the Department of Education for 1984, the latest date for which they are available.
34. Statistics in *Investment in education* chapter 9, pp. 225-264, and T. Kellaghan and L. Gorman, 'A survey of teaching aids in Irish primary schools' in *Irish Journal of Education* Vol 2, No 1, 1968, pp. 32-40.
35. *Ibid* p. 253.
36. *Ibid* p. 260.

37. Department of Education, *Circular, 22/61*.
38. Áine Hyland, 'Shared areas in Irish national schools' in *Proceedings of the Educational Studies Association of Ireland* Galway University Press, 1979, pp. 175-199.
39. *Investment in education report* p. 264.
40. *Dáil Debates* Vol 217, c 1968, 21/7/65.
41. *Ibid.*
42. *Investment in education* p. 337.
43. *Dáil Debates* Vol 220, c 1719, 16/2/66 (Deputy O'Flanagan).
44. *Dáil Debates* Vol 220, c 1719, 16/2/66.
45. *Ibid,* c 1783.
46. T. J. O'Connell, *A hundred years of progress: the story of the INTO 1868–1968.* Dublin: INTO, 1969, p. 448.
47. *Dáil Debates* Vol 263, c 1326, 9/11/72.
48. Aine Hyland, 'Shared areas in national schools', p. 187.
49. INTO, *Report of the working committees on shared areas in Irish primary schools* Dublin: INTO, 1979, p. 6.
50. *Dáil Debates* Vol 220, c 1752, 17/2/66.
51. W. Hyland, 'Effect of retardation on national school pupils' in *Oideas* 2 (1969), pp. 50-55, and *Investment in eduation, annexes and appendices* IX, Table c 2, p. 575.
52. Department of Education, *Circular 10/67*.
53. Tom Kellaghan and Seamus Holland, 'The Rutland Street project' in *Oideas* 3 (1969), pp. 28-32.
54. 'Education facilities for the children of itinerants' in *Oideas* 5 (1970).
55. Department of Education, *Circular 27/85*.
56. For a statement of current policy, see *Programme for action in education, 1984–87* chapter 4, ('special education'), pp. 19-21.
57. Statistical Reports for the Department of Education for 1960–61 (p. 75) and for 1981–82 (p. 36).
58. *Annual Reports of the Department of Education* 'The work in the schools', 1960–64.
59. John Macnamara, *Bilingualism in primary education: a story of Irish experience* Edinburgh University Press, 1966.
60. *Second programme for economic expansion* p. 197.
61. *Dáil Debates* Vol 216, c 958, 16/6/65.
62. Seamus de Buitlear, 'Curaclam nua le h-aghaidh na bunscoile', in *Oideas* 3 (1969), pp. 4-12, p. 12.
63. *Ibid,* p. 4.
64. Background paper of the steering committee on the planned White Paper on education, unpublished, 1967, p. 40.
65. *Ibid,* p. 85.
66. Kathleen McDonagh (ed), *Reports on the draft curriculum for primary schools* Dublin: Teachers' Study Group, 1969.
67. *Report of the Pupil Transfer Committee* (Pl 686), Dublin: Stationery Office, 1982.
68. *Dáil Debates* Vol 256, c 943, 3/11/71.
69. *Dáil Debates* Vol 258, c 2010, 20/1/72.

70. *Dáil Debates* Vol 287, c 1134, 19/6/75 and Dr Aine Hyland 'The process of curriculum change in the Irish national school system 1868 – 1986', paper delivered at ESAI conference, Galway, March 1986, p. 12.

71. *Report of the Committee on In-service Education* (Pl 2216). Dublin: Stationery Office, 1984, pp. 52-54.

72. *Programme for action in education*, p. 35.

73. Aine Hyland, 'Curriculum change', p. 12.

74. *Dáil Debates* Vol 303, c 1096, 8/3/78.

75. Curriculum and Examinations Board, *Issues and structures*; *Primary education*; *In our schools* Dublin: Curriculum and Examinations Board, 1985 – 86.

76. Report of the Primary Committee to the Curriculum and Examinations Board, June 1986, p. 11 (unpublished).

77. Letter from Cardinal D'Alton to the INTO, 24/10/54, quoted by O'Connell, *History of the INTO*, p. 442.

78. Labour Party, *Challenge and change in education* Dublin: Labour Party, 1963, p. 5.

79. Fine Gael, *Policy for a just society – 3. Education* Dublin: Fine Gael, 1966, p. 19.

80. Catholic Bishops Pastoral Letter, 1969.

81. Yvonne McGrath, 'The role of parents in education' in *Oideas* 9 (1972), pp. 37-42, p. 39.

82. Sean Kelly, 'Teachers' attitudes to parent – teacher relationships' *Irish Journal of Education* Vol 1, No 2, 1967, pp. 107-112.

83. *Dáil Debates* Vol 245, c 1971, 1972, 23/4/70.

84. *Dáil Debates* Vol 245, c 1312, 15/4/70.

85. *Dáil Debates* Vol 268, c 376, 23/10/73.

86. For an account of the emergence, aims and approach of this movement see *Dalkey School Project*. Dublin: Dalkey School Management Board, 1976.

87. Department of Education, *Circular 7/85*.

88. Green Paper, *Partners in education: serving community needs* Dublin: Stationery Office, 1985.

89. *Dáil Debates* Vol 220, c 1550, 15/2/66.

90. *Dáil Debates* Vol 259, c 869, 2/3/72.

91. T. Kellaghan, G. Madaus, P. Airasian and P. Fortes, 'Opinions of the Irish public on innovation in education' in *Irish Journal of Education* Vol 15, nos 1, 2, 1981, pp. 23-40.

92. For an account of developments in second- and third-level education, see John Coolahan, *Irish education: history and structure* Dublin: Institute of Public Administration, 1981.

93. *Dáil Debates* Vol 259, c 878, 2/3/72.

94. NESC, *Educational expenditure in Ireland* (John Sheehan), Dublin: NESC, 1975, p. 22.

95. *Ibid* p. 10.

96. Dale Tussing, *Educational expenditure in Ireland*, p. 162.

97. Dale Tussing, 'Priorities in social policy: education' in D. Nevin (ed), *Trade union priorities in social policy*. Dublin: FWUI, 1981, pp. 87-96, p. 88.

98. *Programme for action in education* chapter 3, p. 14.

3

Official Perceptions of Curriculum in Irish Second-level Education

D. G. Mulcahy

It is evident from the scholarly literature of the past decade that secondary education has become the object of increased concern in Western societies. Ireland is no exception. Accordingly, the question arises as to what policies one might develop to deal with these concerns. In this chapter, I shall focus upon the curricular aspects of this issue, and in particular upon what I shall term 'official' perceptions of curriculum. By official perceptions I do not mean merely the perceptions of the government or of the Department of Education but of those various bodies, boards and committees established by the government or the Department of Education to inquire into and report upon relevant matters. My intention is, firstly, to consider the ways in which curriculum has been understood in second-level education in the Republic of Ireland and, secondly, to consider the adequacy of these perceptions or understandings to provide curriculum policies for dealing with problems that have been identified and concerns that have been expressed. Particular attention will be paid to the most recent official Irish statement of curriculum viewpoint, namely, that set forth in the report of the interim Curriculum and Examinations Board, *In our schools*.[1] While the Curriculum and Examinations Board itself seems to have come to an end, an apparent successor has been appointed in the form of the National Council for

I wish to acknowledge the helpful comments of Dr Pádraig Hogan, Department of Education, St Patrick's College, Maynooth, on an earlier draft of this chapter.

Curriculum and Assessment, the purpose of which seems largely
to carry on with the unfinished business of the Board. In any event,
the final report of the Curriculum and Examinations Board, *In our
schools*, represents the only complete official curriculum statement
of any substance sine the 1960s; it also merits attention in its own
right.

The areas of concern in second-level education include:

the ambiguity of purpose and role of second-level education in
Western societies;
the pervasive effects on teaching and learning of examinations
and certification;
the influence of third-level institutions in shaping and
determining according to their own legitimate interests the
curriculum of second-level schools;
the impact of bureaucracy in education and of the prolongation
of formal education;
the motivation of pupils and the suitability of existing
programmes for all pupils;
the relationship between education and preparation for work
and employment.[2]

The emergence of a more conservative emphasis in the educational
thinking and policies of Western societies such as England and
the USA during the 1980s has deflected some attention from these
concerns. Yet grounds for concern and underlying problems still
exist and, if anything, may be exacerbated by policies implemented
or planned in the 1980s at the beckoning of the so-called 'back
to basics' movement.

Basic Perceptions

Secondary education and vocational education

In Irish second-level education the secondary tradition has been
the dominant one. The curriculum which emerged in secondary
education during the early years of the new state, and which
continued to dominate official thinking at least up until the 1960s,
was one in which the literary and academic subjects occupied a
central role. The various subjects were seen as the basic units of
the curriculum, and progress in the curriculum was measured

largely by performance in the public examinations. The view was also taken that there should be a core of subjects which would be required of all pupils. Only by following the kind of programme which was envisaged, it was thought, could the central purpose of the secondary school, namely, the provision of a general education, be secured. The public examinations were closely associated with the curriculum in the official mind and in the public mind alike, and, in practice, they acted as an unyielding support for and determinant of the curriculum of the day.

The distinctive characteristic of second-level education which existed in the vocational education system, and which was known as continuation education, was that general education was not considered to be so heavily dependent upon the study of the literary subjects alone, and should include the study of such subjects as woodwork, metalwork, domestic and rural science, and commercial studies. This view became the basis upon which the programmes of continuation or general education in the vocational schools were conducted and upon which, from the early 1950s onwards, the day group certificate examination was firmly based. A further notable feature of this model of general education was the way in which it allowed for variety in meeting the requirements of the curriculum. All pupils had to study Irish, English and mathematics and there was provision for religious instruction. In addition, pupils were required to follow a group of related practical subjects. The group could be different, however, for different pupils.[3]

What is of particular significance in the evolution of continuation education is that it established an alternative perception of the second-level school curriculum in Ireland, one in which the idea of direct preparation for working life was highlighted. Of significance also is the fact that this alternative view was very much a minority view and even a disdained view in some quarters. It was a view, moreover, which was to lose ground to the dominant secondary view of the curriculum in the rather hectic changes of the 1960s.

Curriculum and organisation

Unlike preceding decades, the decade from the mid-1960s to the mid-1970s saw considerable change in the organisation and

structure and some expansion and change in the curriculum of
second-level education in Ireland. While it was such developments
as the introduction of comprehensive and community schools, the
introduction of so-called free secondary education, and the raising
of the school leaving age from fourteen to fifteen that attracted
major attention during these years, change in the curriculum was
potentially as far-reaching. The main changes in the curriculum
included the introduction of common courses and common
examinations in secondary, vocational and comprehensive schools
and, when they had been established, in community schools and
colleges. This enabled schools to provide a somewhat wider choice
of subjects and it enabled pupils to study traditional secondary
school subjects and traditional vocational school subjects together.
New subjects were introduced, others were changed in content
and a few were even eliminated.[4] These changes reflected the
proposals for the reform of second-level education announced in
May 1963 by the Minister for Education, Dr Patrick Hillery.[5]
The introduction at this time of a number of multi-syllabus subjects
which offered pupils alternatives in the content and methods of
approach to subjects is perhaps less easily attributable to the Hillery
proposals.

An important feature of the changes in curriculum and
examinations which took place since the mid-1960s, however, was
the extent to which the established perception and patterns of
organisation and control of the secondary school curriculum were
maintained and spread to the vocational and newer sectors. This
severely restricted the types of curriculum reform introduced in
the 1960s and 1970s.[6] It was during this time also, and, it would
appear, in response to a critical evaluation of the leaving certificate
examination in 1970, that the method of grading the intermediate
and leaving certificate examinations was altered. Instead of
awarding grades of pass and honours a new literal scheme for
marking was introduced. In addition, pass courses and examinations
became known as ordinary level, and honours became known as
higher level.[7]

Pedagogical innovation

While the established pattern of curriculum and examinations had
not been altered significantly in the 1960s, some old patterns were

challenged during the 1970s. This challenge came in the form of innovations largely of a pedagogical kind and it arose, at least in part, in response to changes already introduced in second-level schools: the fact that pupils were now coming from a wider range of educational and socio-economic backgrounds; the introduction of free secondary education; the raising of the school-leaving age from fourteen to fifteen; and the impact on second-level schools of a new primary school curriculum for which they were ill prepared. As a result there were changes in the ability range of pupils, in educational attainment, and in aspirations and motivations. It soon became necessary to develop initiatives which would respond to this new situation.

Speaking in 1970 of the introduction of such initiatives, the Minister for Education, Pádraig Faulkner, said that the emphasis in educational change was 'passing from that of quantity to quality − from concentration on an expansion in the number of students in attendance at educational institutions to particular concern with the diversity of opportunity provided, the suitability of curricula, and long-term planning for the future'.[8] Among the developments to take place at this time were the setting up of the social and environmental studies project (SESP) based in Shannon Comprehensive School and a number of curriculum projects of the Curriculum Development Unit in Dublin. The publication of *The ICE report* in 1975, a report which contained many new ideas on the examinations in Ireland, also reflected this new emphasis. Later on, in co-operation with the EC, projects of a work-related nature were introduced.[9]

There is some evidence of a continuing challenge in *In our schools*. This is not true of the report as a whole, as I shall argue presently, but it is evident in various views expressed in the course of the report. In chapter 2 of *In our schools*, prominent mention is given to such matters as continuity, breadth and balance, differentiation, relevance and flexibility in the curriculum as guiding considerations in curriculum design and planning.[10] Attention had been given to principles of this kind before though they had not featured as prominently as on this occasion. Throughout *In our schools*, moreover, there are specific measures proposed which indicate ways in which flexibility or differentiation among pupils might be provided for in the curriculum.

The general stance adopted in *In our schools* on the matter of assessment and certification is also an important development on the traditional one, and it incorporates some of the thinking of *The ICE report*,[11] which had never been acted upon. Thus, notwithstanding the cautious approach of *In our schools*, there is an acceptance of the view that examinations and assessment follow from the curriculum, and not the other way around, and that assessment takes precedence over certification.

There is a further significant area in which the perception of curriculum presented in *In our schools* is a development of previous official perceptions of curriculum in Irish second-level education. It is recommended in *In our schools* that all pupils in the junior cycle be exposed to a core of educational experience in the following areas: arts education (including creative and aesthetic studies); guidance and counselling; language and literature (including Irish and English and other languages); mathematical studies; physical education; religious education; science and technologies; and social, political and environmental studies.[12] At the present time the compulsory subjects for all at junior cycle are Irish, English, mathematics and civics.[13] It is true, however, as *In our schools* itself points out, that the areas of experience which are recommended therein for all pupils at junior cycle may be realised through the study of existing subjects. For that reason one cannot draw a sharp distinction between the existing subject requirements for junior cycle pupils and the proposed areas of experience in *In our schools*.[14] The recommendations of *In our schools*, nonetheless, represent a departure in the way in which school knowledge and subjects are perceived and, for this reason, one which could lead to a wider curriculum. Of significance also is the fact that in the recommendations of *In our schools* regarding the curriculum of the junior cycle there is a much greater continuity of studies envisaged as between the primary school curriculum and the post-primary school curriculum. There have been many complaints regarding the breakdown of continuity in this area in recent years. This is one of the more concrete proposals to emerge which attempts to re-establish a kind of continuity which existed in earlier times.

An Appraisal of Official Irish Perceptions

To point to some positive features of *In our schools*, and to indicate areas in which it appears to develop the existing perceptions of curriculum in Irish post-primary education in a way that could be to the benefit of second-level education in Ireland in the years ahead, is not to suggest that it provides a policy basis for dealing with the full range of issues with which second-level education in Ireland is faced at the present time. As the most recent statement of official thinking on curriculum issues, however, *In our schools* may reasonably be seen as an official reflection upon the existing dominant perceptions as well as a measure of their adequacy. It is also an expression of the current perceptions being brought to bear on the curricular issues facing second-level education today and in the years immediately ahead. In turning, then, to an appraisal of official perceptions of curriculum in Irish second-level education it will be appropriate to address a fundamental question which is raised in *In our schools*.

General education

Central to the major official pronouncements on second-level curriculum in Ireland has been the often fuzzy notion of a general education. The reason for this concern with general education has been a desire to deal with the central question of aims and purpose in education, an issue upon which second-level education in Western societies is once again called to clarify its stance. The idea of a general education itself is not highlighted in *In our schools*. In seeking direction for its curriculum thinking, attention is focused instead upon setting forth 'a general aim of education' and in elaborating upon that. This leads the authors to the notion of 'areas of experience' as a guiding principle for curriculum design.

The general aim of education as set forth in *In our schools* is:

> To contribute towards the development of all aspects of the individual, including aesthetic, creative, critical, cultural, emotional, intellectual, moral, physical, political, social and spiritual development, for personal and family life, for working life, for living in the community and for leisure.[15]

From a technical point of view, and given that it is a summary statement, this is acceptable. It is considerably more specific and concrete than those purported statements of aim which still appear with annual regularity in the *Rules and programme for secondary schools*.[16] Unlike these statements it indicates a direction which the various forms of development ought to take. But if, in summary, the aim of education is to develop pupils for personal and family life, for working life, for living in the community and for leisure, the question must be asked as to what constitutes appropriate development for these purposes, be it intellectual, political or spiritual. It is easy to slip into the habit of thinking that just because we hear a good deal of talk about the need to prepare people for working life or for leisure that what these are is self-evident. But this is not so, and many questions need to be asked and answered before we can even begin to understand what these notions entail. By what criteria, for example, is one to be considered prepared for family life or for leisure? Is there just one ideal of what constitutes working life or life in the community? By what values are these various forms of life to be characterised? And, most importantly, what kind of school programmes ought to be designed and implemented so as to ensure that pupils will be prepared in these various respects?

Sadly, no such questions or any discussion of such matters is found in *In our schools*. It is true that, as in other respects, some remarks made in the course of *In our schools* might be alluded to in support of the claim that this is not so. Thus, there is reference to the importance of encouraging creativity, initiative and a sense of responsibility. Many would agree that such qualities are important features of preparedness for adult life, community life and working life. But while it is true that the ideas of responsibility, creativity, initiative and the like are held up as desirable values in *In our schools*, no attempt is made to show how these might relate to preparation for community life, adult life or any other aspect of life. And, just as important, no attempt is made to indicate how and when they would be catered to in a curriculum devised to provide such preparation.

Because these sorts of questions are not addressed in *In our schools* the question of purpose is not adequately dealt with. Without some characterisation of what development for working life or for leisure, for example, amounts to, furthermore, what constitutes a suitable curriculum to promote such development cannot be properly ascertained. The notion of areas of experience, perhaps, has something to contribute to this characterisation and to suggesting curriculum possibilities. But if it has, this is not shown.

Indeed, the notion of areas of experience is not at all well developed in *In our schools*. Notwithstanding the expressed wish that pupils in schools should be given opportunities to undertake responsibilities and challenges, the areas of experience as portrayed do not highlight activity, the taking of initiative, or engaging in practical undertakings, all of which one associates with working life and living in the community and which themselves are lauded in *In our schools*. Actually, one of the disappointing aspects of the notion of areas of experience as it is set forth in *In our schools* is the lengths which are gone to in order to demonstrate that this idea can be accommodated without any significant departure from the existing subjects on the curriculum. A table is even drawn up to show this.[17] But if this is the case, and if it is accepted that there are genuine concerns about the existing curriculum, of what value is the notion of areas of experience if it accommodates so readily to existing practice? Given the passivity on the part of students which is associated with the existing curriculum, is there not a strong likelihood that the curriculum will remain largely an area for passive experience unless clear indications are given as to how objectives which are sought after, such as the undertaking of responsibility, are to be provided for in the curriculum? After all, in developing policy it is not enough merely to express the wish that, for example, pupils will learn to undertake responsibility or become creative. What is needed is a conceptualisation of the curriculum in such a way that it explicitly incorporates provision for the kinds of learnings which are being sought. The introduction of vague new concepts or language which fails to do this will cut little ice and will only lead to further confusion than already exists.

No adequate explicit provision is found either in the traditional view of the curriculum. The *Report of the Council of Education on the curriculum of the secondary school* failed to provide a satisfactory characterisation of what kind of development in pupils it sought to promote and to argue from that to a suitable curriculum. The closest one comes to any such characterisation is in *Memo V. 40*. There, some attempt was made to consider such questions as what does preparation for working life mean in practice, and to move from there to draw up a curriculum framework which reflects working life. It was as a result of such inquiries that, eventually, the old group system emerged in the curriculum of the vocational school.

Tied in rather closely with the whole question of aims and purpose in second-level education is the relationship between second-level and third-level education and the place of assessment and certification and its place in determining the passage of pupils from second-level to third-level education. In Irish secondary education, from its beginnings, there was a clear recognition that one of the guiding objectives of the second-level curriculum was the preparation of pupils for university education. It was as if the curriculum was shaped by the university ideal of academic education. Thus no important place was given to studies or subjects which did not exist in the university, subjects such as home economics or domestic science and secretarial studies – largely 'girls' subjects' to boot – and ample provision was made for classical languages. While metalwork and woodwork were included in the secondary school curriculum in the early years, in time they disappeared. Not until the changes of the 1960s, and the emphasis on education for economic growth, did this begin to change.

The situation was quite different in the vocational view of the curriculum. Never bound by any aspirations to prepare pupils for entry to universities, the vocational sector viewed and shaped its curriculum from the point of view of preparing pupils for entry to work in the trades, in the secretarial sphere, and in a variety of manual jobs. In doing so, however, it never lost sight of its view of the broader purposes of general education and this was reflected in the subject groupings of its programmes. This too was to change, however, as the original vocational view of the curriculum was abandoned during the 1960s. It was abandoned not in the pursuit of a new educational ideal but rather to the force of an economic pragmatism – and highly publicised appeals to the principle of equality of educational opportunity – that ushered in the era of unified post-primary education. It was a unity, however, which lacked definition and a clear sense of direction.[18] In the confusion, and in the competition for places in higher education generated by an almost universal belief in the benefits of higher education, matriculation requirements for entrance to university were to provide the main sense of direction for the school curriculum. Lost sight of almost entirely was any explicit idea of vocational education or even of general education.

A philosophy of education

During this period the system of public examinations, and notably the leaving certificate examination, played a central role in the selection of students for entry to third-level education. In the absence of any other convincing curriculum idea at senior cycle – with Irish the only compulsory subject of study in the leaving certificate programme – the leaving certificate increasingly became a university (or third-level) matriculation examination. As a result, the education of those uninterested or unable to go to third-level education, as well as the idea of second-level vocational education, remained largely unaddressed. And this is more or less the position at the present time. It is an issue which one might reasonably have expected the Curriculum and Examinations Board to address. But did it?

Already I have said that the position taken on the matters of assessment and certification in *In our schools* demonstrates a clear understanding of the subordinate role of assessment and certification in relation to the curriculum, a view which has not been strongly in evidence in the past. This stance is important in itself in that it constitutes a view of the role of assessment and certification in education which sees assessment as having a central role in providing feedback for the guidance of pupils in their learning. But it is practically important also both in the specific context of Irish second-level education and in the context of concerns which have been expressed regarding the distorting role of certification in education. The leaving certificate examination has long been considered to have had a major influence in determining the shape and content of education in Ireland; and much the same is granted in respect of educational systems and practices in other countries. In the view of many, such assessment has become anti-educational; it has promoted assessment and certification – and the 'coverage of content' which leads to such certification – at the expense of worthwhile schooling.[19]

If it is granted that assessment and certification ought to follow from rather than determine the curriculum, that is to say that if the role of assessment and certification is subordinate, then it is imperative that the curriculum itself is well grounded in a guiding philosophy and set of aims, and that any guidance is reflected in appropriate curriculum structures and principles. It is the legitimate educational interests of second-level education which should be guiding the second-level curriculum. Unless this is so, factors external to the curriculum and to the school are likely to determine the philosophy, principles, content and structures of the curriculum.

How adequate is *In our schools*, then, in providing such guidance, in providing such a philosophical underpinning for the curriculum? In discussing the issue of the purpose and role of second-level education earlier on, I suggested that the implications of the notion of areas of experience and the stated general aim of education are not adequately pursued in relation to curriculum content, structures and principles. This is particularly so at the senior cycle. Unlike the possibilities alluded to in respect of the junior cycle when discussing the notion of areas of experience, possibilities with the merit of providing coherence, balance and some sense of direction for the curriculum, here no new ideas of any substance are developed and set forth on what ought to constitute the curriculum. In its place there is reference to transition-year programmes, vocational preparation and training programmes, a broadened leaving certificate programme and the desirability of leaving certificate programmes which 'will continue to cater for the majority of senior cycle students in schools' not needing third-level education. Programmes, it is said, should 'therefore be adapted to cater for the increasingly diverse needs of students'. Indeed they should. And indeed there is a 'need to rationalise the curriculum'. But what are to be the educational grounds for this rationalisation? What educational ideas or principles are to be drawn upon, and most importantly, what general shape should programmes take?[20]

In regard to transition-year programmes, it can be said that the Curriculum and Examinations Board has set forth its ideas in a separate publication. In respect of the leaving certificate programme – the programme that is seen as remaining the main programme – and indeed other possible programmes, next to no discussion, let alone guidelines, is presented. Sadly, too, the subsequent publication of the Board, *Senior cycle*, for all its talk of integration and co-ordination, structures, levels and committees, fails to deal with the central issue of the essential character of the major senior cycle programme, the leaving certificate course.[21] The discussion is replete with advice to committees, to structures and even to the Board itself, as to how they should set about adapting the existing leaving certificate programme but little is said of the form and justification of this adaption, if adaptation it must be.

In its failure substantially to address these matters, *In our schools* has failed to present any view of substance on the nature and general shape of what is seen as the major programme at senior cycle. It has added little or nothing to the old perceptions of the curriculum, the inadequacy of which the very establishment of the Curriculum and Examinations Board itself acknowledges. Not until these deficiences are corrected − notwithstanding the admirable stance adopted in *In our schools* in relation to assessment and certification, or even the thinking regarding the new senior cycle courses other than the leaving certificate course − can one expect that there will be any serious defence erected against the influence of external pressures on the school curriculum and the continued abuse of assessment and certification. Until then also the educational needs of the 'majority of senior cycle students in schools' will probably go unattended and the leaving certificate programme continue as before, unchanged.

Bureaucracy and education

With the growth and development of education systems in this country as elsewhere, bureaucracy and institutionalisation in education have been on the increase. Legal measures, such as the raising of the school-leaving age to fifteen, and the continuing tendency for pupils to stay in school longer, all contribute to this trend. Believing that institutionalisation and bureaucracy in education is overdone and has led to large-scale mis-education, many writers of the 1960s and 1970s argued against the prolongation of school education. Indeed it was in opposition to the growth of bureaucracy and institutionalisation in education that the de-schooling movement, spearheaded by Ivan Illich's *De-schooling society*, took root.[22] It was a movement which raised questions regarding the tendency to equate education with formal schooling, professional teaching bodies and formal certification, as if education and learning which took place independently were of no value. Torsten Husen, the noted Swedish educationalist, has suggested that the ideas of bureaucracy and education are mutually incompatible. This is so, he has suggested, because in education there is a need for direct communication, strong personal relationships, work in small groups, and a high level of sensitivity to the feelings and attitudes of others. In bureaucracy, personal considerations take second place; the system becomes the centre of concern; decisions are made at the centre and transmitted outwards; and there is little room for spontaneous and immediate reactions to novel situations.[23]

The Irish tradition of secondary education has something in common with the critics of bureaucracy and excessive institutionalisation in education in that it has not claimed, at least expressly, to provide for the entire education of the young; the fact that, by and large, Irish secondary schools were small also made a difference. In the *Report of the Council of Education on the curriculum of the secondary school*, clear recognition was given to the place of the family and the Church alongside the school in the education of youth. Likewise, religious education, which was always held to be a central part of the education of the young, was never the subject of state assessment or certification.[24] Thus the formal school curriculum was seen, at least implicitly, as providing for only a part of education.

While this may long have been the official view, increasingly practice is very different, and seemingly in line with the wishes of educationalists and the population at large; few in this country have argued for the reduction of time at school. When we turn to the percepton of curriculum provided in *In our schools* we see that institutionalised education is taken for granted. There is, it is true, the indication that schools might co-operate with other institutions. This would be the case particularly in respect of work-preparatory programmes, to which *In our schools* is prepared to give its blessing without proposing any startling new' ideas or expressly departing from established institutional structures. Most importantly, however, it must be said that in *In our schools* little awareness is shown regarding the issues of bureaucracy and institutionalisation as they affect education. This being so we cannot expect to find there any explicit basis provided for policy making on the matter.

Motivation and learning

Motivation of pupils to learn has been a perennial problem of schooling. The proponents of de-schooling would argue that it could not be otherwise. Their point would be that the very notion of schools as places of education is itself a barrier to motivation. Given the nature of the adolescent pupil, and given that institutionalisation brings with it, as a minimum, some element of compulsion, adherence to regulation and the acceptance of authority structures, one cannot but expect that institutionalisation will be a disincentive for some adolescent pupils. At the same time many pupils are clearly interested in learning in schools even during adolescence. But how one motivates the disenchanted remains a problem, and one with few if any clear-cut solutions.

In the absence of such clear-cut solutions educationalists have been striving for relevance. *In our schools* itself emphasises the notion of relevance: relevance to the interests and needs of pupils as well as relevance to the needs and interests of society.[25] In earlier times, in the secondary tradition, less consideration was given to motivation and relevance. The vocational school tradition, because of the practical and real life focus of its programmes, seemed to provide a greater degree of relevance in many cases. Indeed, it is a common view that many students who are not interested in schooling have a practical bent and can be retained in school by teaching them practical subjects of the kind one used to find in the vocational school curriculum.

If it is accepted that motivation may be a problem for many pupils in second-level schools, and if there are no clear-cut solutions to the problem, where does one look for answers? It has been suggested that greater attention be given to the use of contemporary modes of communication, such as television and computer-assisted instruction. It has also been suggested, for example by Ernest Boyer in *High school*,[26] that school programmes should be challenging and, in particular, that pupils ought to be given the opportunity to follow legitimate personal interests. While many are prepared to accept guidelines of this kind, traditionally school authorities have had difficulty with a theory of school education which does not include a compulsory or mandatory core of general education studies. And this, very often, is where the biggest difficulty arises: in compelling pupils to study certain subjects. There is, then, an apparent impasse between the curriculum requirements of general education and a curriculum which some pupils find to be intrinsically unmotivating or objectionable.

In the perceptions of curriculum which obtain and which have obtained in Ireland one sees little that can help us out of this impasse. Activity-oriented programmes and programmes which allow considerable latitude to pupils to follow their own interests have not been particularly prominent, especially outside of the vocational sector. *In our schools* makes an attempt to recognise the issue of providing for individual interests at the senior cycle of the post-primary school. Such a commitment is not so evident in the junior cycle; granted that the recommendations regarding curriculum time for the junior cycle allow a great deal of latitude, one cannot say that such opportunities are non-existent.[27] But there is little by way of positive guidance.

It should be said that in *In our schools* says a great deal about the importance of teacher initiative and self-directed learning. This makes some provision for responding to what students consider interesting or what might be more suitable for them. Much of the same can be said of the emphasis in *In our schools* on flexibility and differentiation of programmes. Again, however, these are but broad enabling provisions; they do not indicate specific ways in which to provide for motivation and more suitable curriculum experiences.

In dealing with the issue of motivation one is brought back again to the questions of the institutionalisation of education and the 'hidden curriculum'. Cognisance should be taken of the fact that, as institutions, schools often incorporate features that inhibit learning. Those charged with the task of developing policies for school curricula and school programmes would be well advised to be sensitive to the factors that inhibit learning. These include: the nature of compulsory schooling, curriculum structures, patterns of authority and discipline, and the requirements of core curricula and how they affect pupils' perceptions of schooling and learning. These are not easy matters to deal with sensitively and satisfactorily, and it is difficult to know the most appropriate approach to take. New ideas and perspectives are urgently needed. However, in its recommendations and proposals on the curriculum of second-level education in Ireland, *In our schools* does not offer anything new to those seeking policies to address these issues.

Education and work

The main question of the last ten years in regard to the second-level curriculum is the question of the extent to which second-level institutions are preparing pupils for work. When we look at the perceptions of curriculum in Irish post-primary education since the foundation of the state we find that in the vocational sector the principle of preparation for work was central. This was clearly the case in regard to the programmes of vocational schools and it reached its fulfilment in the group certificate programmes. The vocational emphasis was largely non-existent in the secondary sector. This is not to say that the education which secondary pupils received did not prepare them for positions in the public service, in commercial and business life and the like. But at no time was secondary education committed to the principle of vocational education. In fact, the secondary sector, as reflected, for example, in the *Report of the Council of Education on the curriculum of the secondary school*, was very much against the principle of secondary education being a vocational education.[28]

In more recent years a central guiding theme for the state has been that of education for economic growth and development, a theme which in the view of some has been given an unduly narrow and vocationalist interpretation by Irish policy officials and others. This theme was adopted as a guiding principle by ministers and by governments during the 1960s and 1970s. Despite this it was never reflected fully in the rules and programme for schools. Even the vocational sector in this period drifted from its vocational emphasis.[29] The irony was that it was during this time also that the call went out as never before for second-level schools to become more conscious of the need to prepare pupils for work and for employment. Thus on a number of occasions during the past ten years employer groups have attempted to bring pressure on the Department of Education to shape programmes more towards preparing pupils for work. This was quite evident in the *White Paper on educational development* published in 1980.[30] It was also evident in the thinking of the EC and the manner in which it sponsored work-preparatory programmes in Irish schools. Not surprisingly, then, the idea re-surfaces in *In our schools*. But in the area of preparation for work, as in other areas, *In our schools* fails to make strong and reasoned policy recommendations in regard to the curriculum even at senior cycle. It is true that some recognition is given to vocational preparation and training programmes but this is given not so much as a lead for future developments as an acceptance of the fact that such programmes are underway at the present time and should, perhaps, be continued as long as they are found to be worthwhile.

In any event education for work entails a great deal more than immersion in post school-leaving training programmes or the study of so-called vocational subjects while at school. The whole question of the nature and kinds of work which exist, the significance of work in the life of the individual and of society, are but some of the major issues which need to be addressed. So also do a range of attitudinal issues regarding unemployment, mothers working outside the home, acceptable and unacceptable work, which have had little official airing in Irish curriculum circles in recent times. There has been a failure, then, to face in a fundamental way the serious curriculum issues involved in education for work as an integral part of general education in the second-level school. Hastily conceived work-training programmes under external funding hold out little promise of developing a suitable approach to the question of preparation for work, and they speak poorly of officialdom in its dealing with this issue in recent times; at the same time there is little in recent official views on the curriculum that holds out any better promise in this area.

Education and responsibility

Smith and Orlosky have suggested that the failure to integrate pupils into adult society and to prepare them for adult living, that is for participation in community life and for the responsibilities of adult living, is as serious a threat as is the threat to society of environmental disruption.[31] To what extent, then, can we be satisfied that our post-primary schools, and the perceptions of curriculum that guide our post-primary schools, cater to the adequate preparation of pupils for the responsibilities of adult life and for their integration into the community? In the vocational sector there was some attempt to integrate pupils into working life. In the secondary schools, however, this was less evident. In *In our schools* some reference is made to the desirability of students undertaking responsibilities within the school. Some general favour is also expressed regarding work placement. These may be welcome expressions of viewpoint. They cannot be said to provide the basis of a policy position in regard to the integration of adolescents into adult society, however. Neither can *In our schools* be said to represent a significant advance on the positions which have been traditionally adopted in second-level education. Any such advance, in any event, would require a thorough-going reconsideration of institutionalised education in Ireland, and the dependency among adolescents which it very likely generates, two topics on which officials' views are scarce.

Conclusion

The central curriculum question facing second-level education in Ireland today is the question of the general purpose, content and shape of the curriculum. In order to adopt any defensible position on this question it is necessary first of all to adopt a defensible stance in regard to the nature and aims of second-level education. Only then may one set forth a curriculum position to ensure the attainment of the aims or ends in view. These are matters which have exercised the minds of many, including official bodies, in Ireland and abroad in recent years. Yet discussion and debate have not issued in any high degree of consensus as to the best way forward. Accordingly, one cannot speak with any certitude in commenting upon these matters. This is not to say that one should refrain from comment, of course; rather discussion and debate are likely to be a necessary basis for making progress. Granted this, any discussion and debate that has taken place in this country on these matters is to be welcomed as making a contribution. For this reason *In our schools* is to be especially welcomed as a contemporary expression of official thinking on the curriculum, thinking which has been sadly lacking on vital curriculum issues over the past twenty years. It is a publication, moreover, which provides an opportunity to examine the extent to which the view of the curriculum which has obtained in Irish second-level education over the years continues to hold true in official eyes and to examine the views of the Curriculum and Examinations Board as to how the issues with which the curriculum is faced today ought to be handled.

What, then, can be said by way of conclusion on the official

perceptions of curriculum which have grown up in Irish post-
primary education? There are grounds for optimism in the setting
up of the Curriculum and Examinations Board, and of its successor,
the National Council for Curriculum and Assessment, that some
awareness exists regarding the importance of developing a
satisfactory curriculum response to the concerns which have been
expressed regarding the future development of post-primary
education in Ireland. Earlier on I indicated some ways in which
the thinking in *In our schools* represented some developments in
the traditional perception of the curriculum. Given the official
perceptions of post-primary curriculum in Ireland since the
foundation of the state, and more recently in *In our schools*, there
are also grounds for continuing concern, however. For as yet there
has not emerged an official view of the curriculum which is
sufficiently well developed, coherent and imaginative to provide
a basis for policy making which could deal in a satisfactory manner
with all of the issues with which second-level education is faced.

Notes to Chapter 3

1. *In our schools: a framework for curriculum and assessment*. Report of the
   interim Curriculum and Examinations Board to the Minister for Education,
   Dublin: Curriculum and Examinations Board, 1986. For an account of
   curriculum developments in Ireland and abroad published since the
   establishment of the Curriculum and Examinations Board, see Áine Hyland,
   'Views on a core curriculum in the junior cycle of post-primary education
   in Ireland' in *Compass* 15 No 1 (1986) pp. 7-20.
2. For a general overview, see Torsten Husen, *The school in question* Oxford:
   Oxford University Press, 1979.
3. Department of Education, Technical Instruction Branch, *Memorandum V.
   40: organisation of whole-time continuation courses in borough, urban and
   county areas* n.d., c. 1942.
4. See D. G. Mulcahy, *Curriculum and policy in Irish post-primary education*
   Dublin: Institute of Public Administration, 1981, pp. 18-50.
5. Press Conference, 20 May 1963. *Statement* by Dr P. J. Hillery, TD,
   Minister for Education, in regard to post-primary education.
6. See Mulcahy, *Curriculum and policy* pp. 36-37.
7. *Rules and programme for secondary schools* for the year 1968−69 Dublin:
   Stationery Office, 1968, pp. 23, 27.
8. Pádraig Faulkner, TD, Minister for Education, addressing the UNESCO
   General Conference Sixteenth Session, Paris, September, 1970, in Eileen
   Randles, *Post-primary education in Ireland, 1957−1970* Dublin: Veritas
   Publications, 1975, p. 323.

9. *The ICE Report* (report of the Committee on the form and function of the intermediate certificate examination) Dublin: Stationery Office, 1975. Crooks and McKernan give an excellent overview of the many projects and curriculum innovations which were attempted throughout the 1970s and into the 1980s. See Tony Crooks and Jim McKernan, *The challenge of change: curriculum development in Irish post-primary schools 1970–1984* Dublin: Institute of Public Administration, 1984.

10. *In our schools* pp. 13-17.

11. In addition to *In our schools*, see Curriculum and Examinations Board, *Assessment and Certification* Dublin: Curriculum and Examinations Board, 1985.

12. *In our schools* p. 21.

13. *Rules* 1987–1988, pp. 12-13, 21. History and geography are not compulsory subjects of study in vocational schools.

14. *In our schools* pp. 21-22 and 56-57.

15. *In our schools* p. 10.

16. See, for example, *Rules* 1987–88, pp. 12, 15.

17. *In our schools* pp. 56-57. It should be noted here that I am not as generous in my interpretation on this point as is Kevin Williams, though he does admit to some bewilderment as to precisely what *In our schools* has in mind for the core of the senior cycle curriculum. See Kevin Williams, 'Tradition and fashion in curriculum design', *Oideas* 31 (Fomhar, 1987) pp. 67-68. On this point, see also Pádraig Breathnach, 'In our schools – a framework for curriculum and assessment' in *The Secondary Teacher* 15 (Summer, 1986) pp. 17-18.

18. Mulcahy, *Curriculum and policy* pp. 67-72.

19. See, for example, Husen, *The school in question* pp. 145-48.

20. *In our schools* pp. 31-32.

21. Curriculum and Examinations Board, *Transition year programmes* Dublin: Curriculum and Examinations Board, 1986 and Curriculum and Examinations Board, *Senior Cycle* Dublin: Curriculum and Examinations Board, 1986, especially pp. 20-25.

22. Ivan Illich, *De-schooling society* New York: Harper and Row, 1971.

23. Husen, *The school in question* pp. 112-26.

24. *Report of the Council of Education on the Curriculum of the Secondary School* Dublin: Stationery Office, 1960, pp. 88-93.

25. Ernest L. Boyer, *High school: a report on secondary education in America* New York: Harper and Row, 1983, pp. 114-17, 135, 305.

26. *In our schools* p. 15.

27. *In our schools* p. 23.

28. *Report of the Council of Education* pp. 88-93.

29. Mulcahy, *Curriculum and policy* pp. 33-50.

30. *White Paper on educational development* Dublin: Stationery Office, 1980. Con Power, 'White Paper on educational development' in *Journal of the Statistical and Social Inquiry Society of Ireland* 23, Part 3 (1980–81), pp. 84-94.

31. B. Othanel Smith and Donald E. Orlosky, *Socialization and schooling: the basics of reform* Bloomington, Ind.: Phi Delta Kappa, 1975, p. iii.

4

The Evolution of Policy in Third-level Education

PATRICK CLANCY

The rapid expansion of higher education systems in Western society has occurred at the same time as rapid technological and social change and the vigorous pursuit of economic growth. This expansion has been especially marked since the late 1950s, although it is but a dramatic acceleration of a long-term trend. In an analysis of aggregate enrolments in full-time higher education in six Western European countries, Edwards shows that from about 1860 to nearly 1960 there was a remarkably steady exponential expansion of about 2.9 per cent per annum. This rise was deflected temporarily by two great wars and the great depression. During this period of a hundred years, student numbers increased by 2,000 per cent. Edwards suggests that in 1957 there is evidence of a sharp discontinuity and that the average rate of growth accelerated sharply to 8.4 per cent. This rate was maintained consistently for nearly fifteen years; during this time student numbers in third-level education increased by more than 300 per cent.[1]

The explosion of enrolments in the 1960s was accompanied by qualitative changes in higher education systems. In a seminal paper in 1974, Trow proposed a theoretical model which sought to explain the growth and developments of these systems. The essence of Trow's conceptual scheme was that higher education systems in most countries would follow a development sequence similar to that of the United States, passing from 'elite' systems to 'mass' systems and, eventually, developing into 'universal' systems. As quantitative transition points for the various stages, Trow suggested

15 per cent of the relevant age cohorts for mass and 50 per cent
for universal higher education. At the time of its publication Trow's
model seemed eminently plausible, since by the early 1970s many
European systems of higher education were admitting over 20 per
cent of the age cohort and seemed to have made the kind of
institutional changes that such an expansion required. The
significantly slower rates of growth, or in some cases relative
stagnation in student numbers, in the 1970s have caused him to
have second thoughts on the predictive validity of his model.[2]
However, his original formulation contains an accurate and
comprehensive statement of the qualitative changes in modern
higher education systems:

> Mass higher education differs from elite higher education not
> only quantitatively but qualitatively. They differ obviously in
> the proportions of the age group that they enroll, but also in
> the ways in which students and teachers view attendance in
> university or college; in the function of the system for society;
> in the curriculum; in the typical student's career; in the degree
> of student homogeneity; in the character of academic standards;
> in the size of institutions; in the form of instruction; in the
> relationships between students and faculty; in the nature of
> institutional boundaries; in the patterns of institutional
> administration and governance; and in the principles and
> procedures for selecting both students and staff.[3]

The development of higher education in the Republic of Ireland
corresponds with the experience of other Western European
countries. Developments over the past three decades have, in
Trow's terms, changed the system from an elite into a mass system.
There is a difficulty in quantifying precisely the growth in
enrolments because of an absence of comprehensive data prior to
1964. No detailed statistics have been published on enrolments
in professional and technological colleges prior to this period.
Hence, estimates of the pattern of growth prior to the mid-1960s
are based only on enrolments in universities and colleges of
education. Table 1 reveals the general pattern of growth in full-
time higher education in Ireland and in six other European
countries. The Irish pattern of growth is distinguished from that
of our neighbours' by its steady rate of increase, showing less
fluctuations than that in the other countries. The continued rapid

growth in the late 1970s is also somewhat atypical. The fact that this growth has continued over the more recent five-year period is even more striking. Enrolments have grown a further 31 per cent between 1980 and 1985.

TABLE 1

Increase in Higher Education Enrolment
over Five-year Periods in some European Countries
1950−80

	1950−55	*1955−60*	*1960−65*	*1965−70*	*1970−75*	*1975−80*
Ireland	8.0[a]	33.9[a]	38.2[a]	26.7	26.4	26.5
Belgium	23.8[b]	35.5	61.5	48.6	27.9	22.9
France	16.7[b]	32.0[b]	84.2	51.2	29.6	3.6
Germany	18.6	67.1	25.7	35.0	106.7	17.5
Italy	-7.5	27.8	49.4	68.4	42.1	14.4
Netherlands	15.6	48.7	44.9	51.3	24.6	25.0
UK	19.4[b]	41.0[b]	50.6	39.0	21.9	12.9

Notes: [a]Estimate based on enrolments in the universities and colleges of education only.
[b]Estimated figure.
Source: For period 1950−65: *Development of higher education 1950−1967: statistical survey* Paris: OECD, 1970; For period 1965−80: *Tuarascáil statitiúil,* Dublin: Department of Education, (various years) for Ireland; *UNESCO statistical yearbook* 1985 for other countries.

The structural changes in the system of higher education in Ireland over the past fifteen years have been more significant than the numerical expansion. Until the late 1960s, the universities accounted for the majority of total enrolments. The development of nine regional technical colleges, two National Institutes for Higher Education and the growth of the Dublin Institute of Technology and Limerick College of Art, Commerce and Technology have transformed the structure of higher education. The decline in the dominance of the universities is reflected in the steady decrease in the percentage of total enrolments in this sector. In 1969, 78 per cent of higher education students were at university; this figure had declined to 50 per cent by 1985. If we look at the flow of new entrants into higher education, we find that by 1986 only 37 per cent of new entrants were in the universities.[4]

Having briefly reviewed the expansion and diversification of
the system, the remainder of this chapter explores the evolution
of higher education policy in the Republic over the past two
decades. The paper falls into two main parts. The first section looks
at some features of the control and administrative structure, while
the second seeks to identify the main direction of policy over the
period. The scope of this chapter is limited to examining central
policy issues; it does not seek to provide a comprehensive account
of the structure of the system nor does it attempt to provide a
chronology of developments over the period.[5]

Control and Administrative Structure

The quantitative expansion in higher education systems is matched
by a commensurate increase in expenditure. During the recent
decades of expansion, the state has become the main provider of
funds for higher education in all European countries. The centrality
of the state in this provision reflects the expansion of the welfare
state since the second world war. More specifically, the system
of higher education has become an instrument of social and
economic policy in all Western societies. Because the expansion
and development were a function of explicit government policy
and because this endeavour was funded mainly by government,
it is perhaps not surprising that the state has exercised increasing
control over higher education. This interventionist strategy of the
state and its leading to greater government control has been
documented for a variety of national systems.[6]

Government control over higher education is remarkable mainly
because of the previous tradition of autonomy that formed a key
element of the value system. This autonomy imperative has been
particularly strong in the British system and, since much of the
Irish system of higher education in its modern form evolved under
British rule, it is not surprising that the ideal of professional and
institutional autonomy represents an important influence here also.
'The formal limitations upon institutional autonomy in British
universities are minimal', according to Moodie and Eustace.[7]
There is a tradition of non-interference by the state in the affairs
of universities and a widespread belief in the necessity of autonomy.
It is argued that academic freedom is an essential safeguard in a

civilised society; the free expression of intellectual opinion is intrinsically valuable and the right to conduct research in any area, subject only to professional academic judgement, is an end in itself.

The institutional expression of academic autonomy tends to lead to a form of control through the power of professional guilds leading to a type of academic oligarchy. However, from a comparative perspective, Clark points out that this is merely one emphasis, amongst many, in ways of organising and managing systems of higher education.[8] In addition to the power of professional guilds, higher education systems vary in the relative power of political decisions, bureaucratic regulations, and market mechanisms. Whatever the precise relationship between professional, political, bureaucratic and market forces in any country's system of higher education, an essential requirement is that the pattern that is established becomes legitimated. One method used to legitimate any restructuring is that of a commission of enquiry. The report of the Commission on Higher Education helped to fulfil this function in the Irish context.

Commission on Higher Education

In 1960 the Commission on Higher Education was established to 'inquire into and make recommendations in relation to university, professional, technological and higher education generally'.[9] It was, in addition, directed to focus especially on a number of topics of which the most far-reaching were 'the general organisation and administration of higher education and the nature and extent of the provision to be made'. At the time of the Commission's deliberation the higher education system, although expanding, was still a modest enterprise; in 1964 it catered for approximately 18,500 full-time students and 4,500 part-time students. Of the full-time students, 89 per cent were in institutions which were in receipt of public funds.

One of the issues examined by the Commission was the relationship between the state and the institutions of higher education. In its assessment of the existing situation, the Commission recognised that the form of the relationship varies according to the category of institution concerned — the one function it exercises in common in respect of all institutions being that of financial provider.[10] The state provided nearly all the

financial resources in some institutions and in most other cases
the greater part. In relation to autonomy, the Commission noted
that the university institutions are autonomous within the limits
of their charters, and the state had accepted them as such. Similarly,
the state does not interfere with the professional institutions which
are essentially private institutions. On the other hand, the teacher
training colleges, although they are private institutions, are subject
to fairly close control by the state. The colleges within the
vocational education committee system are also subject to a
considerable measure of state control. In general, the Commission
formed the view that under existing arrangements, the state could
not be regarded as a planning authority in higher education. More
fundamentally, it argued, the system as a whole contained no
machinery through which planning could be carried out.

The Commission staunchly endorsed the principle of university
autonomy, noting the views of Dr Hillery, the Minister for
Education, who referred to 'the ancient right of autonomy' of the
universities in his unaugural address to the Commission. It is right
and proper that they should continue to retain it, he said, 'for a
large freedom is of the essence of a university'. In subscribing
to the principle of self-government for the universities, the
Commission noted that in all the evidence received from university
sources 'there was no suggestion that the State unduly interferes
in the working of the universities nor, on the other hand, was there
any call in the evidence for a close supervision of university affairs
by the State' (p. 473). However, the principle of self-government
for institutions was not absolute, the Commission argued;
institutional autonomy must obviously be subject to limitation,
especially where institutions had to rely largely on subventions
from public funds. While the state must obviously be the ultimate
authority for deciding the amount of public resources to be devoted
to higher education, it could only to a limited extent determine
how these resources should be utilised.

A planning and regulating mechanism was needed, the
Commission argued, but it would not be proper for the state to
be the direct authority for planning and financing higher education.
Neither would it be appropriate that the institutions themselves
should perform this function. The Commission recommended the
establishment of a commission for higher education to determine
the appropriate relationship between the state and the institutions

of higher education. In deliberating on the appropriate scope and nature of the buffer agency, the members of the Commission were influenced by the British University Grants Commission (UGC) model which, at the time, and until recently, was commonly regarded as an ideal mechanism by which to facilitate co-ordinated development without infringing on institutional autonomy. However, the recommended commission for higher education was designed to be a more comprehensive planning authority than the UGC, which was seen as being concerned only with the provision of grants to university colleges. The Commission would be concerned with the needs of higher education as a whole and, thus, was expected to preside over the future expansion and diversification of a system which would provide for the community's needs in higher education.

Higher Education Authority

Following the recommendations of the Commission on Higher Education, the government in 1968 established the Higher Education Authority (HEA) on an ad hoc basis. This authority, established on a statutory basis in 1972, corresponds broadly with the Commission's recommendations. It was to be larger than the Commission had recommended. It would comprise a chairman and not more than eighteen members, all appointed by the government on the recommendation of the Minister for Education. At least seven of the ordinary members should be academic members and at least seven non-academic. The Commission had recommended that none of the members be drawn from any of the institutions which came within its scope. This restriction was not maintained in the legislation, although it was specified that none of the academic members be appointed in a representative capacity. The latter distinction, which represents a choice between different forms of corporatism,[11] is highly significant and is designed to ensure an orientation which tilts towards the HEA rather than towards a member's own institution.

In detailing the powers of the HEA, the Act specifies both executive functions and advisory and planning functions. Its advisory and planning functions relate to all of higher education, while its executive functions relate only to those institutions which have been designated under the Act:

The authority has thus a dual function. As an advisory body
to the Minister it must monitor, review, advise and play its part
generally in furthering the development of higher education and
in the co-ordination of State investment therein. Its central
statutory power and function as an executive body is to assess
in relation to annual or other periods the financial requirements
of the institutions of which it is in the funding agency; to
recommend for State grants the capital and recurrent amounts
so assessed; and to allocate to the institutions concerned the state
funds provided.[12]

As a buffer organisation, the HEA needed to establish its credibility
and earn the trust and confidence of both the designated institutions
and the government. In its first years of operation this task was
more difficult with respect to its client institutions, while in recent
years the interface with government has become more problematic.
At its first meeting in 1968 the Minister for Education stressed
that the HEA was 'an autonomous body' and was 'in no way an
executive arm of Government or of any Department of State'.[13]
In the Oireachtais debate which took place at the passing of the
Higher Education Authority Act, the Minister stressed that the
HEA's budgetary procedure would underscore this autonomy. It
was emphasised that the amounts to be received by the HEA
annually would be two global amounts − capital and current −
and that the allocation of sums within these amounts to the
individual institutions would be a matter for the HEA without
further reference to the Minister.[14]

One of the events which enhanced the acceptance of the HEA
by the institutions was its handling of the government's proposals
of 1968 to merge University College Dublin and Trinity College
Dublin and a reconstituted University of Dublin. When the Minister
addressed the HEA at its first meeting, one of the tasks he set them
was to advise him 'on the nature and form of the legislation which
will be required to put into effect the decision already taken by
the Government on higher education'. The HEA considered the
matter in detail, and following many meetings with the institutions
concerned, reported to the Minister in 1971. The HEA advised
against the merger and supported the alternative proposals put
forward by the National University of Ireland and Trinity College
Dublin. It was recommended that there be two separate universities

in Dublin linked by a conjoint board and that there should be an amalgamation of certain schools and departments.[15]

Given the absence of more general work on policy making in Irish education, it is not surprising that the work of the HEA has, as yet, not been the subject of any systematic research. While most participants in this administrative and planning process have 'kept their own counsel', a number have commented on its work. Dr Thomas Murphy, a member of the first authority and subsequently President of University College Dublin, has observed that 'the universities have been very satisfied with the HEA' and has suggested that the HEA's finest achievement has been the establishment of a very large measure of trust between itself and the institutions and organisations with which it has to deal.[16] Perhaps the most nuanced account of the interface between the universities and the HEA is given by O'Cathail.[17] He describes how the budgetary procedure gives the HEA a power of supervision that the colleges cannot afford to ignore. The annual grant received by each college is a block grant and, theoretically, the college may apply the grant as it thinks best. However, in practice, the working budget of each college is discussed with the HEA and, as part of an annual review process, any departures from previously projected lines of expenditure that may have occurred are explored. O'Cathail says 'it is a moot point if a formal ''approval'' of a budget by the Authority must be forthcoming, but it is necessary that there be an understanding'. He also observes that there is now a greater degree of specificity in the HEA's monitoring or supervision of college budgets than there was in earlier years.

Apart from the budgetary procedures which constitute the set-pieces of the university – HEA relationship, O'Cathail mentions two other occasions of interaction between the state and the universities where the HEA is involved but where the effective role lies with government. The first concerns the procedure whereby certain decisions or resolutions of the university colleges' governing bodies have to be incorporated in university statutes and, by law, these statutes must lie for a certain period before the Oireachtas with the right of either house to move that they be disallowed. Since many of the matters dealt with in these statutes have resource implications, this power of veto gives to the state a direct and effective controlling mechanism. A more direct role for government emerges in respect of negotiations on salaries and conditions of employment. In these matters the universities are regarded as falling within the 'public sector' and responsibility for public sector pay is exercised by the Department of Finance. Not surprisingly, perhaps, the government and the college authorities do not always share the same perspective and, on occasions, the colleges in response to a salary claim have to take an attitude with which they would not approve. While the determining role by government in respect of salary and conditions of service has rarely been questioned in recent years (the Irish Federation of University Teachers being the main exception), this practice was previously regarded as a serious infringement of university autonomy.[18]

O'Cathail refrains from offering a personal overall evaluation of the functioning of the HEA as the principal channel for the conduct of state – university relations. However, he does report on the way its operation is perceived (presumably by academics and by university administrators). He intimates that the HEA model would generally be regarded 'as suitable and, indeed, that the procedures for the operation of this model are, in themselves, tolerable, even if occasionally irksome'. However, without adjudicating on their validity, he also lists the complaints made against the HEA. He states that 'there is a view . . . that the Authority . . . has adopted regulatory procedures that are neither necessary nor desirable; that its attitudes are often over influenced by State agencies in the background, for which it becomes the public face'.[19]

The concerns about breaching institutional autonomy in the interface between the colleges and the HEA stem largely from a growing concern that the HEA's own autonomy vis-a-vis government is no longer secure. Some of the stresses and strains in this relationship were outlined by Dominic O'Laoghaire, the then chairman of the HEA at an OECD conference in 1983. To provide one example of the desire for greater financial control of internal allocations, he described how in the revised estimates for 1983, which were prepared by the new government, reductions in grants for HEA designated institutions were announced. More specifically, the announcement by government was accompanied by 'an indication that two specific capital projects would have to be postponed and that, on the current side, practically the whole amount should be borne on pay subheads rather than non-pay subheads'.[20] This government directive involved a significant departure from established procedure whereby the allocation of the two global amounts received by the HEA was at their discretion, without further reference to the Minister.

However, a more ominous indication of the government's desire for greater control over the direction of expenditure was given earlier in the *White Paper on educational development* (1980). This matter was mentioned by Mr O'Laoghaire and has since been addressed by the HEA in its 1974 − 84 *Progress report,* which took exception to the following statement in the White Paper:

> The Government will examine the funding arrangements for third-level education, including the relevant provisions of the Higher Education Authority Act, 1971, with a view to ensuring priority of allocation of resources for such identified areas of national development. In the meantime, the Minister for Education will direct the attention of the Higher Education Authority to the need for ensuring that funds made available by the Government for particular projects should be appropriated accordingly.[21]

In response the HEA expressed its concern that there was some perception in government circles of 'a possible failure of the Authority to co-operate with Government intentions in the appropriation of funds' and that such failure 'might need to be obviated by amending legislation'. The HEA expressed the view that its own actions, for example in relation to the manpower programme initiated in 1979, ought to testify to its responsiveness to government policy. It went on to state its own position that it

> conceives its role to be one of total support for clearly expressed Government policies and, on the other hand, that the Authority considers it essential for itself to be free to offer its own objective assessment of situations at all stages and for its own executive role to be allowed to operate with reasonable latitude.[22]

It is clear from this exchange of views that the government − HEA interface is indeed problematic and that the boundary has proved to be more permeable than had been envisaged. In an earlier progress report, the HEA, interpreting the HEA Act, concluded that it 'entails the devolution to the Authority of certain functions and decisions hitherto reserved to the Minister for Education'.[23]

Subsequent developments reveal a desire on the part of the Minister to regain some of the powers which had been devolved.

Increases in the degree of control exercised by central government on the institutions and on the colleges have also been commented on by the secretary of the HEA. He has argued that the swing back to central control of many activities makes more difficult the colleges' participation in planning and the HEA's taking a leading part in it.[24] Instances of this direct government intervention are legion. They include the comprehensive embargoes on the creation of new posts, the filling of only one in three vacancies and the querying of university statutes which create only the possibility of new posts. An instance of a potentially serious breach of HEA autonomy occurred in 1983 when the Minister for Education, John Boland, initiated direct meetings with the university presidents to learn of their development plans. While the HEA subsequently regained the initiative in this planning exercise, it seems that the direct approach by the Minister to the college presidents, rather than through the HEA, represented a departure from the procedures required under the Act.

The determining role of government in the setting of student fees is a further instance of the erosion of autonomy. While it is true, of course, that in the final instance this, as O'Laoghaire pointed out, 'can only be regarded as an action of the institutions themselves',[25] in practice it is the government which has determined the level of fees in recent years. The strategy adopted appears to be that before deciding on the appropriate annual grant to the HEA the government first decides on the level of fee increase it deems appropriate. The size of the block grant allocated to the HEA is calculated in terms of the necessary supplement to this fee income to enable the colleges to operate. Legally, of course, the universities are free to set their own fee level. However, in a climate of financial stringency, where the total budget is deemed to be much too low, the governing bodies of the colleges have found it necessary to implement the government decision in order to ensure the survival of their institutions.

Most of the examples of a more direct interventionist role by government in directing and controlling higher education refer to matters that have budgetary implications. This intervention has been legitimated by the state's fiscal crisis. The 1988 budget, which heralded the most drastic cuts in higher education, was accompanied by a directive on staffing, which applied to the whole public sector, that the filling of vacancies would have to have the approval of the Minister responsible and the consent of the Minister for Finance. Apart from its immediate effect on the functioning of the colleges, the implementation of this directive would have eliminated institutional discretion in the making of appointments, long regarded as a key element of academic autonomy. Following discussions between the Minister for Education, the HEA and the Committee of Heads of University Institutions, a compromise was reached on the manner in which the government decision could be implemented. Some remnants of institutional autonomy were preserved by the imposition of fixed percentage reductions in the pay bill and in staff numbers. The manner in which these reductions was to be achieved was left to the discretion of the colleges.

The foregoing description of the role of the HEA as the buffer agency designed to structure the relationships between the state and the colleges has been limited mainly to the situation with respect to the universities. However, the executive role of the HEA extends to five other colleges (the National Institutes for Higher Education at Limerick and Dublin, the National College of Art and Design (NCAD), Thomond College of Education and the Royal College of Surgeons of Ireland). It also extends to the National Council for Educational Awards (NCEA) and the Royal Irish Academy. Broadly speaking, the procedures described with regard to the university colleges also apply with respect to the other institutions. Important additional considerations arise, however, with respect to the two NIHEs, the NCAD and Thomond College. These colleges never enjoyed the degree of autonomy which the universities did. In particular, the legislation which established the two NIHEs in 1980, attracted hostile comment because of the degree of direct power which the Minister for Education holds with respect to these institutions. A former Irish Federation of University Teachers president remarked that these Acts provide for an almost unbelievable degree of ministerial interference in the running of the NIHEs. Not only does the Minister appoint the majority of the members of their governing bodies but these governing bodies are subject to ministerial approval of all decisions except in relation to some narrowly defined functions.[26]

One of the consequences of the restrictive nature of the legislation establishing the NIHEs is that many in the universities fear that it might become the model for later legislation. Thus, there is now considerably less enthusiasm than formerly for the new university legislation, which has been promised for almost twenty years, to establish each of the constituent colleges of the National University as independent universities. However, recent developments suggest that the status and statutory position of the NIHEs themselves may soon be altered. For a number of years spokespersons for the NIHEs have sought university status. In 1986, the Minister for Education set up an international study group on technological education to examine the arrangements for technological education outside the universities and to consider the case for a technological university of which the two NIHEs would be constituent colleges. This study group, which was set up under the auspices of the HEA, has presented its report to the Minister, and while the recommendations have not yet been published, it is widely assumed that it will recommend the granting of university status. If such a recommendation is made and if it is accepted by government, it is likely that it will require legislation.

Non-HEA designated colleges

Perhaps the most striking anomaly in the administrative structure of Irish higher education is that the HEA does not have any executive role with respect to a large segment of the higher education system. The colleges of education, with the exception of Thomond College, have not been designated under the Act. Neither the long-established technological colleges nor the newly established regional technical colleges (RTCs) have been designated. Thus, while the HEA has an advisory and planning role with respect to the whole of higher education, its executive role is limited to those colleges which enrolled 59 per cent of all full-time students in 1985. When the Commission on Higher Education recommended the establishment of an administrative and planning body, it is clear that it envisaged that all third-level colleges would come within the scope of this new body.

The rationale behind the pattern of designation and non-designation is unclear. The only college of education to have been designated is the only one in public control. The other eight colleges are private colleges owned by religious authorities. On the other hand, the technological colleges and the regional technical colleges are publicly owned, they are administered by a board of management which operates as a subcommittee of the local vocational educational committee. One interpretation of the failure to designate these colleges under the HEA is that it provides for the incorporation of a more direct role in higher education by the Churches and by local authorities. However, perhaps a more realistic interpretation of the decision not to designate these colleges is that it retains for the state a high degree of control over the work of these colleges. The consequences of this state control is well illustrated by a comparison between the 1986 government decision to discontinue teacher education in Carysfort College and the 1968 government decision to merge UCD and TCD. The government decision in relation to Carysfort was implemented notwithstanding staunch resistance. In contrast, in the case of the university merger proposals, the government failed to implement its decision in the face of institutional resistance and the advice of the buffer agency.

Whatever the rationale for the distinction between designated and non-designated colleges, it is evident that the present structure is perceived by many as being anomalous. In particular, many of those who work in the non-designated colleges would wish to be brought within the ambit of the HEA. For example, Corr has argued that:

> the present fragmentary approach to the co-ordination of third-level education whereby one set of institutions is funded and co-ordinated under the HEA, while another group of Colleges catering for more than 30 per cent of all third-level students is suspended in mid-air somewhere between the Department of Education, the VECs and the NCEA, will have to end.[27]

There is, of course, a compelling logic behind such calls for a unitary planning and administrative structure. However, at least as far as the technological colleges are concerned, the more pressing incentive behind seeking such a change is to escape from the 'vice-grip of the Department' of Education which controls them 'with detailed rules and regulations more appropriate to second-level schools'.[28]

Possible changes in the management structure of the RTCs and other technological colleges have been suggested in a Green Paper, *Partners in education* (1985). The suggested changes for the RTCs and the Limerick College of Art, Commerce and Technology,

involve making the boards of management larger and more
representative, and more independent of the vocational education
committees. Thus the proposed increase in autonomy will be at
the expense of the VECs, although the colleges will retain some
links with the VECs. However, there is no suggestion that they
will be subject to less control by the Department of Education and
it is not envisaged that they be designated under the HEA. In the
case of the Dublin Institute of Technology it is suggested that it
be constituted as an independent institution by legislation, although
no final recommendation has been made as to whether it should
be designated under the HEA.

Interdepartmental committee

The most recent government initiative in the control and
administration of higher education has been the establishment in
1988 of an interdepartmental committee to examine aspects of third-
level education. The committee consists of four senior civil servants
from the Department of Education and one each from the
Departments of Finance, Industry and Commerce, Labour,
Agriculture and Food, and Health together with the secretary of
the HEA. The committee has been asked to set out the priorities
which should guide policy in relation to third-level education and
to make recommendations with respect to:

> rationalisation and other cost-cutting policies;
> the funding of third-level education and research;
> the desirable level of overall higher education provision;
> decision-making procedures for determining desirable level of
> provision in particular disciplines; and
> alternative ways of providing additional places, if required.

It may be that the establishment of the committee is no more than
an exercise in crisis management in the context of the government's
acute fiscal difficulties. However, it does indicate a desire for
centralised and co-ordinated planning by government. What is
perhaps most significant about the establishment of the committee
is that the terms of reference constitute part of the general functions
assigned to the HEA in the Higher Education Authority Act, 1971.
This is the most emphatic indication to date that the government
does indeed wish to regain some of the power which it had devolved
to the HEA.

The Direction of Policy

It is clear from the foregoing discussion that the recommendations of the Commission on Higher Education were influential in the development of a planning authority for higher education. However, its recommendations were less influential in shaping the direction of policy. Specifically, the heavy emphasis on technology and the explicit vocationalism which characterised policy developments over the past two decades do not find their legitimation in the Commission's report. While expansion and diversification of the system were advocated by the Commission its recommendations was for the establishment of a new type of institution to be called 'the new college'. The new college would operate in three major fields – the humanistic, the scientific and the commercial – and would work up to the standard of a pass degree. While it was envisaged that the courses would have a 'stronger vocational bias than would be appropriate to university courses', it was suggested that they be 'planned to provide a broad and balanced education together with a certain measure of specialisation. The humanistic course, for example, would include scientific studies and the science course would contain an arts element'.[29]

It is evident from the description of the new college that its conceptualisation owes more to the university model than to the technical college model. Indeed it was suggested that each new college would be a separate entity with a government and administration of a university type. However, the proposals for the new colleges never seem to have been given serious consideration. Prior to the publication of the report the government had already decided to establish eight regional technical colleges. Although it was initially envisaged that these regional technical colleges would operate mainly at second level they quickly began to offer third-level courses. By 1977 a ninth regional college was added. These colleges began to enrol a significant proportion of all higher education students. The only other new institutional type to be established at third level – the National Institutes for Higher Education – were also firmly located within the technological sector. The Limerick NIHE opened in 1972 and the Dublin NIHE opened in 1980.

The preference for RTCs and NIHEs as opposed to the

Commission's new colleges reveals a distinct vocational emphasis in higher education policy. The different options reflect underlying differences as to the aims of higher education. Such differences become apparent if one compares the Commission's report with more recent government papers. Although, surprisingly, the Commission does not deal explicitly with the question of aims and objectives, it is possible to establish some of the thinking which lies behind the report. For example, the final paragraph of the report suggests: 'Higher education is a means by which individuals fulfil themselves. It is no less a precondition of social and economic progress.' A further insight on this question can be gleamed from the Commission's discussion of whether an expanded provision of higher education should be aimed at for the future. It lists a number of factors which suggest a positive answer: firstly, the demand for more places exists; secondly, national needs in the material sense of the country's requirements of skilled personnel; and thirdly, higher education should be considered a community asset for its own sake. In respect of the latter two factors, the Commission's views are worth quoting in some detail:

> Indeed it would be wrong to view our institutions of higher education, and particularly our universities, simply as professional academies for the training of various categories of skilled personnel; their functions as centres of learning and scholarship and liberal education should not be allowed to become overshadowed by the claims made upon them to provide the country with its requirements of skilled manpower. Likewise, the value of higher education for the community is not alone the content of expert knowledge which a modern community requires to have at its service. Irrespective of service to these needs, higher education must be looked upon as a good in itself, as an intrinsic asset that confers a particular benefit on the community as well as on the individual. The kind of society into which we are moving calls not only for greater numbers of skilled persons but also for an educated community capable of achieving and sustaining the higher purposes of that society in its own life and in its relationship with other peoples.[30]

It is clear, however, that more utilitarian considerations have become paramount in determining policy since the late 1960s. The tenor of this policy emerges unambiguously in two important government reports: the *White Paper on educational development* (1980) and the *Programme for action in education 1984–1987*. In both documents it is assumed that vocational preparation is the prime purpose of higher education and that the main justification for state expenditure on higher education is its contribution to technological development and economic growth. In the White Paper, the government clearly indicates that its priority objectives for third-level education are those which will assist national development. In a similar vein the *Programme for action* states:

> Priority of financial support will be given to those academic developments . . . which are geared to developments in modern society . . . As a corollary, it is to be expected that some courses could be phased out.[31]

The narrow utilitarianism exemplified in these statements of government policy has not gone unchallenged. For example, Lee notes that the chapter on third-level education in the White Paper fails to make a solitary mention of the significance of the quality of social thought, or indeed of any thought, for the well being of society.[32] He has subsequently expanded on this distortion in policy when he suggests that the quality of human resources is a function of the general cultural coherence of a society. He suggests that the main problems confronting this country, including the economic problems, are not essentially economic or technological in their provenance at all: they are primarily political and sociological.[33] The policy emphasis in the *Programme for action* has also been criticised. The Irish Federation of University Teachers noted that nowhere in the chapter on third-level education is there 'any mention of personal development and cultural enrichment, . . . or any recognition that the purpose of economic growth is the improvement of the quality of life in more than a material sense'.[34]

Expansion of technological sector

Whatever the extent of individual reservations may have been, it was not sufficient to check the utilitarian policy emphasis which shaped the rapidly expanding system. The strong vocational emphasis was accomplished by a number of incremental decisions of which, perhaps, the most consequential were the endorsement of a binary structure and the decision to provide for short-cycle higher education courses. By the mid-1960s, when the future structure of higher education was being planned, Ireland already had a binary structure. However, at this stage the non-university sector was but a minor partner and within this sector in 1965/66 the vocational technological colleges catered for less than 5 per cent of full-time students attending state-aided institutions. This was the sector which was to experience the most spectacular growth in the 1970s. Five regional technical colleges were established in 1970 and four more were established between 1971 and 1977. These new colleges, although administered by the vocational education committees, were designed and controlled directly by the Department of Education. With such a high degree of state control it was possible to mould these institutions in a manner which was designed to meet perceived 'national needs'. The brief given to these colleges was elaborated by the Steering Committee on Technical Education in 1969:

> We believe that the main long-term function of the Colleges will be to educate for trade and industry over a broad spectrum of occupations ranging from craft to professional level, notably in engineering and science, but also in commercial, linguistic and other specialities. They will, however, be more immediately concerned with providing courses aimed at filling gaps in the industrial manpower structure, particularly in the technician area.[35]

It was originally envisaged that these colleges would cater primarily for senior cycle second-level courses with a technological orientation, in addition to their involvement in apprenticeship training, together with some third-level courses. However, the colleges quickly shed almost all the second-level teaching and began to concentrate on the provision of third-level courses in engineering and construction studies, business studies, applied science, and art and design. In addition to their strong vocational emphasis, the RTCs' courses are also distinctive in that they are short-cycle or mainly sub-degree-level courses. The majority of courses are of two-year duration leading to the national certificate awarded by the National Council for Educational Awards. There are, in addition, some one-year certificate courses, a significant number of three-year courses leading to a national diploma, and a small number of four-year degree-level courses.

Concurrently with the development and rapid expansion of the new RTCs the enrolments in the five colleges of the Dublin Institute of Technology also expanded. In addition the Limerick College of Art, Commerce and Technology developed rapidly. Taken together these fifteen technological colleges in 1985 catered for 34 per cent of all full-time higher education students.[36] And since these colleges specialise in short-cycle courses, their significance is even greater if we look at the flow of new entrants rather than at aggregate enrolments. In 1986 48 per cent of new entrants to higher education enrolled in these colleges.[37] This emphatic trend towards an increase in the percentage of total higher education enrolments attending colleges of technology is likely to continue. Five new RTCs have been promised by government and although the development of these colleges has been postponed, present policy suggests that any additional colleges which are developed will also follow the RTC model.

In view of this radical transformation in the structure of higher education, it is of interest to compare the distribution of students by course level in Ireland with that of other Western European countries. Table 2 uses UNESCO classification categories which were developed for this purpose, differentiating between sub-degree-level courses (level 5), degree-level courses (level 6), and post-graduate courses (level 7). A striking feature of this table is that with the exception of The Netherlands, Ireland has the largest proportion of its higher education students taking sub-degree level courses. While the Netherlands has 59 per cent of its students pursuing courses at this level, Ireland has 39 per cent, significantly greater than the other countries in the table which range from 29 per cent for the UK to less than 3 per cent for Italy. It is clear that from a comparative perspective, the system of higher education in Ireland is now distinguished by the high proportion of sub-degree-level courses which it offers.

The vocational emphasis in higher education policy is not confined to its impact on the development of the technological colleges. It was also the driving force behind the establishment of the National Institutes for Higher Education and has also influenced course provision in the universities. The initial impetus behind the establishment of the NIHE came from the campaign to establish a university at Limerick. This demand was rejected by the Commission on Higher Education which recommended that

TABLE 2

Percentage Distribution of Third-Level Students
by Programme Level for some European Countries

	LEVEL 5	LEVEL 6	LEVEL 7 Post-
	Sub-degree	Degree	graduate
Ireland (1981)	39.2	52.2	8.6
Denmark (1982)	24.9	75.1	—[a]
France (1982)	16.1	71.5	12.4
Germany (1982)	14.7	83.9	1.4
Greece (1980)	29.2	70.8	—[a]
Italy (1983)	2.6	92.3	5.1
Netherlands (1982)	59.1	40.9	—[a]
Portugal (1981)	10.0	89.5	0.5
Spain (1982)	29.3	58.6	—[a]
UK (1981)	29.3	58.6	12.1

Note: [a]Combined with level 6.
Source: UNESCO statistical yearbook 1985.

a new college be sited there. The Limerick claim for a university
was subsequently referred by the Minister for Education for the
consideration of the newly established Higher Education Authority.
The HEA supported the views of the Commission that 'there is
no national need at present for another university college'.
However, it did recognise another national need, observing that
Ireland was 'to a great extent lacking in a new and increasingly
important form of higher education of which the primary purpose
is the application of scientific knowledge and method'.
Technological education, it argued, had not yet found its proper
level; its content needed to be further upgraded and the scope of
its operation extended. Furthermore, it suggested that technological
and higher technical roles needed to become 'status carrying in
their own right'.[38]

The HEA was impressed by the success of the polytechnics in
Britain and saw this as offering a model for a college of higher
education which would meet both national and local needs. The
new college would combine the 'prestige of degree granting courses
with an extensive provision of certificate and diploma courses'.

From its inception it was envisaged that the new college (to become known as National Institute for Higher Education) would offer courses at a higher level than the RTCs. However, like the RTCs, it has also experienced 'academic drift' and now operates primarily at degree level; in addition, it offers some post-graduate courses up to and including doctorates. Indeed, when the second NIHE opened in Dublin in 1980 it did not offer any sub-degree-level courses. Of the 1,218 students attending the NIHEs in 1985, 36 per cent were pursuing courses in commerce, 31 per cent courses in engineering and a further 9 per cent courses in science, while the remaining 24 per cent were divided among communication and information studies, European studies, art and design, and education.[39]

Like the RTCs, the development of the NIHEs has had an important effect on the shape of Irish higher education. In offering courses at degree and post-graduate level and, with the cultivation of a high media profile, the National Institutes have ensured that technological education is now 'status conferring' as the HEA report felt was necessary. This sensitivity to the prestige function is reflected even in a concern with nomenclature; the directors of the NIHEs have become presidents and some of the senior staff have been given the title of professor. However, it is clear that the success of the NIHEs does not hinge on such tangential considerations. Their graduates, especially in technology, have found ready employment and the strength of client demand for places testifies to the perceived value of their courses. Not surprisingly, the leaders of the NIHEs have emerged as forceful spokespersons for the technological reorientation of Irish higher education. At a recent conference the president of NIHE, Limerick argued that for the foreseeable future the role of the HEA will be the redeployment of resources so as to achieve excellence in areas of strategic importance to the state. He went on to advocate that a priority be given to the new technologies:

> Like it or not, an enthusiastic embrace of the new technologies is the only gesture which will sustain Ireland's economic development. It constantly surprises me that these technologies tend to be treated in such a dismissive way by many traditional Irish educationalists. Can it represent a defensive mechanism arising from a narrow, rather than a liberal, education, which

has provided no foundation for a comprehension of the new technologies? Too often it appears that the new technologies are seen as associated with some inferior intellectual process rather than representing, as I have no doubt they do, the most dramatic manifestation of the capabilities of the human intellect in its upward spiral of evolution.[40]

The increased vocational emphasis in higher education has also affected developments within the universities. One example of the universities' adaptation to vocational imperatives can be found in their willingness to incorporate as recognised colleges the colleges of education which cater for primary teachers and home economics teachers. Similarly, the education of physio-therapists, speech-therapists and more recently that of occupational-therapists have all been integrated into the universities.

However, the universities themselves have also changed and this is reflected in the distribution of students by field of study. In a climate which emphasises a technological orientation and vocational relevance, the universities have been most anxious to develop their engineering, science and business studies programmes. In 1985, 29 per cent of all full-time university students were in the faculties of science and engineering. In contrast, in 1950 only 19 per cent of all students were in these faculties.[41] There has also been a huge growth in student enrolments in commerce and business studies. For example, in the three constituent colleges of the National University in 1985, 12 per cent of all full-time students were in the faculty of Commerce while 13 per cent of full-time enrolments in TCD were in the faculty of Economic and Social Studies. Twenty-five years earlier fewer than 5 per cent of all full-time students in these four colleges were studying commerce or business studies. The strengthening of these faculties represents a gradual evolution of the university's vocational emphasis and, in general, occurred without conflict. Objections arose only when it was perceived that continued development in this direction might only be possible at the expense of the humanities and other 'non-vocational' programmes. The arts faculties in particular have felt themselves under siege and, belatedly, have begun a rearguard action to justify their relevance.

Papers by UCD President Masterson (1983) and by UCC Vice-President Lee (1983) present a strong justification for the continued relevance of the arts degree in an age of rapid technological change.[42] Both authors have addressed the cultural condition of contemporary Ireland. Masterson has identified the problems of 'uprootedness' and 'cultural vertigo' while Lee has pointed out that a people 'who seem to have little else to define a collective identity, inevitably finds that the fetish of technology as ideology, as distinct from technology as technique, threatens whatever little individuality is left'. Both authors assign to the university and particularly to the humanities and social sciences a responsibility to attend to the cultural problem. For example, Masterson argues:

> one of the principal justifications of a university Arts programme is that it provides an indispensable institutional context for the community to achieve a critical and liberating perspective upon this challenge posed to traditional culture by the impact of science and technology.[43]

Policy reorientation in perspective

The previous section has attempted to document the increased utilitarian emphasis which has shaped higher education policy over the past two decades. This policy has been orchestrated primarily by the state. The principal strategy chosen to effect this policy reorientation was to establish new colleges which were more directly controlled by the Department of Education. Taken together, the nine new RTCs and the two new NIHEs catered for 25 per cent of total higher education enrolments in 1983. These new colleges were given an explicit mandate to develop courses which would cater for the labour force needs of an expanding industrial economy. The main alternative strategy, that of a unitary system, best exemplified by the higher education systems of Sweden and Italy, might have been less amenable to such a reorientation of policy. If a unitary strategy was to be successful, it would have required an explicit acceptance of such a policy change by the then dominant and largely autonomous university sector. Indeed, briefly during the mid-1970s there was an indication that the government was going to develop a unitary higher education policy. In 1974, the Minister for Education, Richard Burke, announced that in future all degrees were to be awarded by the universities while the NCEA was to be confined to certificate- and diploma-level work.

This would have required the NIHEs, NCAD, Thomond College and some of the technological colleges to develop close links with the universities. However, the decision was reversed by the Fianna Fáil government when they returned to office in 1977. The NCEA degree-awarding function was restored, thus firmly institutionalising the binary structure.

In choosing the binary option and in targeting the technological sector for more rapid growth, the government has followed a pattern which has found favour in most other European countries. Indeed, the Irish experience fits well into the general sequence of strategies identified by Scott.[44] The first strategy is the 'trust the institution/faculty/department approach'. This involves letting the college or constituent unit within the college make its own judgement about what it can do well and about which of its activities need to be pampered or rationed and which can be provided more cheaply and made accessible to a mass constituency. With this strategy the state provides financial support but exercises what amounts to what Neave describes as a 'self-denying ordinance of non-intervention'.[45] This would seem to describe appropriately the relationship between the universities and the Irish state up to the mid-1960s. The second strategy identified by Scott is to divide national systems of higher education into distinct categories of institutions and to assign to each category a different function. This has clearly been the dominant strategy during the past two decades in Ireland. The Irish experience also demonstrates some of the problems associated with this stratification of higher education. It has, as Scott suggests, stimulated academic drift where such drift is tolerated and academic envy where it is not.

In identifying a third strategy, Scott suggests that we may now be on the verge of a new change when rather crude institutional stratification is replaced by much finer-grained programmatic discrimination. With this third strategy 'national ministries or coordinating agencies begin not only to exercise a much more detailed supervison of higher education systems but also to steer the system in a much more positive and direct way through special programmes'. Scott cites recent examples in Britain such as the special fund established by the government for its information technology initiative and the UGC's programme to establish 'new blood' lecturing posts. In both instances institutions have to compete for money which has been earmarked for special purposes which are not 'the product of any organic academic process but of deliberate political decisions'.[46] It would appear that this is also the strategy which is at present most favoured in Ireland. An example of the use of this strategy was the provision of special funds in 1979/80 to increase as a matter of urgency the output of engineers and computer personnel. An example of a more sustained use of the strategy can be found in the funding of research. It was evident from the orientation of the National Board for Science and Technology that its commitment to stimulate disinterested science was secondary to its commitment to applied research which was perceived as being of strategic importance for national economic growth.

The sequence of strategies identified by Scott reveals a process of progressive intervention by the state. The prevalence of this third strategy in recent years has been documented by Neave in his review of developments in Western Europe's system between 1975 and 1985. Neave concludes that 'what is unprecedented is the degree of penetration, direction and extent to which government policy is now engaged in profiling − and thus determining − the disciplinary dynamic inside higher education'.[47] This intervention can take either a positive or negative form. In its positive form, inducements are offered to encourage the provision of certain courses; in its negative form, it involves budgetary squeezing, differential reductions in funding and in academic staff in those fields or disciplines believed to be less relevant to national needs.

The many parallels between the Irish development pattern and that of other Western European countries point to similarities in the social, economic and political environment within which the different national higher education systems evolved. All European countries experienced rapid growth and technological change during the 1950s and 1960s. Paralleling the economic growth of the 1960s, the political climate supported an expansionist ideology in the interests of achieving greater equality of opportunity. The happy coincidence of economic and political objectives ensured the generous funding of education. In turn the economic recession of the mid-1970s, which deepened further in the 1980s, has led to the decline of the welfare state. In a climate of fiscal stringency claims for expenditure on higher education have to compete with claims for the support of other services such as health and social welfare. The most persuasive claims are those which purport to offer a solution to the country's economic ills.

In a context of growing international competition and a greatly accelerated rate of technological change it was increasingly recognised that higher education occupied a crucial location as the knowledge base, the quality of which would ultimately determine the success of national industrial strategy. Thus, the stimulation of higher technological education became part of the national planning process. On a symbolic level, as Neave has suggested,[48] the university came to be regarded as a surrogate for national economic performance. In addition to the similar problems which confronted politicians, educational administrators and planners, recent decades have witnessed an unprecedented degree of international consultation and deliberation on these common problems. The work of such international agencies as the OECD has been especially influential in developing a consensus in dealing with these common problems.

However, apart from these parallels in the external environment within which educational systems operate, there are, in addition, common internal system dynamics which carry their own imperatives in moulding higher education systems. Mass higher education systems can never be merely elite versions of the same writ large. A recognition of this fact is of course at the heart of Trow's typology. Quantitative change implies qualitative change. Neave has argued that one outcome of the expansion in the size of the system is the emergence of additional bodies to control, monitor and hold accountable a sector of increasing significance in government social expenditure. Such intermediary agencies, he argues, stand as a response to the advent of mass higher education, not an anticipation of it.[49]

Another almost inevitable outcome of system expansion arises in the area of graduate employment. At the elite stage when higher education systems were essentially university systems, the majority of their graduates entered the liberal professions and the state bureaucracy. Even during the initial period of rapid expansion in the 1960s the fast-growing public sector continued to provide employment opportunities for graduates. For example, in the mid-1960s it has been estimated that 40 per cent of British higher education graduates went back into the education system in one form or another.[50] However, this could only be a once-off experience. Even if Western economies were not to experience the recession of the 1970s, the public sector could not have continued to absorb all higher education graduates. Thus, it was inevitable that in all countries where higher education systems had expanded into mass systems they would have had to begin to target an increasing proportion of their graduates towards private sector industry and commerce. Thus, part of the vocational emphasis is a direct function of the expansion of the system.

Whether the increased vocational emphasis of higher education systems is best explained by the internal dynamics of the expanding system, or by the changing external socio-economic environment, it is clear that the concept of higher education as 'human capital creation' has been modified significantly in recent years. During the 1960s the findings of human capital economics seemed to apply to all subjects across the board. The rate of return to the study of literature was as high as those for engineering and accountancy. What seemed to matter was the level of education achieved rather than the subject studied.

> The effects of this belief in Western Europe and North America were profound. It meant that the overall provision of places in higher education could in general be based on the so-called social demand from individual students and the pattern of subjects offered them could be determined by the apparent logic of intellectual developments as perceived by exponents of the various academic disciplines.[51]

All this changed when the graduate job market deteriorated in the 1970s. Quite suddenly qualifications in subjects, such as literature and history, which had been implicitly vocational while there were plenty of teaching jobs available, ceased to have value in the job market. In addition, employers began to be more selective about the type of qualifications they considered suitable to particular job. Thus, graduates with qualifications in what were seen to be relevant subjects began to find it much easier to obtain employment than graduates with less specific skills. It was in this climate that higher education planners and students alike began to give priority to subject areas which appear to offer skills that are immediately applicable in the job market.

It is important to place the discussion on the direction of Irish higher education policy in a comparative framework. It is all too easy for academics and educational analysts to see the new vocationalism in higher education as a monstrous policy aberration.

It should be recalled that in the first instance universities developed in a vocational mould, being built around the professional faculties of law, medicine and theology. Even in their more recent 'golden era', when their cultural mission had been more pronounced, this was never their exclusive remit. Vocational and cultural objectives have always coexisted. Furthermore, it is inevitable that as societies change, the demands made on higher education systems will also change. In addition, as has been argued, the proccess of quantitative change generates qualitative change. The Irish higher education system of the 1980s is a very much larger, more diverse and complex system than that which existed in the 1960s. This diversification implies that it seeks to fulfil a multiplicity of objectives. Perhaps the major dilemma which faces higher education planners is whether this goal enlargement can be achieved without goal displacement. Is it possible to sustain the legitimacy of traditional objectives while also establishing the legitimacy of new objectives?

The achievement of this balance is, of course, especially difficult at a time of acute scarcity of resources. Protagonists in this struggle for legitimacy and for resources are tempted to attack the other side in an attempt to boost their own case. The plea to reduce radically the size of the intake into the university arts faculties to facilitate the expansion of places in engineering faculties has been made in recent years in Ireland.[52] And while this specific advice has not been heeded it would appear that the balance has swung decisively in favour of the technocratic and the utilitarian at the expense of the cultural paradigm.

Neave's incisive analysis of policy in Western Europe aptly describes the present position in Ireland. He notes the tendency to abandon that part of higher education given over to 'honing the political, social and cultural sensibilities and values that go to make up the nation's identities and the place of free moral beings as citizens of that nation'.[53] This critique of present policy does not imply a repudiation of instrumental and vocational concerns. What is being suggested is that goal enlargement ought not to lead to goal displacement. The real potential of diversification in higher education systems is to make possible the simultaneous pursuit of multiple objectives. Higher education institutions are custodians, evaluators and renewers of society's culture, traditions and values. They are no less the creators of the technological knowledge base which is necessary for the achievement of economic growth in the late twentieth century. It is a mistake to view these objectives as mutually exclusive. Indeed, as some of our more perceptive commentators have argued, they are mutually reinforcing. Furthermore the successful achievement of short-term priorities is not possible without simultaneous concern for longer-term needs.

Conclusion

The analysis of the evolution of policy in Irish higher education in this chapter has been limited to a narrow range of issues. Two major questions have been examined. In analysing the evolution of the control and administrative structure, the main focus was on the issue of state control versus institutional autonomy. The analysis of the direction of policy centred on the trend towards vocationalism. Two trends have occurred concurrently. The growing utilitarianism in policy has been achieved by a progressive process of state intervention. The final section of the paper has attempted to provide a perspective within which these policy developments can be understood. It has demonstrated that, in general, the Irish experience parallels the experience in other Western European countries, although some aspects of Irish higher education policy are unique. Specifically, it could be argued that in Ireland over the past two decades the provision of higher education has been supply-led rather than demand-led. The huge growth in the non-university short-cycle sector reflects more the decisions of government than the nature of client demand.

Many important developments and policy issues have not been addressed in this chapter. For example, there has been no examination of the establishment and operation of the National Council for Educational Awards which validates the awards granted by the NIHEs, the RTCs, the vocational technological colleges, the NCAD and Thomond College. Neither has there been any consideration of the transformation of the colleges of education into degree-granting recognised colleges of the universities. A major policy issue which has not been examined is the question of equality of educational opportunity. The social, geographical and gender dimensions of this question have been the concern of many policy initiatives. An assessment of the impact of student support schemes and fees policy is most pertinent in relation to social equality. The effect of regionalisation of third-level institutions is crucial in any assessment of geographical equality. An important dimension of gender equality involves an analysis of the distribution of students by field of study. Data pertinent to each of these issues has been assembled elsewhere.[54] However, the long list of issues that require evaluation signals to the large harvest which awaits policy analysts in Irish higher education.

Notes to Chapter 4

1. E. G. Edwards, 'An analytical view of trends in student enrolents in Western Europe' in *Higher education in Europe* (1891) Vol 6, No 3, pp. 44-66.
2. M. Trow, 'Comparative perspectives on access' in O. Fulton (ed), *Access*

to higher education Guildford: Society for Research into Higher Education, 1981, pp. 89-121.

3. M. Trow, 'Problems in the transition from elite to mass higher education' in *Policies for higher education* Paris: OECD, 1974, pp. 61-62.

4. P. Clancy, *Who goes to college? a second national survey of participation in higher education* Dublin: Higher Education Authority, 1988.

5. See J. Coolahan, *Irish education: history and structure* Dublin: Institute of Public Administration and 'Third level education in modern Ireland: an overview' in *Social Studies* Vol 7, No 3, pp. 163-77.

6. D. Goldschmidt, 'Systems of higher education', in J. H. Van de Graaft et al (eds), *Academic power: patterns of authority in seven national systems of higher education* New York: Praeger (1978): R. Premfors, *The politics of higher education in a comparative perspective: France, Sweden, United Kingdom* Stockholm, University of Stockholm, 1980.

7. G. C. Moodie and R. Eustace, *Power and authority in British universities*, London: Allen & Unwin, 1974.

8. B. Clark, *The higher education system: academic organisation in cross-national perspective* Berkeley: University of California Press, 1983.

9. Commission on Higher Education, *Report of the Commission on Higher Education 1960−1967* Dublin: Stationery Office, p. xxviii.

10. *Ibid*, pp. 467-72.

11. Clark, *Higher education*, p. 172.

12. HEA, *Progress report 1974* Dublin: Higher Education Authority, 1974, p. 4.

13. HEA, *First report 1968−1969* Dublin: Higher Education Authority.

14. D. O'Laoghaire, 1983 'Buffer organisations', paper presented at OECD Workshop, 'Higher education institutions and government: current relations and outlook', Paris: April 1983.

15. HEA, *Report on university reorganisation* Dublin: Higher Education Authority, 1972, p. 59.

16. T. Murphy, 'Higher education: the changing scene' in A. T. McKenna (ed), *Higher Education: relevance and future* Dublin: HEA, 1985.

17. S. O'Cathail, 'Ireland: the university and the state', *Cre-information* No 58 (1982), 2, pp. 44-55.

18. M. Tierney, 'The future of university autonomy', *Studies* (1970), Vol LIX, Autumn, pp. 227-238.

19. O'Cathail, 'University and state', p. 51.

20. O'Laoghaire, 'Buffer organisations'.

21. *White Paper on educational development* Dublin: Stationery Office, 1980.

22. HEA, *Progress report 1974−1984*, Dublin: Higher Education Authority, 1985, p. 77.

23. HEA, *Progress report 1974* p.6.

24. J. Hayden, 'Planning and financing at third-level', *Social Studies* Vol 7, No 2, pp. 178-187.

25. O'Laoghaire, 'Buffer organisations'.

26. B. McCartan, 'The HEA four year plan: an overview' in *University planning and financing* Dublin: Irish Federation of University Teachers, 1982.

27. J. G. Corr, 'The technological colleges: agents for change' in A. T. McKenna (ed), *Higher education: relevance and future* Dublin: HEA, 1985.

28. Corr, 'Technological colleges', p. 65. Calls for a unitary structure are discussed in Hayden, 'Planning and financing' and HEA, *Progress Report 1974–1984.*

29. Commission on Higher Education, *Report 1960–1967* pp. 127-28.

30. *Ibid* p. 118

31. *Programme for action in education 1984–1987* Dublin: Stationery Office, p. 27.

32. J. Lee, 'Culture and society', in F. Litton (ed), *Unequal achievement: the Irish experience 1957–1982* Dublin: Institute of Public Administration, 1982.

33. J. Lee, 'University, state and society in Ireland', *The Crane Bag* (1983) Vol 7, No 2, pp. 5-12.

34. Irish Federation of University Teachers, *Programme for action in education: The IFUT response* Dublin: Irish Federation of University Teachers, 1984, p. 2

35. *Report of the Steering Committee on Technical Education* Dublin: Stationery Office, 1969, p. 11.

36. HEA, Accounts 1985 and 1986 and student statistics 1985/86, Dublin: Higher Education Authority, 1987.

37. Clancy, 'Who goes to college?' pp. 12-13.

38. HEA, *A council of national awards and a college of higher education at Limerick* Dublin: Higher Education Authority, 1969, p. 9.

39. HEA, *Student statistics 1985/86.*

40. E. M. Walsh, 'The higher education business – responding to market' in A. T. McKenna (ed) *Higher education: relevance and future* Dublin: Higher Education Authority, 1985.

41. *Statistical abstract of Ireland* Dublin: Stationery Office, 1950.

42. P. Masterson, 'The arts degree in an age of science and technology' in *The Crane Bag* (1983), Vol 7, No 2; J. Lee, 'Culture and Society'.

43. Masterson, 'The arts degree', p. 36.

44. P. Scott, 'Higher education: the next twenty years', *International Journal of Institutional Management in Higher Education* (1985), Vol 9, No 2, pp. 195-207.

45. G. Neave, 'The changing boundary between the state and higher education', in *European Journal of Education* (1982), Vol 17, No 3, pp. 231-241.

46. Scott, 'Next twenty years', p. 205.

47. G. Neave, 'Higher education in a period of consolidation 1975–1985', in *European Journal of Education* (1985), Vol 20, Nos 2-3, pp. 109-124.

48. *Ibid* p. 118.

49. *Ibid* p. 114.

50. G. L. Williams, T. A. V. Blackstone and D. H. Metcalfe, *The academic labour market* Amsterdam: Elsevier, 1974.

51. G. Williams, 'Graduate employment and vocationalism in higher education' in *European Journal of Education* (1985), Vol 20, No 2-3, p. 183.

52. L. Connellan, Report of paper given at careers symposium, *The Irish Times* 13 November 1979.

53. Neave, 'Consolidation', p. 120.

54. P. Clancy, *Participation in higher education: a national survey* Dublin: Higher Education Authority, 1982; and, 'Who goes to college?'.

5

The Involvement and Impact of a Professional Interest Group

DAVID BARRY

In this chapter the focus of attention shifts to a consideration of the impact on both the process of policy making and the content of policy of a teachers' union, The Association of Secondary Teachers, Ireland (ASTI). The chapter concerns itself with the period from the mid-1960s to the present and in particular with the attempts of government to restructure secondary education during that period and the attempts of a professional interest group to reshape it in accordance with its interests. In order to understand the developments of that period, it is necessary to outline the situation from which they emerged.

Background

The ASTI was founded in 1909 as an association for lay secondary teachers working in secondary schools. By this date secondary education in Ireland had developed certain characteristics which were to remain virtually unchanged up to the 1960s. Secondary schools were private in the sense that they were owned and managed by private groups and individuals. Their private nature was not lessened by an element of public funding, whether through results fees in the nineteenth century or by means of capitation grants on the establishment of the Irish Free State, as the state did not demand any control or involvement in the policy-making process as a *quid pro quo* prior to the mid-1960s. This to some extent was due to the second major characteristic of secondary schools, their denominational character. The vast majority of secondary schools were Catholic diocesan colleges, schools owned by Catholic religious orders, and colleges run by the Protestant denominations, and state reluctance to interfere in an area regarded by the Church as its own was a marked feature of the period prior to the mid-1960s.[1] Such policy issues as the building of new schools, pupil selection, school fees, disciplinary policies, and appointments to teaching positions were matters for the religious order or managerial authority concerned. Professor T. M. O'Sullivan, Minister for Education, in 1928 described the system as 'a mixture of cooperation, of voluntary effort and State support'[2] and his successors continued to uphold this arrangement. Only in the area of curriculum did the state involve itself in the policy-making process. In this area, school authorities had little influence, as the curriculum was determined by the programmes developed for assessment by the state examinations, a tradition that began in the period between 1878 and 1922 when state funding itself depended on the results of examinations set by the Intermediate Education Board. This indirect, yet virtually total control of curriculum by the state was acceptable to the private school authorities because both the Catholic Church and the state saw secondary education in terms of a classical humanist curriculum, and because the state, in the words of General Mulcahy, Minister for Education in 1948-51 and 1954-57, 'unreservedly accepted the supernatural conception of man's nature and destiny.'[3]

ASTI influence prior to the 1960s

In the first fifty years of its existence, most of the energy of the ASTI had been directed at improving the salary, the working conditions, the professional status and security of employment of its members within the private denominational religious-controlled system. The ASTI did not attempt to change either the private nature of secondary schools, their denominational character, or their control by religious orders. Many ASTI presidents in their annual addresses supported vehemently the private nature of secondary schools and warned against state encroachment.[4] To some extent this satisfaction with the private system was due to the ASTI achieving some of its major objectives (for example a superannuation scheme, formal contracts and an appeals procedure)[5] while operating within the state-supported private system. Failure to achieve these objectives might well have led to the ASTI becoming disenchanted with the private system and seeking greater protection from the state. The establishment of a public second-level sector in the form of vocational schools from 1930 on did not lessen ASTI support for the secondary sector; prior to the 1960s, secondary and vocational schools were regarded as offering different forms of education. The ASTI can be seen as reflecting the view of Irish society that secondary education was an area for the Church rather than for the state. Despite the fact that the ASTI was accepted by the religious authorities as the official voice of lay secondary teachers, its influence on the internal policies of schools or religious orders was limited by the fact that, prior to 1960, religious teachers outnumbered lay teachers in secondary schools.

Likewise, in the area of curriculum, the ASTI did not have a major influence. It had some involvement, for example representation on the Dáil Commission on Secondary Education in 1921 and representation on the standardising committees which were established in 1929 to advise on the examination papers of the state examinations. But its influence was limited owing to the centralised nature of state control of the curriculum. Its participation in this process was confined, in the main, to deputations to the Department of Education. In order to secure what it regarded as its rightful professional input, the ASTI pressed continually for the establishment of an advisory body representing educational interests to the government.[6] The fact that when the government did establish the Council of Education in 1950, the ASTI was not officially represented on it, is evidence of the failure of the ASTI to assert successfully its claims to be involved, as of right, in major educational decisions. Within the ranks of the ASTI the general satisfaction with the status quo must have lessened the energy with which it might have pursued its demand for influence. An examination of the reports of the educational committee of the ASTI shows that any requests for change were concerned with the minutiae of subject disciplines rather than with making a critical analysis of the curriculum as a whole. In its submission on the secondary curriculum to the Council of Education, the ASTI found the existing courses, the list of obligatory subjects and the number of optional subjects to be generally satisfactory.[7] The ASTI also agreed with the Council of Education's support for the existing examination system with some minor adjustments. The Council of Education report has been criticised for 'its highly defensive and conservative tone.'[8] The ASTI's virtually complete support for the existing situation renders these remarks applicable to it as well, and may well have contributed to its lack of influence in this area. As the developments of the 1960s and 1970s will show, the ASTI increased its influence when it disagreed with, and reacted actively to, government policies.

State Intervention

If continuity was the characteristic of the educational scene up to the mid-1960s, the period subsequent to that produced major changes and brought education to the forefront of public debate. Given the satisfaction of the ASTI and of the other interests in secondary education with the existing situation, as shown by the report of the Council of Education in 1962 and the various submissions to it, it is not surprising that the impetus for change came, not from these bodies, but from the state. The state adopted a more aggressive role in an attempt to provide equality of educational opportunity. The objectives of the state intervention were both social and economic; they resulted from a heightened awareness of developments in other countries and from Ireland's increased participation in international organisations, in particular the OECD Policy Conference on Economic Growth and Investment in Education in 1961.

Proposals for a common curriculum

Education was now seen as an economic investment and the ideal of equality of opportunity for all was stressed. Linked with the view of education as an economic investment was a growing demand for the provision of technical skills. These were the forces which produced a major press statement by the Minister for Education, Dr P. J. Hillery, on 20 May 1963.[9] He emphasised that some children were deprived of equality of educational opportunity because of the lack of either a secondary or vocational school in some areas of the country, but he aimed at much more than the building of extra schools.

Dr Hillery intended to mould the two disparate systems of education into a unified body. The fact that secondary and vocational schools were 'separate and distinct entities', Dr Hillery regarded as a 'structural weakness'. He did not attempt to abolish the vocational or secondary system, but aimed rather at eliminating some of their differences by changing the curriculum. A comprehensive curriculum and a common examination system were to be developed. The intermediate certificate course would be expanded to include practical subjects and the two-year courses in vocational schools would be extended to three, in order that their pupils could sit for the intemediate examination. Further proposals for the establishment of a technical schools leaving certificate and the provision of a number of regional technical colleges would ensure the higher technical education which was needed by Ireland on the threshold of industrial expansion. The Department of Education realised, however, that the division between the secondary and vocational systems would not disappear because of the announcement of a common curriculum and examination system and subsequently produced plans for structural reform.

Given the commitment of the ASTI to the private nature of secondary schools and the fact that the ASTI represented a single monolithic group — lay teachers working in secondary schools — it is not surprising that the main concern of the ASTI was to maintain the rights and working conditions of secondary teachers. Neither is it surprising that the ASTI viewed with suspicion the structural proposals of the Department of Education. These proposals, whose ostensible aim was to provide a comprehensive curriculum, were seen by many as being inspired by economic rather than curricular considerations.

The first structural change — the establishment of comprehensive schools — was proposed in 1963. Many other interventions followed, including rationalisation proposals, common enrolment, regionalisation proposals and, finally, the community school. In its consideration of these issues, the ASTI was concerned more with the welfare of its members than in helping to construct a system of schooling which would provide secondary education for all. Secondary teachers favoured the retention of the existing system of secondary schools with their individual management, absence of political involvement and high social regard.

The proposal to build comprehensive schools (included in Dr Hillery's press statement of 1963) attracted much attention because, as he rightly claimed, it introduced 'a new principle into Irish education, namely, direct State provision of a post-primary school building.'[10] Dr Hillery attempted to lessen the seeming threat to the existing school authorities which these comprehensive schools posed, by limiting their provision to areas where there were no secondary or vocational schools. Furthermore, the management structure adopted for these schools made it clear that they would tend to be denominational in character. The board of management was to consist of a representative of the local Catholic or Protestant bishop (in line with the denomination of the majority of the pupils of the school), a representative of the VEC and a representative of the Minister for Education. Dr Hillery's successor in Education, George Colley, also reassured existing school authorities that the comprehensive schools were not intended to replace the secondary or vocational system: rather they were 'a kind of pace-setter in post-primary education generally'.[11]

Given the influence of the ASTI in the community school debate a decade later, it is interesting to examine their influence on this first major proposal. The teachers' unions had not achieved the status of bodies which the government considered it had to consult prior to the decision. When the ASTI joined in a common statement with the Vocational Teachers Association (VTA) and the INTO deploring the lack of prior consultation, they received little satisfaction from the Minister who declared that 'there could be no question of submitting such matters to outside bodies, prior to their promulgation.'[12]

The ASTI achieved only limited success in comparison to their later negotiations on community schools, when they attempted to protect the position of secondary teachers who would be affected by these schools. They did not achieve the right of automatic transfer for teachers in a secondary school which closed as a direct result of the opening of Cootehill Comprehensive, but did win an assurance that the application of such teachers would be given precedence. When the ASTI queried the reservation of a post in Shannon Comprehensive for a clerical nominee who would not be restricted to teaching religious knowledge, they were informed that 'the Minister was not prepared to comment on the reasons for his decision in this regard.'[13]

The ASTI's influence had increased greatly by the time the debate on community schools began. This can be seen in the agreements made on the establishment of the comprehensive schools. In 1968 a viable secondary school, Crescent College, Limerick, became a comprehensive; and the Jesuits made a guarantee to the ASTI that the lay staff would be assimilated into the new school.[14] In 1972 the Department of Education agreed that the assimilated secondary teachers in Manorhamilton Comprehensive would have the conditions of their secondary school contracts honoured.

By the late 1960s, comprehensive schools had ceased to be a matter of major concern to the ASTI. Possible reasons included the expectation that they would be small in number and the fact that three of the first comprehensive schools absorbed vocational schools and were therefore more the concern of the VTA. Only one, Cootehill, absorbed members of the ASTI. A more important reason, however, was the initiation of the Colley rationalisation proposals which most teachers saw as far more threatening to the status quo.

Rationalisation proposals

In his early speeches, George Colley stressed the need to avoid duplication between secondary and vocational schools and emphasised the maximum use of existing facilities. But soon it became apparent that the Department aimed at a large-scale rationalisation of the existing school network into junior cycle and senior cycle schools. In a personal letter to the authorities of all post-primary schools, Mr Colley suggested that secondary and vocational school authorities in each locality should formulate proposals on the utilisation of existing accommodation and the provision of new facilities.[15] Later documentation prepared by the Development Branch of the Department of Education and based on the statistics of the OECD report *Investment in education* was more specific. It stated that each post-primary centre should offer both academic and technical subjects; and that 150 pupils were necessary for a viable junior school and 320-400 pupils for a viable senior school. Non-viable schools should close and their pupils should be transported to a viable centre. Regional conferences were to be convened to consider the use of existing resources, propose ad hoc arrangements and consider interchange of teachers or the employment of teachers to serve all the schools in the area.

The Minister did not seek the views of the ASTI. This lack of consultation indicated the union's position in the educational framework at that time. The ASTI merely received a copy of the letter as a matter of information. Not surprisingly, the Minister's letter sent alarm bells ringing in the ranks of the ASTI, as decisions reached at the regional conferences would have major implications for secondary teachers. Initially the Department of Education was not prepared to furnish the ASTI with reports of these meetings, and merely invited an observer from the union. ASTI pressure to correct this situation was successful. The Department agreed to furnish copies of the detailed county plans to the ASTI and the minister agreed to ASTI representation at the meetings.[16]

ASTI opposition to the rationalisation proposals was expressed quickly and forcefully. The kernel of its objections was the threat which the proposals posed to the private system of secondary education and to the working conditions of secondary teachers. The annual convention of the ASTI in 1966 resolved:

> that to guard the independence of secondary teachers, the ASTI under no circumstances agree to an arrangement that would entail a secondary teacher being compelled to teach partly in a secondary school and partly in a school which is not a recognised secondary school or to any other arrangement which might later be used to undermine the secondary teacher's independence of state control.[17]

While the president of the ASTI did accept the need for some rationalisation, in areas where a number of small schools were trying to survive, ASTI statements over the next few years were, in the main, highly critical of the Minister's intentions and aimed at mobilising parental opposition to the plan as well as that of secondary teachers. For the latter the ASTI raised the spectre of the closure of some secondary schools with possible redundancies and the likely disturbance for teachers who would have to move without financial compensation. To parents the ASTI emphasised the long school journeys that would face their children in the event of the two types of school being introduced. ASTI members in the west of Ireland were concerned with the social implications of the Department's proposals. They saw existing secondary schools as focal points of community consciousness and argued that the imposition of journeys of 25-30 miles on children meant taking them out of the community on which their lives were centred and into communities that had little meaning for them.[18] The ASTI was highlighting extreme but possible occurrences. These emotive examples were effective, however, given the tardiness of the Department in allaying fears. Also, the fact that secondary schools were independent of the Department in many aspects limited the latter's ability to give guarantees of redeployment. Another strand in the public opposition of the ASTI was the view by some, including the ASTI president in 1970, Michael Sheedy, that there were essential differences in kind, in teaching techniques and in requirements 'between vocational or technical education and secondary or academic education.'[19] This view was in complete conflict with the government's objective of creating a unified system. A major criticism by the ASTI of the rationalisation proposals was that they proposed the creation of two distinct types of school, one offering a longer cycle of schooling than the other. The senior school would attract the best teachers and parental support, thus hastening the decline of the smaller school. This problem would be solved if pupils could be allocated to the various schools by a central body, but the Department of Education had not the power to effect such a drastic change. The principle of parental choice was one which all the Churches regarded as extremely important, even if the choice for many parents was extremely limited.

Common enrolment

The Department of Education made a proposal in 1967 to overcome the difficulties involved for relatively small post-primary schools in providing comprehensive facilities out of their own resources. This suggestion was 'common enrolment', an advanced form of co-operation between schools; this would be an option where amalgamation or closure was not desirable or practicable. All children would be placed on a common roll and would be catered for as if the two schools formed a single educational unit. For the purpose of payment of grants to the secondary schools involved, it would be necessary to get agreement on the proportion of the total enrolment on which grants should be paid. The principals jointly would have responsibility for arrangements connected with the day-to-day running of the combined schools, while a committee of the managerial interests involved would be responsible for overall educational policy, staff recruitment and financial matters. The Department claimed that this proposal enabled each school to preserve its own managerial system while combining with another school in the interests of the children of the area. Common enrolment did occur in Boyle in 1967, but the ASTI annual convention rejected the concept,[20] thus ensuring that it would not become widespread. ASTI criticisms of the concept included the possibility of absorption into the vocational system, the loss of the individual character of the schools concerned and the implications of the suggested role of the committee for the employment and contractual position of teachers. In the period that followed only two more areas adopted common enrolment − Ballinamore and Rathmore − and the ASTI successfully blocked its proposed introduction in Cobh and Thurles.[21] The ASTI was determined to oppose any proposal, even on an experimental basis, which would change the existing situation. The development of secondary education might have been better served by a more flexible attitude. The fact that, in 1975, the ASTI ameliorated its stance indicated that common enrolment could work in certain areas if it had the support of the teachers involved.

While favouring the community school concept to common enrolment in providing a continuity independent of the personality of individual managers and in providing a greater security for ASTI members, the ASTI annual convention resolved 'that the ASTI adopt an open policy towards the system of common enrolment'.[22] This change of policy was due to a forceful advocacy by teachers who had experienced common enrolment. They pointed out that a small centre was unlikely to be offered a community or comprehensive school and that if a vocational school, with its practical facilities, decided not to continue ad hoc co-operation, small secondary schools might close: thus they argued for a neutral policy in regard to common enrolment. It is unlikely that such an argument would have been acceptable in 1967 when schools were seen as either secondary or vocational, but in 1975 the second-level system had become more complex and less stratified with the establishment of comprehensive and community schools. Prior to 1975 ASTI opposition, coupled with the many administrative complexities involved, had prevented the spread of common enrolment. After that date, the community school concept had become a more attractive one for those seeking a solution based on secondary-vocational co-operation.

The Department's proposal to rationalise second-level schools into junior and senior centres was not any more successful than common enrolment. The threat to the secondary system produced co-operation between the ASTI and the secondary school managerial bodies represented by the Joint Managerial Board (JMB). In 1967 the JMB undertook to protect the interests of lay teachers as far as possible,[23] and a common unity of purpose was established between union and management. An article in the 1968 edition of *Studies*,[24] written by Seán O'Connor, whose function it was to implement the Department's rationalisation proposals, failed to split this accord. Writing in a personal capacity, he criticised the religious authorities in secondary schools, stating that their attitude to co-education had been a major obstacle to the establishment of viable school units. He advocated a lesser role for the Catholic Church in secondary schools, 'I want them in it as partners, not always as masters', and deprecated the position of the lay teacher, 'always the hired man', whose responsibility ended at the classroom door. His article created suspicion among religious orders of 'nationalisation by stealth'.[25] There is no evidence that his advocacy of upgrading the position of the lay teacher weakened the unity of purpose, vis-a-vis the rationalisation proposals, between the ASTI and the religious managers. On the contrary the ASTI and JMB agreed to show a united front at rationalisation meetings. It was also decided that the JMB would send to the ASTI a list of their convenors of the various county committees of secondary headmasters/headmistresses and that the ASTI would ask its local representatives in each county to contact these convenors.[26]

In 1972 the Department attempted to persuade some post-primary schools to have a common timetable at leaving certificate level and proposed an informal council of managers and principals of the secondary and vocational schools in question. The ASTI feared that this was but a step to these councils actually employing teachers, thus changing the contractual position of secondary teachers. The ASTI warned the Department that their existing willingness to cooperate with local vocational schools on a voluntary basis would be put in jeopardy if any new structure was imposed on the ASTI without consultation.[27] The proposed councils were never established. Some rationalisation did take place.

In 1975 the Department withdrew recognition of senior cycle classes in some small secondary schools, but later, under ASTI pressure, suspended this decision for three years. The ASTI had now accepted that closure was inevitable for some small schools and its annual conference in 1973 demanded twelve months' notice and a disturbance allowance. While threatened redundancy, due to school closure, was a major issue in the ASTI from the mid-1970s on, it was due more to the internal policy decisions of religious orders than to Department rationalisation. Overall the widespread rationalisation envisaged in the Colley letter of 1967 did not take place. To some extent this was due to the 25 per cent increase in secondary school pupils between 1968 and 1974[28] which had been facilitated by the introduction of 'free education' by the Minister for Education, Donogh O'Malley, in 1966, as this ensured that many small schools increased their numbers. A major factor, however, in preventing widespread rationalisation was the opposition of the ASTI and the managerial authorities.

The desire of management and unions in the secondary and vocational schools to retain the status quo was displayed when a proposal by the Minister for Education, Richard Burke, in 1973 to introduce regionalisation of administration failed to make any progress. The chairman of the representative committee established by the Department of Education to further this proposal declared, in frustration, that delegates only accepted proposals in so far as they did not affect their particular organisation.[29]

The suspicions of the ASTI and the JMB in connection with rationalisation proposals also affected proposed changes to the curriculum. In 1967 the Department established a committee to examine the structure of the leaving certificate course and examination. The ASTI was represented on this committee. One of the committee's major recommendations was to organise related subjects into five groups — language, science, commerce, technical studies and social studies. This proposal was given a qualified acceptance by the ASTI, who recommended a slight widening of the subjects in some groups in order to prevent over-specialisation.[30] When, however, in May 1968 the Minister formally announced the introduction of subject groupings on a voluntary basis from 1969 and on a compulsory basis from 1972, the ASTI response had changed. Believing that the proposal to group subjects was an attempt to bolster the rationalisation proposals, as only large schools could offer all the groups, the central executive council resolved:

> That in the light of information now available, the ASTI is opposed to the inflexible grouping of subjects at leaving certificate as educationally questionable and socially undesirable.[31]

The Department responded to ASTI pressure and, in a letter to the general secretary of the ASTI, stated that while the Minister would continue to support grouping on a voluntary basis, he had withdrawn the proposal for compulsory grouping at leaving certificate level in 1972. This decision delayed the development of scientific, commercial and technical subjects. Had the ASTI maintained its original stance and used its influence to persuade the Department to provide the necessary resources, it would have facilitated curriculum development in accordance with the needs of society.

Community Schools

The next major initiative by the Department of Education in its attempt to rationalise second-level education was on community schools. It was to be the subject of educational controversy for ten years. The concept of the community school was first mentioned by Seán O'Connor in his article in the 1968 *Studies*, where he viewed the rationalisation attempts as a 'drive for community schools'. In 1970, legislation essential to the operation of the later community school arrangement was enacted. The Vocational Education (Amendment) Act 1970 enabled vocational education committees to contribute towards the cost of shared facilities on the basis of their being jointly owned and managed by the vocational education authorities and another education authority.

The Department of Education issued a document on community

schools in the same year. The document made it clear that the concept was a new attempt to attain government objectives that had remained constant since 1963:

> the elimination of barriers between secondary schools and vocational schools;
> the creation of a unified post-primary system of education;
> the provision of comprehensive facilities in each area in order to provide equality of educational opportunity for all children of varying aptitudes and abilities.

In 1971 the Department of Education produced specific proposals in regard to trusteeship and management of community schools. The site and building would be vested by the minister in three trustees nominated by the bishop, one of whom would be taken from names furnished by the local VEC. The proposed board of management would consist of six members: four to be nominated by the authorities of the secondary schools (including two parents) and two by the VEC. By conceding majority representation for secondary school interests, the Department's proposals clearly aimed to attract the support of the Catholic hierarchy. By seeming to make this proposal in the context of amalgamations, which would normally incorporate two secondary and one vocational school, equity of managerial interests could be claimed. The Department, however, moved quickly in establishing new community schools in 'greenfield areas', i.e. Tallaght and Blanchardstown, and applied the proposed trustee and management structure to these schools, even though no secondary school was amalgamated in these areas.

The determination of the Department of Education to achieve success in this latest rationalisation proposal was demonstrated by the fact that twelve community schools were built and forty-two planned before ever a formal deed of trust appeared. This created pressure on all interests to come to an agreement. The formal deed of trust was published in 1974, but the official signing of the deeds for the majority of community schools did not take place until April 1981. The negotiations between 1974 and 1981 included a ministerial ultimatum that the schools would be managed by the Department of Education,[32] a threat that the religious orders might leave Tallaght community school,[33] a rejection by the Bray VEC of the deed of trust as 'totally incompatible with the 1970 Vocational Education Act',[34] and threats of industrial action by the ASTI and the TUI. The length of the negotiations was, in part, due to the difficulty in satisfying all the vested interests involved: the Department of Education, bishops and religious orders, vocational education committees, the teacher unions, and parental organisations. It was also due, however, to the many complex issues arising from this attempt to merge a private denominational sector with a public undenominational one. The length of the negotiations in itself was a cause of further delay; as the passing of time produced new issues, changing responses from the various pressure groups, and differences in their influence.

The ASTI which confronted the community school issue was stronger and more powerful than the ASTI which had witnessed the first rationalisation proposals in 1967.[35] The increase in secondary school pupils had led to an increase in teachers of 40 per cent between 1968 and 1974. Lay teachers, by that date, amounted to 73 per cent of the total number of secondary teachers. The ASTI responded to this new situation. A full-time post of organiser/negotiator was created in 1971, and a recruitment drive among new entrants to the profession was initiated, with marked success.

ASTI membership increased from 1,800 (55 per cent of all full-time lay registered secondary teachers) in 1968 to 5,809 (96 per cent) in 1974. This increase can be attributed partly to an energetic recruitment policy. The main factor was the felt need for trade union organisation in a period that had witnessed a major salary dispute and strike in 1969 and constant pressure from the Department of Education to rationalise second-level education. This pressure was seen by ASTI members as a threat to their contractual position and working conditions.

ASTI membership continued to increase, reaching 9,700 (98.5 per cent of teachers eligible for membership) in 1982.

It might seem surprising that the ASTI failed to recruit religious teachers during this period. The ASTI thus opened itself to a charge of discrimination as well as limiting its potential membership. Although religious teachers had declined to 17 per cent of the total by 1982, they still numbered over 2,000 teachers. The repeal of the rule in the ASTI constitution which confined membership of the ASTI to lay teachers was on the agenda of the majority of ASTI annual conventions between 1970 and 1984, but the issue never achieved the necessary support. The main reason for the continuation of the ban was the perception by lay teachers that religious teachers had neither an identity of working conditions nor an identity of interests with themselves. Lay teachers were assistants and employees: they saw their religious colleagues as actual or potential principals and managers. The establishment of posts of responsibility in 1971 did not change this situation as religious orders continued to appoint to principalships from within. The position is now beginning to change owing to the role model of lay principals in community and comprehensive schools, and to the establishment of boards of management and a growing number of lay principals in secondary schools. This new environment may produce majority support within the ASTI for opening membership to religious, but for the period under review the ASTI remained a lay organisation albeit one which had improved considerably in organisational strength.

Even in 1970, it was clear that the Department of Education considered that the ASTI had a right to be kept fully informed. This attitude was in sharp contrast to the Department's attitude in 1963. In 1970 when the Department was organising meetings of interested parties in eight areas to consider the establishment of community schools, the ASTI was invited. Also the Department submitted to the ASTI in strict confidence a list of centres where the Department considered community schools might be set up.[36] In 1977 the Minister for Education, John Wilson, informed the Dáil that the teacher unions were a full party to the deed of trust negotiations, and that he did not intend to sign any deed of trust pending the outcome of discussions with the unions and the managerial bodies.[37] This greater union involvement stemmed from the organisational changes in the union and in the growth of trade union influence generally. But it also stemmed from changes of policy within the ASTI and a more aggressive pursuance of policies.

The ASTI's initial response to the concept of the community school was governed by its commitment to the secondary school system and its suspicions of government policy stemming from earlier rationalisation attempts. As time progressed the stance of the ASTI was influenced by various decisions of their convention arising from developments in regard to community schools and also by pressure from its own members working within community schools.

The first outline of the community school concept proposed by the Department in 1970 produced a defensive response from the ASTI. The general secretary of the ASTI warned that any effort on the part of the state to dilute the values of traditional secondary education would have to be carefully watched.[38] Various ASTI sub-committee reports all favoured the dual rather than a unified system. They repeated fears expressed in response to earlier Department initiatives. These included a possible lowering of standards, the impersonal nature of large schools, and the difficulties for pupils involved in long travel. An ASTI press statement warned that the Department of Education might concede to an international finance agency (i.e. the World Bank) 'the right to discuss the structure of Irish education, dictate the size of schools and impose an alien educational philosophy'.

The ASTI was critical of the proposed management structure, which would, in its view, lead to extra bureaucracy and higher administrative costs. It favoured the immediacy of an individual manager for each secondary school because this system facilitated ready communication between manager and staff. If, however, boards of management were to be established, ASTI would insist on teacher representation. The 1971 annual convention resolved:

> that the ASTI demands representation on the management boards of the proposed community schools, should they be established, in accordance with the social teaching of Pope John and the stated policy of ICTU.[39]

As community schools were built, the ASTI's attitude became less one of opposition in principle and more one of dissatisfaction with the details of the proposed arrangements. In 1972 the ASTI annual convention resolved:

> that while the ASTI welcomes in principle the genuine Community School concept for social and educational reasons, it rejects the arrangements envisaged for the control and management of the proposed community schools at Tallaght and Blanchardstown.[40]

It would seem also that the ASTI came to see the community school as less a threat to the secondary school tradition and ethos than other departmental proposals, such as common enrolment. In 1974, the ASTI preferred a community school to the latter option in Cobh and was party to the decision to have a community school in Clonakilty.

The ASTI's attitude to the community school was changing because the ASTI was changing; it was no longer a union of teachers in private secondary schools only. It now included in its membership a sizeable and growing number of teachers in comprehensive and community schools. The ASTI had developed structures to cater for these interests: an annual meeting of representatives in comprehensive and community schools and a standing advisory committee with access to the top officials in the association. These structures facilitated the emergence of a community school 'voice' in the ASTI which was more influential than their numbers merited. Indeed in 1979, the year when negotiations on the deed of trust were most intense, the advisory committee, believing that the union leadership was not sufficiently aggressive or clear in its opposition to the deed, called a special convention of the ASTI, the decisions of which, according to the Department of Education, would determine whether community schools would continue in the future.[41]

Negotiations on the deed of trust did not take the form of a roundtable conference. The Department negotiated with each group in 'secret diplomacy' and inter-group negotiations were conducted where differences between two groups emerged. Thus the ASTI had many meetings with the Conference of Major Religious Superiors as well as with the Department of Education. The ASTI achieved a considerable amount. Its efforts to achieve transfer of members to comprehensive schools from secondary schools affected by their establishment bore fruit when in the first document of the Department on community schools there was a clause which stated that in the case of amalgamations, permanent teachers in the schools being amalgamated would be offered assimilation on to the staff of the community school.

The 1974 draft deed of trust contained sections on the suspension and dismissal of teachers,[42] but the ASTI insisted that such contractual matters were for negotiation between the Department and the unions, and the Department agreed to take them out of the deed of trust. To cater for threatened redundancy, the ASTI also succeeded in having a clause inserted into the deed which allowed for the waiving of the procedure for teacher appointments in the event of a redeployment scheme being agreed to by the trustees and the Minister.[43] By agreeing to these proposals, the Department lessened the fears of secondary teachers in relation to the proposed community schools. The ASTI had some success in the area of management, though clearly on this point the strongest cards were held by the secondary and vocational managerial bodies. The draft deed in 1974 was more clearly a partnership of interests in the areas of trusteeship and management than the proposals of 1971, which had reflected a stronger Church participation. In the case of an amalgamation of a vocational school, a brothers' school and a convent school, each of the three school authorities would nominate a trustee for appointment by the Minister for Education. The trust property would be for the purposes of a school, the objectives of which would be the provision of a comprehensive system of post-primary education, combining instruction in academic and practical subjects and on-going education for those living in or near the area, and 'contributing towards the spiritual, moral, mental and physical wellbeing and development of the community.'[44] The composition of the trusteeship represented a partnership between religious authorities and the VECs. Likewise, as regards management, the VEC would nominate two and the religious orders one each. The decrease in religious representation from the 1971 proposals represented increasing influence by the other interests and in particular the increase in influence of parent organisations. The parents of children attending the school would now elect two members to the board of management. As no person 'employed for the purpose of the school' could be a member of the board,[45] representation of the teachers in the school was ruled out specifically. In subsequent negotiations the ASTI succeeded in having this clause omitted.

The CMRS/Episcopal Commission insisted on trustee nominee majority on the board, and both they and the Department would not accept union representation. Under pressure from the ASTI they did accept teacher representation and the amended draft deed in 1979 had a board of management consisting of three 'order nominees', three VEC nominees, two parents and two elected teacher nominees. The principal of the school would be a member of the board but in a non-voting capacity. The Minister for Education pointed out to the ASTI that while he could not agree to the teachers being union representatives, they would be such de facto.[46] Subsequently the ASTI and the TUI devised a structure to ensure that such would be the case.

This co-operative approach was not typical of union relations on community school matters. Inter-union tension was caused by the fact that both unions competed for members in community schools and by the different traditions that had moulded the attitudes of the two unions. The issue of posts of responsibility exemplified this; the TUI favoured open competition and the ASTI believed that seniority should be a significant factor in appointments, as in secondary schools. Resolution of issues such as this was left, wisely, to negotiations outside those of the deed of trust.

While the ultimate composition of the board represented the outcome of a struggle by each group to secure maximum representation for its particular interests, the attempt to unify the secondary and vocational sectors in a new partnership that was the essence of the community school concept produced more emotive and controversial issues than that of board representation. This was inevitable given that what was involved was a partnership between the denominational secondary sector with that of the non-denominational vocational one. In 1971, the Catholic bishops had made it clear to the ASTI that the Catholic character of the schools would have to be retained in an amalgamated situation and that the schools should be voluntary rather than public or state schools.[47] Such a view inevitably led to charges of a take-over of the vocational system. The bishops made it clear in reply that amalgamations into community schools were occurring because of a Department of Education policy of insisting on one single type of post-primary school.[48]

The ASTI believed that denominational groups had the right to develop schools of their own, if they had objections to sending children to schools of other denominations, even if it meant the existence of parallel systems of education.[49] It stated that minority religious denominations were entitled to the same privileges and protection from the state as the majority denomination. In the subsequent negotiations, the religious orders and the Catholic bishops tried to ensure what they regarded as essential for the religious and moral upbringing of the children, and what they regarded as necessary for the proper carrying out of their own responsibilities. The main areas of dispute concerned the position of teachers of religion, the so-called 'faith and morals' clause and the issue of reserved places. As each of these matters had implications for serving teachers, the ASTI was a major force in the negotiations. It had some success on two of the three issues.

In the 1974 draft deed, one of the clauses stated that 'no teacher shall at any time do or say anything which may offend or weaken the religious belief or the moral training and practice of pupils in the school.'[50] The ASTI opposed this as unacceptable and too wide-ranging. Subsequently it was re-written in a more specific form: 'a teacher shall not advertently and consistently seek to undermine the religious belief or practice of any pupil in the school'.[51] The ASTI still feared that this clause might be used by management to dismiss a teacher.

The ASTI did raise the issue subsequently with the Minister but his officials saw that the CMRS were insistent and that, while the clause had no legal validity, it was an expression of concern that would be demanded by society.[52] Similarly, ASTI pressure produced an agreement concerning teachers of religion, which if not totally satisfactory to the ASTI was sufficient for it to accept the operation of the deed. According to the 1974 draft deed, teachers of religion were appointed by the board of management, but subject to the approval of the 'competent religious authority'. Should such a teacher fail to give 'religious instruction efficiently and suitably or in accordance with the teaching of that religious denomination as determined by the competent religious authority',[53] the authority would require the board to remove the teacher. The ASTI believed that teachers of religion should be subject to the same conditions as teachers of other subjects, and under the same departmental control. Officials of the Department, however, did not favour a departmental inspectorate of religion.[54] Responding to ASTI objections, the Department and the CMRS proposed the equivalent of the situation which existed in vocational schools. There the teacher of religion had a second subject and could be moved 'sideways' if the religious authorities were not satisfied with the teaching of religion. The Minister for Education gave a commitment to the ASTI that if a catechetics teacher did not have a second subject, provision would be made to qualify him or her for this.[55]

The most controversial section of the 1974 draft deed was the one which entitled the provincial or mother superior of the order involved to nominate a number of the members of their orders as teachers, provided that the board of management was satisfied with their qualifications.[56] The importance of the issue lay in its being a precondition of the involvement of religious in community schools. The religious felt that these places were essential to their contributing to the community school as a religious order, and essential to their community life in that a certain amount of mobility would be necessary in moving religious personnel from one community to another. Thus to the CMRS opposition to reserved places meant opposition to involvement by religious. The ASTI distinguished between the two and opposed 'reserved places' in the negotiations. The ASTI believed that religious teachers should have the same rights to assimilation as lay teachers in an amalgamated situation, but that equally both lay and religious should have to undergo the same procedures for appointment to non-assimilated positions. The ASTI also mentioned the practical difficulty involved if a religious teacher of one subject was replaced by a teacher of a totally different subject. The advisory committee for community/comprehensive schools of the ASTI collected the necessary signatures of ASTI members to call a special convention to oppose 'reserved places'. There were three motions on the agenda:

Motion 1: That the A.S.T.I. oppose the guarantee of reserved teaching posts to religious orders in community schools.

Motion 2: That the A.S.T.I. seek legal advice and take appropriate legal action on the constitutionality of reserving teaching posts for members of religious orders.

Motion 3: That the A.S.T.I. take industrial action if any deed of trust for community schools is signed which provides for reserved positions on the teaching staff for members of religious orders.[57]

As the CMRS had linked 'reserved places' to their continuing involvement in community schools, the first motion had huge implications for the future development of post-primary education. The debate on this motion, in its record length and number of contributors, bore witness to this. Union officers informed the convention that the Department of Education had taken a decision that, if the motion was passed, seven schools due to open would become section 21 schools, i.e. schools run by boards of management but operating under the vocational education committees. Speakers who opposed 'reserved posts' saw them as deeply discriminatory, and emphasised that all suitably qualified people, whether lay or religious, should be entitled to apply for all teaching posts, should go through the same appointment procedure, and should be appointed on merit. A less frequently mentioned objection was the fear that religious might close small secondary schools in the West to take up reserved posts in urban areas.

It might seem strange that a large number of union representatives was prepared to jeopardise the community school proposal because they saw in the concept of 'reserved places' a denial of the principle of equal opportunity, while at the same time upholding the independence of secondary schools where the religious could reserve as many places as they wished and where teachers did not participate at all in the management structure. In this view, self-interest and ideology were uneasy bedfellows. Its proponents believed that if a new system based on partnership of interests and state funding was being constructed, it should be a genuine partnership without privilege for any group: but it also believed that the best conditions of service for its members were to be obtained in the secondary system.

Speakers who opposed the motion stated that parents in Ireland wanted religious involvement in schools; that if the religious were not involved, the VECs would take over the schools, an event which would not be advantageous to the employment prospects of ASTI members.

The debate was heated and intense. The motion was narrowly defeated, by 107 votes to 103. The fear that all future schools might be vocational schools, with its implications for union membership and members' prospects, had narrowly won the day against the view that the concept of reserved places was a deeply discriminatory one. Motion 3 was withdrawn. Motion 2 was passed, but the ASTI officers already had a legal opinion that reserved places were not unconstitutional. The defeat of Motion 1 had clearly signalled to the Department that the ASTI would no longer be an obstacle to the signing of the deeds, and the ASTI was unable subsequently to get any major change in the deed. Nevertheless, the issue had spotlighted the enormously increased power of the ASTI from that of 1966. Although the ASTI was not a signatory to the deed of trust, its opposition to reserved places had placed it in a position of having de facto veto on the continuation of community schools. The position of the ASTI for future negotiations on issues concerning its members had been strengthened enormously and the ASTI had become a significant element in the policy-making structure.

The community school represented the most successful intervention by the Department of Education in its many initiatives to break down the barriers between the secondary and vocational sectors. By 1982 forty-one community schools were in existence. The Department had shown a greater determination than in its previous efforts, and its officials by skilful negotiation with the various interests had, in time, produced an agreement which was reasonably satisfactory to all. ASTI satisfaction with community schools was demonstrated in 1981 when the president in his address to the annual convention stated that they had gained widespread parental support, attained high standards in academic and technical subjects, participated fully in curriculum development projects, and provided an adult education service that was second to none.[58]

Another development, which may be quite significant for the future development of second-level education, occurred without any involvement by the Department of Education. In the late 1970s a number of community colleges had been established. These colleges were administered by the vocational education committees but had boards of management similar to those in community schools. Traditionally, teachers in vocational schools had been organised by the TUI. During the 1980s a number of secondary schools, either by direct transformation or by amalgamation, had become community colleges. The ASTI had continued to represent its members in these schools and the VECs had negotiated with the ASTI, realising that ASTI support for community colleges or even neutrality in the community school/college debate would facilitate an expansion in the number of VEC schools. In 1982, the disputes committee of the Irish Congress of Trade Unions, despite TUI opposition, upheld an ASTI claim to the right to recruit and represent members in new 'greenfield' community colleges as well as community colleges which arose from the absorption of secondary schools into the VEC system.[59] This decision removed reservations, based on the rights of recruitment, which the ASTI had concerning community colleges, and is likely to mark a major step forward in the elimination of barriers between secondary and vocational schools.

For this reason the attitude of the ASTI is likely to be more pragmatic and less ideological on any future proposals for restructuring second-level schools. Government policy at present does not favour any particular sector. The recent *Programme for action in education 1984—1987* aims 'at the rational and complementary development of the secondary, vocational and community/comprehensive sectors'.[60] Thus, in the future, disputes concerning the type of second-level school are less likely to occur.

Conclusions

The topic of structural reform was not the only issue of concern in education circles in the last twenty years, but it was a prominent one throughout the period and is likely to remain so in the immediate future given the present emphasis on the need to curtail public expenditure. Thus it is a useful vehicle for analysing the change in the policy-making process since 1960, an analysis which may be of use to the policy makers of the future.

At the beginning of the period under scrutiny, the policy-making process was simple, unambiguous and had been unchanged for decades. Decisions on most aspects of secondary schooling were a matter for the school authorities, usually religious, while the Department of Education kept a firm grip on the curriculum. Other interests, including the teacher unions, had the opportunity to convey their views, mainly in the form of written memoranda, but were not regarded as sufficiently significant to be a major consideration in the calculations of the policy makers.

The next twenty years, however, witnessed a widening of the policy-making process and a much more active participation in policy making by the ASTI. When the comprehensive school was launched in 1963 by ministerial initiative, the sending of a memorandum after the official announcement was the only input from the ASTI. No meeting with the minister occurred and the ASTI did not seem to be in a position to demand this. The ASTI took a more aggressive stance towards the Colley rationalisation proposals in 1967 and gained the union the right to attend rationalisation meetings. While it had not gained an input into policy making, the ASTI had acquired a say in the development of its operation at school level. By 1979, when the most intense negotiations on the deed of trust for community schools took place, the ASTI had become a full party to the negotiations, which included policy making on a variety of issues. Its views were sought at every stage, both by the Department and by the religious authorities. Proposals were submitted to the ASTI and negotiations took the form of meetings with departmental officials of assistant secretary and principal officer status. When agreement on various issues was not reached, the ASTI sought a meeting with the minister as a final attempt to achieve the incorporation of ASTI views into departmental policies. Ministerial willingness to meet the ASTI when requested was based on an unspoken agreement that such meetings would not be requested too regularly and only when every attempt had been made to resolve issues at a lower level of negotiation.

Ministers met union representatives at the beginning of a period of government as a public relations exercise. This enabled the union to bring major matters of concern to the Minister's notice which would then be explored in depth at a lower level. In regard to the deed of trust, the agreement of the ASTI, or at least a union willingness not to oppose actively, was regarded as essential to implementing policy. This status was acknowledged formally when the Minister for Education, John Wilson, TD, informed the Dáil that the teacher unions were a full party to the deed of trust negotiations. The extension of the policy-making process to include the ASTI was a byproduct of the attempt by the state to control and to mould secondary education as well as the resulting vociferous and active stance of the union attempting to safeguard the interests of secondary teachers.

What effect did this widening of the policy-making process have on government policies? The opposition of managerial and union interests had effectively prevented the implementation of many of the structural initiatives of the 1960s. The rationalisation of second-level schools in the form of a two-tiered structure did not occur and the proposed regionalisation of educational administration did not progress beyond the opening gambit. The state could not easily progress from being a support agency to a position of complete control. Though the ASTI was only one of the conservative bodies that was effective in maintaining the status quo, the alliance of management and union in defending the existing secondary school situation proved an obstacle that the Department could not easily overcome, especially in the fight for public opinion. The Department was forced to bring the various interest groups into the policy-making process. By thus widening the process, while maintaining its thrust for structural reform, the Department eventually brought about a partnership that broke down the rigid divide between secondary and vocational school structures. The involvement of interest groups in the policy-making process meant that the emerging community school structure was not that of the original proposal, but one which bore the imprint of the various groups involved. The impact of the ASTI on the community school model can be seen in a number of ways. The management structure was a wider, more representative one than it would otherwise have been. Teachers as well as trustees and parents participated in management. Another result of ASTI pressure was that the deed of trust was less religiously authoritarian; it was more suitable for a school that was open to all the children of the community, as evidenced by its successful demand for changes in the proposed 'faith and morals clause' and in the arrangements for teachers of religion. In this area of negotiation, the stance of the ASTI helped to produce a compromise which facilitated the agreement of the vocational system to this partnership of the denominational and undenominational sectors. The widening of the policy-making process did not necessarily mean the formulation of a division between the state and the interest groups. On this issue the ASTI stance helped, rather than hindered, the creation of a structure that was in line with government policy.

What are the implications of the impact of the union for Irish educational policy making? The place won by the union in the policy-making process will not be easily surrendered. If any large-scale reform is to take place, the ASTI will have to participate in the process. The history of structural reform has shown that outright opposition by the union, particularly if this coincides with managerial interests, would make it extremely difficult for the Department to implement proposals. Participation by managerial and union groups in making a policy is a precondition to implementation. Such a process is a more complex one than that of the 1960s, but there is greater likelihood of lasting change, given forceful but imaginative and flexible negotiation by all. The developments of the last twenty years have shown that the major motivation of the ASTI is the determination to represent its members' interests rather than any political or educational ideology. Interests and ideology may overlap as when in the 1960s the defence of the private secondary system seemed to the union to be the best way of forwarding its members' interests.

The debate within the union on the issue of 'reserved places' in community schools was perhaps the only example of an ideological position coming near to forcing a decision which was against the narrow self-interest of the union. The ASTI is both a professional association and a trade union, but the issues studied in this chapter do not throw any light on a possible conflict between these roles. Because secondary teachers believed that the secondary school programme/ethos provided the best education, and that their conditions of service were safeguarded by the continuation of the secondary school system, professional and trade union interests coincided on these issues. The dispute within the union on 'reserved places' could not be regarded as a conflict between the professional and trade union roles because the matter was more a political issue than an educational one.

The fact that the union's stance has in the main been pragmatic rather than ideological is likely to mean an avoidance of insoluble conflict and a greater possibility of emerging solutions within the wider policy-making process that now exists. Another important feature for those involved in decision making to note is that the union tends to reflect general societal attitudes, as is evident by the opposition to state control in the 1960s and the more secular approach to the deed of trust in the 1980s.

It is clear that in its participation in policy making, the ASTI will seek to ensure the welfare of its members rather than work objectively to create a good education system, where these objectives are in conflict. This may well be true of other groups in the policy-making process. The Department of Education, whose function is to construct an education system that best serves the needs of the children, will be mindful of this. Yet the analysis in this chapter has shown that despite the primacy of self-interest, greater progress in the implementation of state objectives occurred when the policy-making process was widened to include the union and the other interest groups. As the ASTI represents the vast majority of second-level teachers, proposed reforms are more likely to succeed, gain greater acceptance in society and put down deeper roots if union views can be incorporated into their structure.

Notes to Chapter 5

1. John H. Whyte, *Church and state in modern Ireland 1923 — 1970* Dublin: Gill and Macmillan, 1971.
2. Daniel C. O'Connor, 'Secondary education in Ireland 1878 — 1969' unpublished MA thesis, St Patrick's College, Maynooth, 1971, p. 23.
3. Whyte, *Church and state* p. 20.
4. T. J. Boylan, 'Presidential address', ASTI Annual Convention (henceforth Presidential address), 1942, p. 10.
   Patrick J. O'Reilly, 'Presidential address', 1955, p. 5.
5. Patrick J. N. Riordan, 'The Association of Secondary Teachers, Ireland 1909 — 1968. Some aspects of its growth and development' unpublished MEd thesis, University College, Cork, 1975.
6. John Coolahan, *The ASTI and post-primary education in Ireland, 1909 — 1984* Dublin: Cumann na Meán-mhúinteoirí, 1984, p. 120.
7. *Official programme of the annual convention of the ASTI* (henceforth *Official programme*), 1956, p. 65.
8. D.G. Mulcahy, *Curriculum and policy in Irish post-primary education* Dublin: Institute of Public Administration, 1981, p. 13.
9. Eileen Randles, *Post-primary education in Ireland 1957—1970* Dublin: Veritas Publications, 1975, pp. 328-337.
10. *Ibid.*
11. *Ibid* p. 178.
12. *Dáil Reports*, Vol. 203, col 598, 30 May 1963.
13. *Correspondence* with the Department of Education, 2-9 May 1966.
14. *Correspondence* with the Jesuit Order, 11-13 July 1968.
15. Randles, *Post-primary education* pp. 338-342.
16. *Official programme* 1967, pp. 66-67.
17. *Ibid* p. 24.
18. *Ibid* 1972, p. 82.
19. Michael Sheedy, *Presidential address* 1970, pp. 5-9.
20. *Minutes of the annual convention of the ASTI* (henceforth *Annual convention*) 1968, p. 16.
21. ASTI *Press statement* 2 December 1974.
22. *Annual convention* 1975, pp. 25-27.
23. *Minutes of the standing committee of the ASTI* (henceforth Standing committee) 4 July 1967, p. 1.
24. *A Studies symposium, post-primary education, now and in the future* Dublin: Talbot Press, 1968, pp. 9-16.

25. *Ibid* p. 58.
26. *Letter* from the General Secretary of the ASTI to each member of the Central Executive Council, 17 December 1968.
27. *Official programme* 1972, p. 81.
28. Coolahan, *ASTI* p. 272.
29. *Official programme* 1973, p. 129.
30. *Standing committee* 23 March 1968, p. 1.
31. *Minutes of the Central Executive Council of the ASTI* (henceforth *CEC*), 18 January 1969, p. 4.
32. *Irish Independent* 7 October 1979.
33. *Ibid* 26 April 1978.
34. *The Irish Times* 12 July 1979.
35. Coolahan, *ASTI* pp. 273 and 355.
36. *Standing committee*, 1 May 1971, p. 3.
37. *Dáil Reports*, 11 May 1978, col. 932-6.
38. *The Secondary Teacher* (December 1970), p. 11.
39. *Annual Convention* 1971, p. 20.
40. *Ibid* 1972, p. 16.
41. *Minutes of the Special convention of the ASTI* (henceforth *Special convention*), 20 April, 1979.
42. *Draft Model Lease for a Community School* (henceforth *Model Lease*), 1974, Section 7(c), (d) and (e) of the Second Schedule of the Articles of Management.
43. *Ibid* July 1979, Section 7c(vi) of the Second Schedule, p. 22.
44. *Ibid* 1974, p. 1.
45. *Ibid* p. 13.
46. *Standing committee*, 8 December 1979, p. 7.
47. *Report* of meeting between ASTI and the Episcopal Commission on Post-Primary Education, 8 May 1971.
48. *ASTIR*, February 1972.
49. *Report* of ASTI Sub-Committee on Community Schools, 25 May 1971 and 29 May 1971.
50. *Model Lease* 1974, Section II (vi)(b) of the Second Schedule of the Articles of Management.
51. *Ibid* February 1979, Section II of the Second Schedule of the Articles of Management.
52. *ASTIR*, December 1979, p. 3.
53. *Model Lease* 1974, Section II (i)-(vi) of the Second Schedule of the Articles of Management.
54. *Report* of meeting with officials of the Department of Education, 8 May 1979.
55. *Standing committee* 8 December 1979.
56. *Model lease* 1974, p. 20.
57. *Special convention* 20 April 1979.
58. David Barry, *Presidential address* 1981, pp. 8-9.
59. *Official programme* 1983, p. 143.
60. *Programme for action in education 1984–1987* Dublin: Stationery Office, 1984, p. 22.

6

Central Initiatives
and Local Realities:
Curriculum Change in the County
Cork VEC Schools, 1963 – 1983

Timothy J. Owens

Economic considerations greatly influenced educational planning during the 1960s and the 1970s as the Department of Education sought return from its investment. It sought this return in terms of a workforce which would be geared towards the needs of an expanding industrial economy; it also sought to eliminate overlap and duplication in the provision of buildings, teachers and equipment, so that the available financial resources would be best utilised.

This viewpoint led to a review of existing policies on school provision. It led to the development of policies such as amalgamations and sharing of facilities and the consideration of the post-primary centre as distinct from the individual school. It also meant that, in an effort to increase the number of students studying subjects of a technical nature, an expanded common curriculum and common intermediate and leaving certificate examinations were made available in both secondary and vocational schools.

This chapter deals with the attitude of the Cork County VEC towards these developments and the extent to which it accepted, or modified and ignored, the wishes of the Department of Education. Attention is also given to a consideration of the extent to which the tradition of vocational education came under pressure

The author wishes to acknowledge the facilities for research extended to him by R. Ó Buachalla, Uasal, CEO, Cork County VEC.

to adapt itself increasingly to the 'secondary' model of post-primary education at a time when the state itself was arguing for a stronger link between post-primary education and the economy. The chapter attempts to highlight the need for central policy making to take cognisance of interests and expectations which are likely to arise at the school implementation stage.

VEC Influence

Amalgamations, and sharing of facilities

In a letter to the authorities of all post-primary schools in January 1966, the Minister for Education, George Colley, suggested that there should be a pooling of resources between vocational and secondary schools, collaboration, and, where possible, amalgamations in order to provide a comprehensive curriculum for all pupils.[1] Following this letter, the Department began talking in terms of the post-primary centre rather than individual schools. It encouraged amalgamations, and the sharing of facilities. Two amalgamations did occur in County Cork, in Dunmanway and Ballingeary; each involved the amalgamation of a small secondary school with the local vocational school.

Dunmanway was a relatively straightforward case. The headmaster of a two-teacher boys' private school wrote to the VEC suggesting amalgamation. The Department approved and the two teachers in the secondary school became employees of the VEC and classes were continued at the local vocational school. The Ballingeary amalgamation was more contentious. At the time of the amalgamation, classes had been abandoned at the local vocational school owing to lack of numbers. A local, privately owned secondary school requested the use of some facilities at the vocational school. When the Department of Education was informed, an amalgamation was suggested. The teachers in the private secondary school were opposed to the idea. When the owner and headmaster of the secondary school died, however, his wife agreed terms with County Cork VEC and the amalgamation, or 'take-over' as the teachers in the secondary school referred to it, occurred.

More difficult and complex situations were soon to emerge and

Mr Colley's proposals on co-operation and sharing of facilities ran into serious problems. Passage West was a case in point, where an arrangement for co-operation between the vocational school and a local secondary school which had operated since 1970 was terminated in 1978.[2]

Community schools

If Department of Education proposals on amalgamations and sharing of facilities received less than enthusiastic support at school level, it was soon apparent that the Department had no intention of abandoning plans for the rationalisation of post-primary schools. Seán O'Connor, then assistant secretary in the Department of Education, outlined the next stage of the rationalisation drive in an article in *Studies* (Autumn 1968) entitled 'Post-primary education: now and in the future'. According to this article, the Department of Education felt that 'single community schools are the rational requirement in most centres outside the large urban areas'.[3] This was the first occasion that the concept of the community school was mentioned. The precise meaning of the title 'community school' was not fully explained, however, until October 1979 when the Department issued a document on community schools. The schools were to have enrolments of between four hundred and eight hundred pupils and were to provide a comprehensive curriculum. School facilities were to be made available during out-of-school hours to voluntary organisations and the adult community generally. A board of management consisting of representatives of the secondary school managers and the local vocational education committee and possibly parents or industrial/commercial interests would govern the school. The capital costs involved would be met in full out of public funds, subject to an agreed local contribution, and the current costs of running the school would be met by the state. Community schools would, in effect, be state-run schools.

The community school issue was discussed by the Cork County VEC at a meeting in June 1971. The committee's response to the proposals for community schools was negative. It stated that the proposed management structure for the schools was unacceptable and that the schools were too large and not realistic in the context of the smaller rural districts. Anger was expressed at the manner in which the community school proposals were announced. One member did express the opinion that it was premature to come to any decision on the matter of community schools; his was the only dissenting voice in the chorus of condemnation.[4]

In an effort to develop a uniform policy on community schools, the issue was discussed again in January 1973. In the intervening period, some members of the committee had visited the new community school at Tallaght, County Dublin and were obviously impressed. Several members, including some of those who had strongly opposed the community school proposals when they were first discussed in 1971, now spoke in favour of community schools. These members urged that the committee should abandon its policy of non-co-operation and agree, in principle, with the concept of community schools.

At the first meeting to discuss the community school proposals in June 1971, none of the eight clerical committee members present is recorded as having spoken on the issue. Faced, over a year later, with considerable support for the community school concept, they made their contributions to the debate. One senior member expressed the opinion that the Tallaght example was an argument for a well run vocational school. In his opinion, the continental experience had shown that the community schools were a failure. They failed, he said, because they tried to mix different systems of education. Management, he claimed, was not the issue. He felt that:

> the committee should examine each particular case on its own merits and should be content to maintain the *status quo* especially where viable new secondary and vocational school buildings were already in existence.[5]

Another felt that the concept of measuring education in economic terms, which had originated with the OECD report, had gone too far. Education, he felt, was to train people for life and in pursuit of this aim the curriculum should be restricted and studied in depth. Tallaght, he contended, contained fringe benefits only and much of the work described by those committee members who had visited the school, such as pastoral care and career guidance, had been going on for years in the vocational schools and secondary schools.[6] Following a long debate, it was eventually decided not to make any specific decision for or against community schools and to consider each case on its merits as it came before the committee.

Opportunities to judge cases individually were soon to arrive. During the early 1970s the Department of Education proposed that community schools be built in four centres in Cork County, and that this would involve the merger of vocational schools with other post-primary schools. These centres were in Cobh, Clonakilty, Millstreet and Castletownbere. The vocational education committee's response to the Department's overtures to build community schools in these centres is indicative of what 'judging each case on its merits' actually came to entail.

Clonakilty There were three schools in Clonakilty in 1972/73: the Convent of Mercy, which had 416 pupils; the vocational school, which had 208 pupils; and St Mary's, a private secondary school, which had 102 pupils. At a meeting with representatives of the three schools in May 1972, Department of Education officials proposed that a community school be established in Clonakilty. The VEC and the private secondary school representatives agreed with the proposal but the convent authorities stated that they were unwilling to give up control of their school.[7]

In the course of subsequent discussions with the Department, the Conference of Major Religious Superiors suggested that, as an alternative to the community school proposal, post-primary education in Clonakilty should be organised on a two-school basis, a girls' school (the convent) and a boys' school. In January 1973, the secretary of the Department gave an undertaking that post-primary education in Clonakilty would be re-organised on this basis. A public meeting to discuss the future provision of post-primary education in Clonakilty was held in the town on 8 May 1973. Present were representatives of the three schools, the Vocational Teachers Association (VTA), the Association of Secondary Teachers, Ireland (ASTI), and members of the general public.

The departmental representatives stated that a community school would best meet the future educational requirements of the town in the Department's view. In view of the convent's refusal to enter into such an arrangement, however, the Department was anxious to ascertain the support locally for the alternative two-school proposal. Representatives of the VTA objected to this proposal on the grounds that they would not be prepared to abandon the principle of co-education. Representatives of the ASTI also favoured the original community school proposal. The Department of Education representatives pointed out that facilities which could be provided in a community school of some eight hundred pupils, such as gymnasium, language and science laboratories, could not be made available to the same extent if two schools of four hundred pupils were established. If the two-school proposal was adopted, it would mean a new vocational school would have to be built to accommodate the influx from St Mary's College. A new vocational school near the convent was suggested with sharing of facilities between the schools but the departmental representatives informed the meeting that where this type of arrangement had been tried, it had not worked satisfactorily.

Despite the Department's urgings, the convent school authorities remained adamant: on the grounds of ownership and management, they were not prepared to go along with the community school proposal. They wished to retain the convent as a separate school. The VTA's representatives urged the Department not to abandon the community school proposal as a result of the convent's decision.[8]

Support for the convent's stance, however, came from within the VEC. At the County VEC meetings of June 1973, it was pointed out that the nuns had provided secondary education in Clonakilty since 1906: and that 'the convent was a viable unit and that the nuns felt they should be free to continue with an enrolment of pupils'.[9]

It was agreed by the VEC that a deputation should approach the Department and the private boys' secondary school, St Mary's, regarding the problem of accommodation for boys in the town. By doing so, it acquiesced in the convent's rejection of a community school, and gave no reason for arriving at their decision other than the convent's objection to a community school.

In July 1974, the Minister for Education wrote to the VEC and St Mary's College stating that he had decided on an amalgamation of the vocational school in Clonakilty with St Mary's College to form a community school. This solution, however, was not acceptable to the vocational school teachers. They felt that as one of the town's private secondary schools had opted out of a community school, and as the other was due to close in any case, the new school should be under the control of the Cork County VEC. The Department eventually conceded the point and decided that the new school should be referred to as a community college, should be under VEC control and should be managed by a board of management to be established under section 21 of the Vocational Education Act 1930.

Cobh Another centre where the Department's proposals to build a community school in line with central policy met with rejection was Cobh. There were three post-primary schools in the town in the early 1970s: a vocational school, a Presentation boys' school and a girls' convent school. For some years, the Cork County VEC had planned to provide a new school in the town.

In July 1972, the committee received notice from the Department of Education that they proposed to build a community school in Cobh. At a subsequent committee meeting, the committee was reminded that their first duty was to implement a scheme of vocational education in the county and in this connection their priority was to provide a new technical school in Cobh. It was also stated that it was most uneconomic to embark on the provision of a new community school, when a new technical school, which would adequately cater for the children of Cobh, would only cost one-third of the amount being allocated to a new community school. Similar sentiments were expressed by other speakers and the committee proceeded to reject the Department's proposal for the provision of a community school in Cobh.[10]

The managers of the two religious secondary schools in the town also rejected the community school proposal. When this news was conveyed to the VEC, they decided to request the Department's permission to proceed with the building of a vocational school in Cobh. This was the eventual outcome, and once again the Department of Education was thwarted in its attempt to provide a community school in a Cork County centre.

Rejection at local level of departmental proposals for community schools did not always occur, however, and a consideration of two cases, namely, Millstreet and Castletownbere, where such proposals were accepted and acted upon, throws some light on the possible reasons why departmental proposals were rejected by local authorities and the way in which deviation from central planning occurred.

Millstreet The provision of a technical school in Millstreet in 1964 brought to three the number of post-primary schools in Millstreet. A private boys' secondary school had been in existence since the early 1940s and girls were catered for in the local convent school. When Millstreet was earmarked by the Department as a possible community school centre, the principal of the vocational school approached the principals of the town's other post-primary schools with a view to calling a meeting to discuss the issue. Both were agreeable and a meeting was convened under the chairmanship of the local parish priest. Representatives of the three schools attended and agreed that a community school should replace the existing schools.

The first official indication the VEC received that the Department intended to proceed with its plans to provide a community school in Millstreet came in a letter from the Department in November 1972. The Department requested the committee to nominate a person to the board of management of the new school. The committee was perturbed that it had not been consulted prior to the decision to proceed with construction. The VEC members were especially upset because 'they had built a vocational school which had cost a lot of money not too many years ago, which would now cease to exist'.[11] They wanted to know if it was proposed to close the vocational school in Millstreet and what right the Department had to dispose of the committee's property. The committee refused to nominate any members to the board of management of the new school.

One must remember that at this time the VEC was rejecting the Department's proposal to build a community school in Cobh and was requesting the Department to proceed with the building of a new vocational school for the town. Confrontation, therefore, seemed inevitable in the case of Millstreet where the VEC had built a new school less than a decade previously. In view of its stance in relation to the Cobh development, it seemed certain that the VEC would reject the proposed new community school and seek the retention of vocational education in the town. At its February 1973 meeting, however, the VEC considered a letter from the Department indicating that the three schools in the area were in favour of a community school. Without further protest, the VEC agreed to nominate two members to the board of management and thus ended VEC dissent on the issue. The school was built and opened to pupils in September 1973.

The willingness of the religious authorities in Millstreet to enter into a community school arrangement would appear to have been the major factor influencing the VEC's decision not to oppose the provision of a community school for the town. The one major difference between the Millstreet case and those of Cobh and Clonakilty was the attitude of the religious authorities. If the decision against the community school was made on any grounds other than the attitude of the religious, Millstreet, with its new vocational school, was a most likely case. If, as one VEC member stated, it was uneconomic to build a new community school in Cobh when a cheaper vocational school could be provided, then it was even more uneconomic in Millstreet, where the new vocational school had been provided only eight years previously. If, as had been remarked in relation to the Cobh proposal, the primary aim of the committee was to implement a scheme of vocational education, then surely it was wrong to agree to the disposal of the committee's own new school in Millstreet.

Castletownbere   That the attitude of the religious authorities was a likely major influence on the decision to accept a departmental proposal for a community school in any particular area, is further supported by the case of Castletownbere. In the early 1970s there were two post-primary schools in Castletownbere, the Convent of Mercy secondary school and the local vocational school. In November 1973, a report on post-primary facilities in Castletownbere was submitted to the committee. The report stated that the staff of both schools had been jointly involved in assessing the adequacy or otherwise of the facilities in the two schools and had decided to request that 'a new school incorporating full facilities for academic, technical, cultural and recreational disciplines' be provided.[12] The report, as presented, was endorsed by the meeting, and the CEO was instructed to invite officials of the Department of Education to meet the mother general of the convent, a member of the VEC and himself with a view to seeing a new post-primary development in the area. Following negotiations with the Department it was agreed by all to build a community school in Castletownbere, and a community school was subsequently provided. Once again, the attitude adopted by the VEC corresponded with that of the religious secondary school involved in the merger.

In the early 1970s the VEC supported the provision of community schools in two centres in the county and objected to their provision in two other areas. A variety of reasons, including overt statements that it had been because a religious order objected, were given as to why community schools were not in certain cases acceptable.[13] The inconsistency of approach is hard to explain, other than to point out that in no centre did the VEC oppose the decision of the religious order involved when judging 'each case on its merits'. Whatever the reasons for the VEC decisions, however, their decisions, locally made, did have the effect of considerably modifying departmental policy on community schools at the point of implementation.

Personal Influence

New vocational school provision

Pending the outcome of the post-primary surveys being conducted in the Department of Education during the early to mid-1960s, there was a moratorium on the provision of new vocational school buildings in Cork. Following the completion of the surveys, the main emphasis of departmental policy was on the provision of community schools. These schools were not envisaged for every area, however. During and immediately following the completion of the surveys, therefore, there was a period when schools in areas other than those designated as possible community school centres suffered from a degree of neglect as far as the provision of facilities was concerned. It so happened that this neglect occurred at a time when vocational school enrolments were rising at an unprecedented rate owing to the commencement of free education and the introduction of the leaving and intermediate certificate examinations into the vocational schools. Between 1966/67 and 1976/77, vocational school enrolments in Cork County rose by 89 per cent, from 2,716 pupils to 5,141 pupils. As a short-term solution, the Department of Education suggested that the accommodation crisis be solved by the provision of pre-fabricated buildings.

Following the completion of the post-primary surveys, the stage was set in the early 1970s for further development of the vocational system in the county. This development was, however, to occur with a different hand at the helm in County Cork, for in 1972 the

CEO of twenty-five years standing, Liam Mulcahy, retired. The new CEO, Bobby Buckley, took office in October 1973. A change in administrative style soon became apparent as Mr Buckley quickly set about tackling the problem of school provision. He initiated a survey of the adequacy of existing school provision. It was envisaged that on the basis of the results a plan for future school development programmes would be prepared.

The main conclusion drawn from the resource study was that there was an urgent need to provide new schools. In pursuit of this objective a programme of school building to cover the 1975—78 period was drawn up by the VEC: eight new school buildings were planned for completion by 1978. To describe the programme of school building as ambitious would be an understatement. Many of those involved in vocational education in the county were sceptical that the programme would ever be completed. Since 1957 only two new vocational schools had been built in the county. It was now proposed to build eight in four years. Usually, it took that long for plans to reach the drawing stage. Scepticism seemed justified in the circumstances.

In October 1978 the CEO presented a document, 'School building programme (Phase 2) 1979—1982', to the committee for their consideration.[14] This document contained a review of the progress of phase one of the building programme and set further targets for the 1979—82 period. It showed that work had started on six of the eight new schools. It proposed that all eight schools be completed and that the planning of major extensions should proceed for all but three of the remaining schools in the county. By 1982 these objectives had been achieved.

By national standards eight new schools in County Cork in eight years is an impressive achievement. Between 1974 and 1981 only twenty-five new vocational schools were provided in the country as a whole. While it may be held that the new CEO arrived in Cork at the opportune time, in that existing facilities were overcrowded and the virtual embargo on new school building in existence since the 1960s was lifted, much of the credit for the new school developments must be accorded to Mr Buckley.

The role of a chief executive officer is very much dependent on the occupant of the post. Rather than slotting into a position of reactive administration, Mr Buckley chose a proactive, a leadership role. Appointing a back-up team of education, finance, development, youth and sport, and personnel officers, the CEO projected the Cork County VEC to the forefront of the vocational education stage. With a keen sense of perception, he gauged the mood and attitude of the Department of Education towards educational developments ensuring that if new projects or innovation were in the pipeline, Cork County VEC was ready to submit well researched detailed applications for financial consideration. While other VECs were passing resolutions on the need for various services (for example remedial teachers, guidance counsellors, physical education teachers, computer facilities), County Cork VEC was acquiring them. A CEO can either await directions from a VEC or he or she can formulate policy and plans and present them to a VEC for their approval. Mr Buckley adopted the latter approach.

This is not to imply that the VEC was just a rubber-stamping body. It had the power to reject the proposals of the CEO. The VEC is, however, a body composed mainly of churchmen and politicians, each with major interests other than vocational education. Many of them sit on a variety of committees. On the other hand, the CEO is a full-time paid official who has the time and back-up services to formulate plans and decide policy. The initiative, or lack of it, of a CEO can greatly affect what happens to Department of Education plans at local level. Mr Buckley's entry to the educational scene in County Cork as CEO in 1973 demonstrates the power of even one individual at local level to implement or expedite − and conceivably impede − central policy.

Enrolment

One of the main reasons the common intermediate and leaving certificate courses were introduced to vocational schools in the mid-1960s was to encourage greater attendance at these schools, thereby increasing the proportion of post-primary students studying subjects of a technical nature. At a VEC meeting in early 1982, it was proposed that headmasters be allowed to curb the number of pupils permitted to enrol each year. The proposer of the motion spoke of the swing away from an academic education and the burden this was placing on vocational schools. He added that the Cork County VEC was a victim of its own success. While the motion did not receive much support, the CEO made a comment on the discussion stating that 'what was being highlighted was the huge demand for vocational education'.[15] If the VEC were under the impression that there was increased demand for vocational education in the county, they were undoubtedly correct. An analysis of enrolment trends throws important light on the nature of this increased demand, however. As already stated, between 1966/67 and 1976/77, enrolments in County Cork vocational schools rose by 89 per cent. This percentage increase is undeniably impressive. It must be remembered, however, that during this period the length of the vocational school course was extended from two to five years, free education and free transport were introduced, and the school leaving age was increased to fifteen years. To a large extent, therefore, the increase between 1966 and 1976 occurred because children were staying on longer at school. Since 1976, all vocational schools in the county have been teaching the leaving certificate course, and between 1976/77 and 1983/84 there was an 18 per cent rise in overall enrolment. Since 1976, first-year enrolments have remained fairly constant showing little sign of substantial increase (see Table 1); thus indicating that this 18 per cent rise is largely due to an increasing retention rate after junior cycle.

TABLE 1

First-year Enrolments in County Cork Vocational Schools 1976/77 to 1983/84

Year	Number of pupils
1976/77	1,253
1977/78	1,248
1978/79	1,292
1979/80	1,283
1980/81	1,289
1981/82	1,239
1982/83	1,176
1983/84	1,301[a]

Note: [a] does not include figures for new community colleges at Schull and Dublin Hill

The best way to establish the success or otherwise of the Department of Education's policy to encourage greater attendance at vocational schools is to compare the 1965/66 first-year enrolment figures with present-day figures (1965/66 was the last year that pupils enrolled in vocational schools without the option of proceeding to third year). The number of students that enrolled in first year that year for full-time day classes in County Cork vocational schools (excluding for comparison purposes those schools no longer part of the scheme) was 1,127 pupils.[16] Comparisons between that figure and the first-year enrolment figures since 1976 (Table 1) indicate that there has been an increase of 13.4 per cent in first-year enrolments since 1965/66.

This finding has important implications. People in the vocational sector are apt to point to a large increase in enrolment figures in vocational schools since the introduction of the intermediate and leaving certificate examinations as being indicative of a greater acceptance by the general public of the system. The indications are, however, that in terms of the numbers of students who enter the system as first-years in County Cork, the increase has not been exceptional. In that sense, therefore, the introduction of the intermediate and leaving certificate examinations has not achieved the goal of attracting substantially more pupils to the vocational schools in County Cork.

Introduction of Intermediate and Leaving Certificate Courses to Vocational Schools

The intermediate certificate course was introduced to vocational schools in September 1966. The leaving certificate course was introduced three years later to some of the bigger vocational schools: and the first VEC students sat the leaving certificate examination in 1971. According to the *ICE Report*, the introduction of these examinations led to a lessening of the time devoted to traditional vocational subjects and to a decrease in continuation education.[17]

For the purpose of this study, curricular and examination patterns in County Cork vocational schools for the 1978–82 period were studied to gauge the extent, if any, that the phenomena mentioned in the *ICE Report* occurred. As well as showing what education in Cork vocational schools has come to entail since the introduction of the leaving and intermediate certificate courses, such a micro study also highlights factors at school implementation level which can frustrate the best efforts of national planners to achieve their objectives.

Clear trends emerge in the subjects most heavily subscribed in the leaving certificate examination in County Cork schools between 1978 and 1982 (Table 2). With the exception of 1978, when slightly more pupils sat for geography than technical drawing, the seven most popular subjects have been in this order: mathematics, English, Irish, biology, technical drawing, geography, engineering workshop theory and practice. Of these subjects, mathematics, English, Irish, biology and geography were also the most heavily subscribed at national level for all post-primary schools. Technical drawing and engineering workshop theory and practice, however, did not rate highly at national level.

To be eligible to sit for the leaving certificate examinations, pupils are required to take only one specific subject, namely Irish, as part of their course. Pupils must study at least five subjects to be eligible to sit for the examination and they are recommended to sit for no more than seven subjects. English, Irish and mathematics are studied at leaving certificate level by almost all pupils. A certificate without these subjects is regarded as deficient. Indeed in reality, it turns out to be so, if measured in terms of third-level entry regulations and employer expectations. After these three, the next most heavily subscribed subject in County Cork is biology, by far the most popular of the science subjects. The dominance of biology over the other science subjects can be explained by the fact that in the pre-intermediate/leaving certificate era rural science was the science subject taught in the schools. The teachers who taught this subject had qualified as rural science instructors, through courses organised by the Department of Education. Naturally, these teachers sought to promote either biology or agricultural science as these were the subjects most akin to rural science.

Manpower considerations therefore determined that these were the subjects that would be pursued. The relevant teachers were in the schools, and graduates in other science areas were quite thin on the ground in the vocational schools when change was being brought about. Of course, this does not explain why biology, and

TABLE 2

Number of Candidates Sitting Various Subjects in Leaving Certificate Examinations in County Cork Vocational Schools 1978−1982

Subjects	Number of Candidates				
	1978	1979	1980	1981	1982
English	292	311	275	302	378
Mathematics	282	288	266	288	372
Irish	271	271	254	275	343
Biology	211	202	179	187	227
Technical drawing	162	177	173	159	180
Geography	164	154	149	153	155
Engineering workshop theory and practice	117	124	136	110	148
French	79	95	90	71	106
Business organisation	65	57	63	72	83
Accounting	63	65	59	47	77
Building construction	47	65	48	79	69
Home economics (general)	40	34	49	51	57
Home economics (soc. & sc.)	42	47	35	39	45
Economics	35	55	16	24	42
History	32	31	41	56	62
Physics	21	41	21	64	102
Agricultural science	29	30	39	37	33
Chemistry	24	28	19	22	20
Art	17	21	16	19	25
Mechanics	10	2	3	6	—
Physics and chemistry	18	17	21	—	10
Economic history	6	—	—	—	—
Music	—	—	2	—	1
Agricultural economics	8	1	2	9	—
Applied mathematics	—	—	2	4	—
Computer science	—	—	—	—	10

not agricultural science, became the dominant science subject. A possible explanation is that when the leaving certificate course was introduced to vocational schools, biology was considered more suitable, especially for girls, as it opened the way for entry into the nursing professions. Agricultural science probably suffered because it was not a matriculation subject in the early 1970s.

The fifth most heavily subscribed subject, and the most heavily subscribed subject of a technical nature, is technical drawing. Indeed, the subject is much more important in County Cork vocational schools than might be apparent from Table 2. The greatest number of girls to take the subject in any one year in the period studied was thirteen, so it can be deduced from the subscription figures that the vast majority of boys take technical drawing in the leaving certificate examination. Apart from any belief which may or may not exist as to the innate value of technical drawing, the relatively high subscription rate is no doubt influenced, as in the case of biology, by personnel considerations. Up to 1969 all schools employed one or more teachers of both woodwork and metalwork. These teachers would also have taught mechanical drawing to group certificate level. Following the addition of a senior cycle, a strong lobby of teachers pressed for the introduction of technical drawing. It made good timetabling sense to use the available personnel. Add to this the view held in vocational schools that technical drawing is a necessary complementary subject for anybody studying engineering workshop theory and practice or building construction, and its high subscription rate is not surprising. These factors may offer some explanation for the sharp contrast between the County Cork vocational school rate and the rate at national level where less than 11 per cent of students sat the subject in the leaving certificate of 1983.

It was mentioned that technical drawing is almost exclusively a boys' subject; home economics, on the other hand, is almost totally a girls' preserve. The highest number of boys, during any one school year over the period studied, who studied home economics was six while the percentage of girls taking home economics over the period never fell below eighty-four per cent. The schools divided fairly evenly over the period studied in terms of which home economics syllabus was offered, with slightly more students opting for general courses (see Table 2). In contrast, at national level, 76 per cent of the girls who took home economics in the leaving certificate in 1983 did the social and scientific course; this is more widely recognised for university matriculation purposes than the general course.

Geography is the next most heavily subscribed subject. The subscription figures for the County Cork schools compare to the national average for children from all types of post-primary schools. This is surprising when one considers that the number of schools which offered the subject in the period reviewed never exceeded twelve out of a possible nineteen schools in any one year. This would seem to indicate that in those schools where geography is offered, the level of subscription is high. The fact that many of the schools do not offer the subject at all, while it is a fairly heavily subscribed subject in the remainder, points to unresolved questions in the county as a whole as to what form the leaving certificate course should take. The question could arise: should a traditional academic subject such as geography, which (unlike Irish, English and mathematics) does not seem to have an over-riding claim for inclusion, be included in the curriculum of schools which are committed to providing a technical or commercial education?

The seventh most heavily subscribed subject has been engineering workshop theory and practice. Even more so than technical drawing, this subject is a male preserve. Only two girls studied the subject during the 1978−83 period while a minimum of 75 per cent of boys took the subject each year. Even by vocational school standards, however, the percentage of students in County Cork studying engineering is high, for only 52 per cent of vocational school boys nationally studied the subject in 1980/81.[18] Engineering workshop theory and practice is seen as the natural progression at senior level from metalwork at junior level. It is by far a more popular option than building construction, which (though wider in scope than woodwork) is seen as the follow-on subject from woodwork at junior level. Generally twice as many students sit for engineering in the examination than for building construction (see Table 2). Students usually have to choose between one subject and the other. In fact, in only two schools in the county in the period studied have students been able to study both engineering and building construction. This might come as a surprise to those who are under the impression that vocational schools offer pupils the opportunity to pursue a wide range of technical subjects.

All but four schools in the period studied put forward students for examination in a continental language. The significance of a continental language is that, according to the National University of Ireland regulations, one cannot matriculate without having studied a third language. In the five years 1978–82, 37 per cent was the highest percentage in any one year of pupils who could possibly satisfy university matriculation regulations. Of the remaining subjects, accounting and business organisation are the most heavily subscribed. Girls account for the great proportion of pupils studying these subjects. By adding the total number of girls studying the most heavily subscribed commercial subject in each school, it was calculated that a minimum percentage of girls doing at least one commercial subject was 75 per cent.

Curriculum at Junior Level

In September 1966 vocational schools were allowed to organise courses in preparation for the intermediate certificate examination. As the course leading to the intermediate certificate spanned the first three years after primary schooling and the day group certificate examinations covered the first two, it was decided to phase in the latter as two-thirds of the former. Syllabuses were amended so that pupils might sit for a group certificate at the end of the second post-primary year and take the intermediate at the termination of the third. This re-organisation of the examination structures worked to the detriment of the day group certificate examination. It was perhaps inevitable that an examination course viewed as being the equivalent of two-thirds of another would suffer in prestige.

The more prestigious intermediate certificate examination became the main target of achievement in County Cork vocational schools. Group certificate subjects which could not be taken in the intermediate certificate examination fell in popularity. There is little doubt that in County Cork schools, as in other vocational schools nationally, success in the intermediate certificate examination came to be the goal of junior level pupils. Schools in the county take a number of different approaches to the examination. These approaches could be categorised as follows:

1. only the weaker pupils, after three years of schooling, take
    the group certificate examination; and take the intermediate
    certificate examination after four years;
2. all pupils take the group certificate after two years and take
    the intermediate after three;
3. all pupils take the group certificate after three years and
    take the intermediate after four;
4. the better pupils take the group certificate in second year,
    the weaker pupils in third year; each group does the
    intermediate examination a year after the group certificate;
5. girls only do the group certificate;
6. boys only do the group certificate.

This multiplicity of approaches points to the fact that the day
group certificate is no longer important as a terminal examination.
Its original purpose, to testify that a pupil had successfully
completed a continuation course and thus to provide a passport
to employment, became obsolete. The day group certificate now
fulfils a number of functions, such as providing an incentive to
students to study during the second year; an initial experience of
an externally controlled examination; success or qualification for
weaker pupils who might not achieve as much in the intermediate
certificate examination.

While the day group certificate is no longer an important terminal
examination in County Cork vocational schools, however, it would
be incorrect to give the impression that technical subjects are no
longer important in the junior cycle curriculum. Indeed with the
exception of one school which resulted from an amalgamation
between the vocational school and a private boys' school, where
not all boys studied metalwork and woodwork, all of the boys at
junior cycle in all of the schools in 1982/83 studied mechanical
drawing, woodwork and metalwork. With one exception, all of
the girls in the county vocational schools in 1982/83 studied home
economics at junior level. Commerce was studied in all schools
in 1982/83 and, with the exception of four schools, was studied
by all of the girls in the schools. While technical subjects are still
important at junior cycle, it must be admitted that subjects
traditionally considered to be of an academic nature are making
inroads.

TABLE 3

Number of Students Sitting Intermediate Certificate Examination
in County Cork Vocational Schools 1980–82

	YEAR		
SUBJECT	*1980*	*1981*	*1982*
Irish	570	642	716
English	591	704	783
Mathematics	588	710	767
History	408	503	506
Geography	419	511	537
French	221	219	231
Spanish	27	24	23
Science 'A'	28	171	127
Science 'E'	536	517	637
Home economics	177	170	225
Metalwork	423	463	529
Mechanical drawing	422	506	553
Commerce	186	248	314
Art	37	29	104
Woodwork	421	502	521

Though not specified subjects for the intermediate certificate examination in vocational schools, history and geography have made significant inroads into the schools. By 1978/79, they were studied by all junior level pupils in twelve of the nineteen schools in the county. Only three schools did not offer these subjects. During the 1970s a continental language was introduced into all schools at junior level. Therefore, what has resulted, in terms of curriculum at junior level, is that certain core academic subjects are married to certain core technical subjects, with one or two extra options making the balance. The academic core can be identified as Irish, English, mathematics and science. Mechanical drawing, woodwork and metalwork form the technical element for boys, home economics and commerce for girls. An extra subject or subjects will be chosen from a continental language, history and geography, art, mechanical drawing for girls and commerce for boys. Because there are more subjects to be studied, the technical content of the curriculum has declined. Certain technical subjects – magnetism and electricity, and mechanics – are no longer approved subjects. On the whole, however, technical subjects still have a high profile at junior level. While not as much time is devoted to them, mechanical drawing, woodwork, metalwork, commerce and home economics are still regarded as essential curricular components. Therefore, at junior level the child is introduced to a range of academic and practical subjects with the latter being regarded as an integral part of the curriculum. This differs from what occurs at leaving certificate level where less time is devoted to technical studies. At this level, Irish, English, mathematics and a science subject form an academic core, and while there will be a technical element, the academic core is also likely to be supplemented by other academic studies such as geography or a continental language. Therefore, whereas at junior level, technical studies are viewed as being as essential a part of the curriculum as the academic core, they are less so at senior level where they are regarded more as additions to an academic core.

Factors Affecting the Curriculum in County Cork

While one can only speculate as to how the curricular pattern outlined has developed in the Cork County schools, one can point to the factors that have influenced the curriculum:

state departmental regulations, particularly at junior level;
external influences, such as matriculation and job-entry requirements;
inertia within the system resulting from traditional practices and resources in terms of teachers and facilities.

None of these factors could in themselves be considered dominant. Rather a curricular pattern developed as a result of a juxtaposition of these variables. Up to 1967 most of the teachers in County Cork vocational schools were specialist. Even if a particular school wanted to bring about major curricular change following the restructuring of the post-primary system, it would have proved quite difficult. Schools had a plentiful supply of teachers of metalwork, woodwork, domestic science and rural science. These particular subjects entailed a relatively high capital investment in terms of specialist facilities and equipment. Even by national vocational school standards, County Cork is very well equipped with metalwork rooms. During the 1970s much money was spent in the county on re-furbishing home economics rooms. Schools equipped with these types of facilities could not easily justify their positions if they chose not to do some practical subjects at leaving certificate level. Indeed it may well be that practical subjects owe their survival on the curriculum to inertia caused by teachers, facilities and traditional practices, rather than to any philosophical justification for their continued existence.

There can be little doubt that the matriculation requirements of the National University of Ireland exercised a strong influence on the emerging senior cycle curriculum of County Cork vocational schools in the early 1970s. To prepare students adequately for possible university entry would mean that they would have to spend time on academic studies, time which they might otherwise allocate to studies of a technical nature. To do otherwise, and to ignore university matriculation requirements, would be damaging in terms of their appeal to prospective pupils. It would also mean turning their backs on something they had long fought for, namely an avenue to the most prestigious sector of third-level education, the universities.

In the early 1970s the vocational schools, so long accustomed to a Cinderella-like role in Irish education, were determined to display their capabilities now that they had officially been raised to a position of equal status within the second-level sector. Individual schools which found themselves in competition for pupils with neighbouring secondary schools were determined to take up the challenge. While hard to quantify, the level of competition, mistrust, even jealousy, between schools of different traditions in County Cork towns in the early 1970s, now that they were competing for the same market, should neither be underestimated nor ignored. In this climate, those involved in the vocational school sector were anxious not to give substance to claims of being second-rate by denying pupils the opportunity to matriculate. It would be incorrect to give the impression that the over-riding concern of vocational school authorities in the county in planning leaving certificate programmes in the 1970s was to comply with matriculation requirements. As mentioned earlier, no more than 37 per cent of County Cork students in the period studied took a third language in any one year in the leaving certificate examination. On average, approximately 50 per cent of the schools do the home economics general course. If schools were overconcerned with matriculation requirements, they would opt for the social and scientific syllabus. Following the introduction of the leaving certificate to the schools, however, the majority of vocational school headmasters wanted to be able to answer yes to the query 'can my child go to university on leaving school?' Therefore, headmasters were obliged to offer a third language and a sufficient choice of academic options to enable students to matriculate, if they so desired. In providing a sufficient range of academic subjects, schools inevitably reduced the amount of time available for studies of a technical nature. The fact that technical drawing, building construction, and engineering theory and practice were not recognised matriculation subjects during the 1970s contributed to this. Their equivalents at junior level — mechanical drawing, woodwork and metalwork — had long been, and continue to be, bulwarks of technical education in County Cork vocational schools. Not alone did the new technical subjects at leaving certificate not contribute to a points total for matriculation purposes but by studying them to the exclusion of other subjects a prospective university candidate might not have the requisite six subjects for matriculation.

The senior cycle curriculum in the vocational schools has also been greatly influenced by the manner in which the Department of Education chose to re-organise the second level system. According to Mulcahy, the attempted reforms were introduced almost entirely within the existing framework of the secondary school curriculum and examination system.[19] To many people, all the restructuring entailed was the upgrading of the vocational school system. Far more was made of the fact that vocational school pupils could now sit for the traditional secondary school examination than the fact that secondary school students could take subjects of a technical nature. Had the Department of Education instituted new examinations, a different attitude might have prevailed; but the secondary schools traced their very roots and owed their origin to the intermediate examination. The Irish tradition in post-primary education is one in which secondary rather than vocational schools enjoyed status and prestige. Little wonder, then, that when the opportunity to do the intermediate and leaving certificate examinations was afforded to the vocational schools, they tended to emulate the secondary school model. The aims of vocational schools as set forth in the Vocational School Act 1930, or in Memo V. 40, were no longer relevant in an expanded system. But if they were not, 'nothing by the way of a clearly worked out and well formulated overall rationale of the development of vocational ... education was presented'[20] in their place.

Pressures were thus brought to bear on the sector to comply with the traditional secondary academic model. Some have characterised today's vocational schools as schools which provide neither an adequate academic nor a truly technical education.[21] It is a charge worth considering. Despite their size (twelve of the schools in Cork County have less than three hundred pupils enrolled and only three have more than five hundred), all the schools, with one exception, strive to provide a range of academic and technical studies. While there is breadth in each curriculum, it might be held that there is a lack of depth. One school took a conscious decision in 1978 to provide a technical studies based curriculum. A third language is not taught in the school even at junior level; nor is history or geography. The subjects on offer since 1978 were Irish, English, mathematics, physics, engineering workshop theory and practice, technical drawing, building construction, business organisation, home economics (social and scientific) and, up to 1981, mechanics. Boys had the opportunity of taking — and were encouraged to take — the three practical technical options. The curriculum could truly be described as technically oriented. It is an example of the type of curriculum that vocational schools might have adopted following the restructuring of the post-primary sector.

This school has been an exception in shunning the academic trappings of the widened curriculum. The other schools have adopted a broader approach. Whether this has been to the detriment of studies of a technical nature is debatable. If other schools nationally had adopted this approach when the leaving certificate was introduced, vocational education in the country might have been pushed to the periphery of mainstream post-primary education as has been the experience in many other countries. What is clear is that the manner in which the re-organisation of post-primary education at national level was conducted was not conducive to the introduction of technical studies, even though a major policy objective was to increase participation in studies of a technical nature.

Conclusion

The County Cork experience would seem to suggest that the government failed to assess the complexity of the educational change it proposed in the post-primary sector in the mid-1960s. Too many variables at school implementation level, such as staffing, competition between schools, curricular resources, were ignored. Exhortations to schools to share facilities fell mainly on deaf ears. Efforts to amalgamate schools to form new community schools succeeded only in cases where the local interests and special interests involved favoured such moves. In the absence of necessary support structures, the introduction of the intermediate and leaving certificate courses to vocational schools did not have the effect of attracting a greater proportion of the school-going population to these schools. Irish vocational schools have found it difficult to evade the influence of the longer established secondary schools, a difficulty which the national planners failed to appreciate fully when introducing changes in the mid-1960s.

Notes to Chapter 6

1. George Colley, Minister for Education, 'Letter to the authorities of secondary and vocational schools', January 1966.
2. Eileen Randles, *Post-primary education in Ireland, 1957–70* Dublin: Veritas Publications, 1975, p. 47. Randles outlines some of the factors that hindered co-operation: 'A simple practical difficulty in many places was the distance between the Secondary and Vocational schools. Moving pupils from one school to the other would entail loss of pupils' hours. Problems in insurance, of identification with a particular school community, of discipline, of time-tables, of co-education. . . .'.
3. *Studies* Vol 57, No 227, Dublin: Talbot Press, 1968, p. 247.
4. Cork County Vocational Education Committee, 'Minutes of proceedings at monthly meetings', June 1971, pp. 11-12.
5. 'Minutes', January 1973, p. 8.
6. *Ibid* p. 9.
7. Department of Education, 'Outline of Clonakilty case' p. 1, n.d. circa 1972.
8. See account of meeting in 'Minutes', May 1973, pp. 9-12.
9. 'Minutes', May 1973, p. 12.
10. 'Minutes of a special meeting to discuss post-primary provision in Cobh', 27 July 1972, pp. 1-4.
11. 'Minutes', November 1972, p. 2.
12. 'Report on post-primary facilities in Castletownbere, minutes', November 1973, pp. 2-3.
13. May 1973 (p. 12) and July 1973 (p. 9) meetings of the VEC.
14. Cork County VEC, *School building programme (Phase 2) 1979–82*, 1978. An additional school, Schull Community College, not contained in the building programme, was opened in 1982.
15. 'Minutes', February 1982, p. 7.
16. See *V35s, statistical returns for 1965–66*. These returns give the numbers in each class in each school.
17. Committee on the form and function of the intermediate certificate examination, *The I.C.E. Report* Dublin: Stationery Office, 1975.
18. Department of Education, *Report for the school year 1980–81* Dublin: Stationery Office, p. 55.
19. D. G. Mulcahy, *Curriculum and policy in Irish post-primary education* Dublin: Institute of Public Administration, 1981, p. 67.
20. *Ibid* p. 67. See also Cork County VEC, *Resources study* 1974.
21. Dale Tussing, *Irish educational expenditures: past, present and future* Dublin: Economic and Social Research Institute, 1978, p. 39.

7

The Interface of Research, Evaluation, and Policy in Irish Education

THOMAS KELLAGHAN

Prior to the 1960s, empirical research in Irish education was confined to sporadic incursions by students in search of data for theses. If one were to believe the statement of one Minister for Education, one might be led to the conclusion that the state's involvement in policy making was also unknown before the 1960s. Richard Mulcahy said in 1956 when he was Minister for Education that he did not see he had a duty 'to philosophise on educational matters'. Rather, his position was that 'of a kind of dungaree man, the plumber who will make the satisfactory communications and streamline the forces and potentialities of the educational workers and educational management in this country'.[1]

While it may be true that Ministers for Education had not been noted for their philosophical statements, a cursory reflection on the history of education in this country would surely have brought many examples to the Minister's mind of government involvement in policy making and planning in education. From as far back as the sixteenth century, when parish schools were founded in the reign of Henry VIII, the educational system has been used as an agent to promote government aims relating to linguistic, cultural, social, and political interests. The use of education to promote such aims continued through successive administrations and, though the aims may have changed, government efforts to direct education

The author is indebted to Mary Lewis for comments on an earlier version of this paper.

towards definite goals following independence were no less strenuous than prior to it.

What did change in the 1960s, and it was a change which is also to be found in other Western industrialised nations, was that the state's interest in education broadened (particularly to include economic considerations), its financial contribution to education increased, and it became committed to planning. This resulted in government departments becoming involved to a greater extent than they had in the past in specifying courses of action to achieve policy objectives.[2] A number of reasons have been advanced for this development of interest by governments; these include a growth in the belief that educational investment contributed to economic development, increasing interest in social problems (particularly poverty), and the expansion of education to involve ever-increasing numbers of students. This expansion raised a number of issues, such as equality of opportunity, the democratisation of education, the appropriateness of curricula, and the distribution of financial resources in the system.

As a basis for planning, decision makers needed information on the current situation; this, in turn, indicated a need for research. It was no coincidence that the first major state-sponsored research project in Ireland was the *Investment in education* survey in 1965 which placed education squarely in the forefront of policy making.[3] Research would also be needed to evaluate the effectiveness of any specific actions that might be taken.[4]

While from the 1960s onwards there was an increase in activity in policy and planning on the one hand and research and evaluation in education on the other (a development which was accompanied by efforts to build up viable research communities, mostly outside universities in this country), in practice, it is difficult to identify a close relationship between and among policies, planning, research, and evaluation. Often the activities seem to have run in parallel rather than in any clearly identifiable interactive mode. Although I shall attempt to identify linkages and interactions in this chapter, this is not easy as the relationships between policy, planning, research, and evaluation can take many forms and in each form the relationships are exceedingly complex. Furthermore, since policy making is not usually carried out in the public arena, it is difficult to obtain information which might identify factors which contributed towards its formation. There has been little by way of study of the relationship between policy making and research in this country and, although there have been a number of analyses and discussions of the research – social-policy relationship,[5] education has received little attention in these analyses. While there has also been at least one study of the effectiveness of policy making in a government department,[6] there have been no attempts in this country, as there have been in the United States, to conceptualise the uses of research by policy makers[7] or to study empirically how research and evaluation findings are used.[8]

Definition of Terms

It would be helpful if I could provide clear definitions of the terms policy, research, and evaluation that might be generally acceptable. A difficulty in doing this is that these are all areas of continuous study and understanding of the terms is changing rapidly. However, something about the general areas covered by the terms is necessary. When I speak of *policy*, I will be referring to general principles and courses of action designed to achieve some educational purpose.[9] Policy makers comprise politicians (members of government and members of parliament), senior administrators in ministries and government agencies, and their advisers. Information on policy may be found in official statements, legislation, White Papers, regulations, ministerial speeches, and specific policy documents. In Ireland, there is relatively little legislation relating to education; hence, one has to rely on other sources. Indeed, such other sources are not very plentiful either and do not always contain explicit and comprehensive statements of the objectives of educational policy.

I shall use the term *research* to apply to the systematic investigation of educational phenomena. While distinctions can be made between different kinds of policy research,[10] I shall use the term in a broad sense to refer to any kind of research undertaken to produce evidence related to issues of policy. Such research is usually carried out in research institutions, universities, and government departments. Most educational research in Ireland, as elsewhere, over the past twenty years has been carried out in an empirical tradition, in which the traditional methods and assumptions of the social sciences (which in turn were based on those of the physical sciences) were applied to educational phenomena. Historical and philosophical research has also been undertaken but, as yet, there has been little evidence of the approaches which are being proposed elsewhere as an alternative to empirical research, such as interpretive studies (analytic, phenomenological, and hermeneutic) and critical theory (neo-marxist). The lack of popularity of such approaches may arise at least in part from the fact that their use raises a host of problems for researchers and policy makers who have grown up in more empirical traditions.[11]

While educational research dates back to the turn of the century, *evaluation*, as we know it today, developed in the United States in the 1960s. At first, it seemed to some observers that while there were obvious similarities between evaluation and educational research in terms of content and methodology, there were also fairly clear distinctions between the two activities relating to problem selection and definition, the ability to generate hypotheses, the role of value judgments, the generalisability of findings, and the ability to control variables.[12] As evaluation studies became more common in the 1970s, the distinction between them and research became more blurred, not only because evaluation was changing but also because research was changing.[13]

In this paper, I shall not usually distinguish between research and evaluation studies as the two types of study are sufficiently similar in many respects to be regarded as comprising one category. However, the general point may be made that there has been an increase in evaluation studies in recent years in Ireland. Further, there has been a move away in such studies from the use of more traditional research paradigms towards more qualitative studies, in the belief that such studies are more likely to provide the kind of information needed by policy makers in making decisions.[14] It is not possible to say precisely how much of a shift there has been in the absence of a categorisation of studies. Besides, evaluation studies are often not reported in the literature in the way that research studies are, because they may not be of general interest or because the reports which they generate are confidential to clients. However, the impression one gets is that, while evaluation has not received the form of official approval that it has in the United States (in which most federal social programmes have an evaluation component), programme evaluation is becoming more common in Ireland, while research activity seems to have declined since the mid-1970s.[15]

In the rest of this chapter, I shall examine the interface of research, evaluation, and policy primarily from the point of view of research and evaluation. An examination from the point of view of policy might have led to a very different approach. For example, while I shall describe the types of methodology used in research and evaluation studies, somebody approaching the topic from the point of view of policy might have focused on types of policy. Following this, I shall describe some research projects which were designed to monitor policy and then I shall outline a variety of ways in which research and evaluation findings enter the policy-making process. Finally, I shall consider some of the problems in the interface of research, evaluation, and policy, an awareness of which may help to improve the interface. Throughout the paper, I shall confine my attention to research which had implications for policy as I have defined that term. Thus, I shall not be dealing with the considerable amount of research carried out in Ireland which had as its primary focus issues relevant to classroom teaching and school practices.

Types of Research and Evaluation Studies

A variety of types of research and evaluation studies has been used in policy-oriented research in Ireland. At the risk of doing an injustice to this variety, studies can be considered under six major headings, based on the typology of Rossi, Wright and Wright.[16] Since the categories are somewhat arbitrary, not every study will fit neatly into a single category; the inclusion of a study under one heading does not mean that it might not also fit under another. I will provide a brief outline of the categories, together with some examples from research in Ireland.

A form of research that appears from time to time in the literature on educational research involves an *analysis or review of policy and/or practice*. The approach adopted in this type of research may not be strictly empirical though it may draw on empirical data as well as on a variety of other modes of analysis and criticism, including philosophy, history, and literary criticism. Many studies contain brief reviews of aspects of policy and some have attempted to explicate basic concepts, such as equality of opportunity, which may underlie policy. The most extensive study of educational policy has been Mulcahy's analysis and evaluation of curriculum provision for the purpose of general education in post-primary education in Ireland.[17] A study of educational practice, more empirical than Mulcahy's, but also with important implications for policy, was Madaus and Macnamara's study of the quality and reliability of the leaving certificate examination.[18]

The second category of research is based on a paradigm which is common in the physical sciences and involves *research and development (R & D)*. Three steps are involved in this process: basic research, which is followed by the application of the findings of the research to meet everyday needs, which in turn is followed by the development of appropriate technologies. Attempts have been made to apply a similar paradigm in the social sciences in general and in education in particular. Such studies are rare in Ireland. One example involved the use of linguistic research on the Irish language to develop programmes for use in primary schools.[19]

A third category of research called *parameter estimation* has as its aim the provision of precise information about the nature and extent of existing conditions and involves the collection of information on the distributional characteristics of policy-relevant phenomena. Usually, parameter estimates focus on one variable of interest, which may be an input parameter (for example the availability of teaching aids in primary schools) or an output parameter (for example achievement in mathematics at sixth grade). As well as data which are explicitly collected to examine issues, data which are routinely collected by the Department of Education and presented in its reports are an important source of information on the system (for example numbers of schools of different types, numbers of students and teachers, students' examination performance). Individual researchers may make use of such data or of other unpublished statistics collected by the Department to examine issues of interest. Alvarez has estimated that 16 per cent of the studies which he examined in his review of educational research in Ireland had used public data, such as government statistics.[20]

A wide variety of aspects of the educational system at all levels was examined in the *Investment in education* study.[21] There also have been several less extensive studies of parameter estimation. As well as several surveys which have been carried out by the Department of Education on achievement in Irish, English, mathematics, environmental studies, and music, other institutions have carried out studies of achievement in spoken Irish[22] and in mathematics.[23] Since 1980, concern about unemployment among young school leavers has given rise to annual surveys of a sample of school leavers to obtain information on their educational attainment, aspects of their home background, and their career paths in their first year out of school.[24] The purpose of the studies is to help policy makers reach decisions on measures to assist the young unemployed in general and school leavers in particular.

A logical extension of parameter estimation is *monitoring*, that is, the following of trends in parameters over time. The index used to identify such trends is sometimes termed an educational indicator, which is really a form of social indicator, a term inspired by the use of economic indicators (such as gross national product and consumer price index). Indicators, which are intended to provide a broad indication or a general overview of the state of a system, have two main characteristics. Firstly, they are always quantifiable (that is, they represent in numerical form some aspects of the system) and secondly, since a particular value of an indicator will apply to only one period or point in time, several observations are required to interpret indicators fully.[25]

As in the case of parameter estimation, monitoring may be based on official statistics, although the use of such statistics for monitoring is limited in a number of ways.[26] In addition to using official statistics, information may also be specifically collected to examine the functioning of the system. One of the earliest educational research studies carried out in this country was prompted by 'an awareness of the need for ... an objective yardstick for measuring progress in reading comprehension in Ireland'[27] and was designed to be the first of a series of studies which would monitor the reading achievement of Irish school children.

Examples are to be found of two ways in which indicators have been used in research in Ireland. In the norm-referenced (or synchronic) approach, a comparison is made with another educational system. Alvarez, for example, has noted that about half of the studies of reading which he reviewed had established some sort of comparison with standards in other countries, particularly in Britain.[28] In self-referenced (or diachronic) comparisons, a comparison is made between indicators obtained at different points in time for the same system. Such comparisons are used to monitor changes within the system and in Ireland have been made on the basis of census data,[29] Department of Education statistics,[30] and information specifically obtained in surveys of reading achievement.[31]

Research which does not go beyond parameter estimation or monitoring is likely to be of limited value to a policy maker. Indeed, some commentators would not regard census data or the fact-gathering activities of many surveys as research at all, since such activities are divorced from the traditional disciplines of the social sciences, except for their methodology.[32] Since they are likely to lack a theoretical or even conceptual framework, the data they provide may do little to further understanding of the phenomena which the data represent. And, in the absence of such understanding, it is argued that it is difficult to prescribe ameliorative action.

Research which makes some attempt at *modelling social phenomena* is more likely to be of value to the policy maker in illuminating the processes which generate policy-relevant parameters and trends. Such research is not very much different from basic social research except that the kinds of problems investigated in policy-oriented research are likely to be selected because of their relevance to policy and the kinds of variables chosen are likely to be ones which are amenable to policy manipulation. Further, so as to be intelligible to clients, the models and methods of analysis used will often be less complicated and more commensensical than those used in basic research.[33]

Many Irish research studies, even ones which have been concerned with parameter estimation or monitoring, have included an estimation of relationships between variables in an attempt to increase understanding of the phenomena being investigated. Thus, for example, Harris's study of spoken Irish, which can be classified as a study of parameter estimation, also considered the extent to which variance in achievement in spoken Irish could be predicted from a range of demographic, administrative, and instructional variables.[34]

The final type of research which has been used in education is *experimentation and quasi-experimentation*. Experiments are the bread and butter of the physical sciences. Because they involve the manipulation and control of variables, they provide the strongest basis for drawing inferences about cause − effect relationships. Some of the behavioural sciences, particularly psychology, also accepted the experiment as the ideal, if not always feasible, procedure for research. In the wake of increasing criticism of the artificial nature of psychological experiments carried out in laboratories, suggestions have been made to bring the experiment into real-life situations.[35] Because of the difficulties in implementing experimental treatments in social settings, social scientists often use quasi-experiments in which all the conditions required for experimentation (for example the random allocation of subjects to treatments) are not present.

There has been a number of experiments or approximations to experiments in Irish educational research. One evaluation study which attempted to implement a quasi-experimental design was concerned with the effects of an early childhood education programme on children living in a disadvantaged area.[36] More recently, an experimental study, though primarily concerned with the use of standardised tests in schools, also attempted to assess the problems involved in implementing an experimental design in the educational system.[37]

These categories encompass most policy-related studies which have been carried out in Ireland over the past twenty years. The type of research adopted to examine a policy-related issue should ideally be determined by the nature of the issue and the kind of information that is required. In practice, however, because of time or financial constraints, policy makers and researchers may be tempted to opt for strategies which may not be entirely adequate. Social experimentation, compared to other forms of social research, may seem an expensive and time-consuming way of finding answers to policy questions. However, it has been argued that the costs of major experiments are small compared with the costs of social policies that do not work or could be significantly more effective if experimental information had been available.[38] If the findings of social experiments have in the past been less than adequate in meeting the needs of policy makers, the solution may not be to discontinue such experiments but to structure them and to supplement them with information obtained by other means so as to produce information which is more relevant to policy decisions.

The Response of Research to Policy

Very often, it is difficult to evaluate the extent to which a policy is achieving its intended effects because the objectives of the policy were not stated in sufficiently precise terms. Despite this problem, there has been a number of attempts to evaluate broad policy objectives and specific programme initiatives. Two examples will be considered here, which relate to major policy objectives of the 1960s.

Equality of opportunity in education While government policy was not always clearly stated in terms of the criteria of equality, several policy statements indicate that the meritocratic ideal played a major role in its thinking.[39] The meritocratic ideal does not assume that equality of participation (or achievement) will result from policies designed to promote that ideal. All it requires is that educational participation or achievement should not be determined by such characteristics as gender, social class, place of residence, or other variables considered to be educationally irrelevant. Rather, such achievements should depend on an individual's ability, choice, and effort.

One study in Ireland followed in the tradition of American studies of the status attainment process[40] in attempting to determine the extent to which attainment was related to an individual's ability or to educationally irrelevant factors, particularly gender and socio-economic background.[41] Of the factors on which information was obtained when students were eleven years of age, the best predictor of students' persistence in or withdrawal from the system was students' level of verbal ability. This variable also correlated more highly than any other of the initial measures with students' performance in public examinations (intermediate and leaving certificate) and with their occupational status on leaving school.

While the educationally irrelevant variables did not play as significant or consistent a role as ability in predicting the educational attainments of students (and this was particularly true in the case of gender), socio-economic status was found to be an important factor. As had been found in other studies, from the end of primary schooling up to third-level education, the representation of students from the lower socio-economic groups decreased, while the representation of those from the higher groups increased. Further, the loss of high-ability students was proportionately greater among students from non-professional backgrounds than among students from professional backgrounds.

What of the relative size of the effects of ability and socio-economic background for retention in the system? An estimate of this can be obtained from a consideration of reanalyses of the data obtained in this study.[42] These reanalyses can be interpreted as indicating that ability has more than twice the explanatory power of socio-economic status for retention at entry to post-primary school, slightly more throughout the post-primary period, and over nine times as much at the point of transition to third level. To the extent that these findings can be taken as indicative of the operation of meritocracy in the system, it can be said that the system is operating in accord with government policy. However, to the extent that the system is not totally meritocratic, policy objectives are not being achieved. Since policy statements lacked specificity, there is no way of knowing whether or not the position revealed in the study can be regarded as satisfactory in terms of government policy.

Vocational education   Policy relating to the promotion of the role of education in providing students with technical and other applied skills of a vocational kind was examined in a study which used official statistics to determine the extent to which vocationalism had increased in second-level education from the late 1960s to the early 1980s.[43] Trends were examined in the numbers enrolled in vocational schools and in the numbers taking vocationally oriented subjects in public examinations. In both cases, evidence was found of increasing vocationalism. While vocational schools between the early 1960s and 1980s lost their share of junior-cycle students (from 29 per cent to 24 per cent), a trend which obviously goes against increasing vocationalism, their share of senior-cycle students grew very considerably (10 per cent to 23 per cent). In the case of examinations, an increase in participation between the late 1960s and early 1980s occurred in most vocationally oriented subjects which exceeded the increase in the total number of students sitting for examinations. For example, the increase between 1969 and 1983 in the number of students who took the group certificate examination was 38 per cent. However, the increases in the numbers taking nine vocationally oriented subjects were all greater; they ranged from 221 per cent for shorthand to 59 per cent for domestic science. As in the study of equality of opportunity, we cannot say whether or not the situation revealed by these statistics can be regarded as satisfactory from a policy point of view, since no precise targets were set for policy. All that can be said is that the trends in vocationalism for the most part are in accord with policy.

The Response of Policy to Research

Does research affect the decisions of the policy maker? More specifically, do we have any evidence from this country that it does? Since research evidence is likely to be only one element influencing the decision of a policy maker and since policy makers do not usually provide a detailed rationale of the basis on which they reach decisions, it is easy to conclude, as some commentators have, that research rarely has any discernible impact on the policy-making process.[44] No doubt, one could find many examples in which information obtained from research or evaluation studies has been ignored or neglected by the policy maker. However, Marshall Smith, who has considerable experience of working in government in the United States, has observed that 'only those who have not been in state or federal government doubt that information from research affects policy and public opinion'.[45] It may be that research has had a greater impact on policy in the United States, where there is a tradition of politicians employing experts to provide policy-relevant information, than in European countries. In Britain, for example, it has been argued that politicians are likely to be ignorant of social science research and to regard 'practical experience' as the major legitimate source of knowledge.[46] Given the similarities in traditions and attitudes between the bureaucratic structures of Britain and Ireland, we might expect the influence of research in this country to be similar to its influence in Britain rather than to that in the United States.

A major difficulty in assessing the response of policy to research is that the relationship between research knowledge and policy is complex, indeterminate, and unsystematic.[47] In an examination of research utilisation, Weiss has identified seven meanings which can be attached to the term.[48] I shall outline Weiss's categories, identifying where possible, research from Ireland that fits the categories. In an alternative classification by Rich, the first five of Weiss's types involve instrumental use in which changes in policy or practice result directly from research findings.[49] The final two types involve conceptual use; in these, changes in the decision maker's perception and understanding of policies or practice are influenced by the findings of research studies.

We have seen that research and development is a basic procedure in the physical sciences. Utilisation based on this procedure has been identified as *the knowledge-driven model*. Basic research is carried out which is followed in turn by applied research, the development of technologies, and finally their application to the solution of some problem. Weiss points out that few examples can be found in the social sciences of the use of research knowledge in this way. In Irish education, the research that seems to come closest to this model was the linguistic analysis of vocabulary and structure of the Irish language on which primary school programmes in Irish were based (*Buntús Gaeilge*, 1966).

The second type of research utilisation is the *problem-solving model*. In this situation, a problem exists and a decision has to be made. However, the information that is available is not adequate to generate a solution to the problem or to select among alternative solutions. Thus, research is required to clarify the situation and reduce uncertainty and may be commissioned to provide the required information.

This type of research is common. However, it is often difficult to identify the precise role that research information ultimately plays in making a decision. For example, while many features of educational policy in the 1960s and 1970s were reflected in the *Investment in education* report (1965), it is not clear whether the report's findings determined policy or were used to support policy decisions that had already been taken. (If the latter is true, the *Investment in education* findings would fit more properly under the political model of use, described below, than under the problem-solving model.) For example, the amalgamation of small schools was already under way before the study began while the need for increased technical education had been anticipated by the Minister for Education at least two years before the publication of the report.[50]

Evaluation rather than research studies are more likely to fit into the problem-solving model of research utilisation. Over the years, the Department of Education has commissioned several evaluations of school programmes. The first of these was a pre-school programme for three- and four-year old children in a disadvantaged area.[51] More recently, other programmes such as transition year programmes and youth encounter projects have been evaluated.[52]

In the problem-solving model of research utilisation, it has usually been assumed that the research findings will have direct and immediate applicability and will form the basis of decisions. For example, in the early stages of the development of programme evaluation in the United States in the 1960s, it was thought that decisions to continue or discontinue programmes would be made on the basis of evaluation findings.[53] However, time was to reveal that discontinuing social programmes is rare and discontinuing them on the basis of research or evaluation findings is practically unheard of. This is so partly because the findings of evaluation studies are never entirely compelling, but perhaps of greater importance because 'evaluation is in many ways just another political act that occurs in a context where power, ideology, and interests are more powerful determinants of decision making than feedback about programmes'.[54]

A variant of the problem-solving model of research is the problem-creation model. Research in the problem-creation mould, rather than attempting to provide information that might help solve a problem that has already been identified, focusses on aspects of the educational system that may be problematic and in need of the policy maker's attention. Macnamara's study of bilingual education in Irish primary schools fits into this category.[55] While it is not possible to document the precise influence of Macnamara's study, his findings received considerable public attention and he was invited to discuss these with Department of Education officials. It is clear from the experience of Macnamara's study that policy makers are as likely to attend to problem-creation research as they are to attend to problem-solving research.

A third way in which research can enter the decision-making arena is as part of an interactive search for knowledge. The *interactive model* is probably common enough in policy. As indicated above, we would expect decision makers to call on a variety of sources of information and experience, in which the use of research would be only one part of a complicated process, before reaching decisions. Because of its very nature, it is difficult to document the role of research in reaching individual decisions using the interactive model. However, the use of research to clarify issues and support arguments can be seen in government publications. The official document which makes the widest and most effective use of research is the *White Paper on educational development* (1980).[56] In developing its positions on a range of issues, research evidence (particularly research that had been carried out in Ireland) is frequently cited, although unfortunately, citations for the research are not provided in the paper. The research refers to standards in reading and mathematics (p. 25), teachers' views of the 'new' curriculum and its effects (pp. 26-27), problems of disadvantage (p. 32), class size (p. 36), and the development of measures of literacy and numeracy (p. 48).

A less satisfactory appreciation of research is to be found in the work of the policy advisory body, the National Economic and Social Council. Two examples will illustrate this point. The first describes a situation in which the NESC does not seem to understand the implications of research which it cites. In a 1976 publication, it accepts on the basis of a study by Swan,[57] that '30 per cent of entrants to vocational schools had severe reading difficulties'.[58] The conclusion is based on the assumption that students scoring lower than one standard deviation below the mean (15.9 per cent of students) suffer from 'severe reading difficulty'. While Swan's study did show that low-scoring students were overrepresented in vocational schools, the percentage scoring lower than one standard deviation below the mean was a function of the distribution of the scores, not of the level of reading skill demanded by the test. If a normal probability curve fits a distribution of scores, the performance of any group, whether it be at kindergarten or university, will contain 15.9 per cent of respondents with scores lower than one standard deviation below the mean. To assume that such students suffer from a severe reading difficulty is entirely unwarranted. In a later publication, NESC makes recommendations for policy[59] while in fact it should have been making recommendations for research. Its recommendations were that

priority for expenditure of funds in education should be given to
compulsory age groups, 'as this would do most to promote equality
of opportunity in education' (p. 44), and to make adequate provision
for remedial teachers. Apart from the problem that neither 'equality
of opportunity' nor 'adequate provision' is defined, the report fails
to provide any supporting evidence for its recommendations. It
may be that pre-school provision or home intervention would do
more to promote equality in terms of student achievement than
higher expenditure during the compulsory period. It may also be
that similar provision or greater attention to the identification of
pupils with learning problems in the early stages of schooling would
be more effective than providing remedial teachers.

The fourth model of research utilisation is the *political model*.
In this case, decision makers, for whatever reason, have taken
a stand that research is not likely to shake. If research is used,
this will be done, probably in a selective manner, to provide support
for a position that has already been taken. Such a use of research
may seem improper. However, so long as the research is not
distorted or misinterpreted, and so long as it is available to all
parties to the issue, it can serve a useful function in debate.

A fifth model of research use is the *tactical model*. In this case,
the fact that research is being done is used as a tactic for delaying
action.

A sixth method of research use is represented by the
enlightenment model, which, though not an easy concept to
define,[60] is an important one, as it appears to be the way in
which research most frequently enters the policy arena.[61] In this
approach, research is considered to be a gradual and diffuse
process,[62] providing concepts and theoretical perspectives that
permeate the policy-making process; research utilisation then
becomes a 'process through which research penetrates the sphere
of organisational decision-making – the process of understanding,
accepting, reorienting, adapting, and applying results to the world
of practice'.[63] Research, according to this model, is less likely to
affect individual decisions than it is to affect general policy defined
by Cohen and Garet as 'a system of knowledge and beliefs – ideas
about the causes of social problems, assumptions about how society
works and notions about appropriate solutions'.[64] Even if policy
makers do not seek out research findings when faced with a
particular issue and even though they may not be aware of specific

research information, it is still likely that educational and social science findings and orientations shape to some extent the way they think about educational issues. Thus, it is unlikely that policy makers would be unaware of the broad thrust of research on children's learning difficulties, disadvantage, school effectiveness, and the relationship between home background and scholastic achievement, and that their awareness would not have affected the ways in which they define issues and seek solutions.

Though its advantages may be obvious, this model of research utilisation suffers from a number of disadvantages. For one thing, the process is open to oversimplification and distortion and poor research may attract as much attention as good research. Secondly, it is an inefficient way of reaching policy audiences and some important research may never get to the decision maker. These problems point to the importance of adequate communication between the policy maker and the researcher.

A final view of research utilisation regards *research as part of the intellectual enterprise of society*. In this view, research is another dependent variable (rather than an independent variable affecting policy), collateral with policy, as well as with other areas of intellectual endeavour, such as philosophy, history, journalism, legal studies, and criticism. While at one time it was thought that evaluation findings would have a more specific decision-oriented focus than is implied in this view of more traditional research, the history of the use of evaluation findings indicates that evaluation too is often much broader and less specific than early practitioners and clients had envisaged and hoped for. Like research, evaluation plays a co-determinative role with other factors in making decisions, influencing internal priorities of programmes and the way in which programmes are provided, being cited in discussion and debate and being used in pre-service and in-service education courses.[65] General statements about programmes based on evaluation studies, just as research generalisations have, are now entering textbooks.[66]

The promotion of the advancement of knowledge as a cultural aim and as an element in society may properly be regarded as a function of government. One would expect that this objective would be realised primarily through the allocation of funds to universities, while the promotion of research for public planning and operation would be achieved through non-university institutions.[67] In fact, funds for carrying out research in education in Irish universities have been extremely limited. Furthermore, the type of research in which universities have engaged has tended to be of a rather practical nature.[68] Because of this, it is probable that the role of educational research as part of the intellectual enterprise of society, as well as its role in a general enlightenment model of utilisation, has been less than it might have been. At the same time, it would be wrong to assume that research in education as an intellectual enterprise has been entirely neglected or that such work has not contributed to the *Weltanschauung* of contemporary Ireland. In tracing developments from the 'bleakness of the intellectual terrain of twenty five years ago', Lee has pointed out that in 1957 there was still 'no ESRI, with its impressive publications list, no NIEC or NESC, no Foras Forbartha, no NBST. There was no *Crane Bag*, no *Irish Economic and Social History*, no *Irish Educational Studies*, no *Irish Journal of Education*, no *Irish Jurist*, no *Scríobh*, no *Studia Hibernica* ...'[69]

However, perhaps it is a measure of the quality and influence of thought on educational matters during the period that in the volume in which these words were written, *Unequal achievement: the Irish experience 1957–1982*, the subject of education did not merit a chapter.

The evidence that is available from studies which have been carried out in other countries indicates that research use in policy is likely, using the categorisation of Rich,[70] to be conceptual rather than instrumental. Weiss has concluded that in the United States knowledge that derives from systematic research and analysis is only sometimes used in a direct and instrumental fashion in the formulation of policy; rather, it is more likely to be used as general guidance affecting the development and modification of policy in diffuse ways.[71] In European countries also, Husén and Kogan have found the diffusion and enlightenment uses to be most common.[72] It is unlikely that the situation is different in Ireland.

The enlightenment or conceptual role of research in policy becomes clearer when we consider how policies and policy-decisions come about. If it were normal practice for policies to be formed and decisions reached only after a problem had been formally identified and systematically deliberated on by a group of authorised decision makers weighing the alternative options, then research might have a more instrumental role. Most policy, however, does not come about in this way. The process is less rational; in Weiss's terminology, it tends to 'accrete' with little conscious deliberation.[73] In this situation, it is easy to see why the enlightenment or conceptual use of research has been deemed to be most influential.

Problems in the Interface

Although the extent of research and evaluation activity in the Irish system of education may not be great by international standards, nevertheless, over the past twenty years, a variety of issues relevant to policy, using a wide range of techniques and approaches, has been investigated. Policy makers, for their part, seem to take into account the contributions of research in their deliberations. This is not to say that problems do not exist in the interface of research, evaluation, and policy in Irish education, that policy makers are always adequately informed, or that researchers can always provide relevant information. Few of the problems, however, are specific to Ireland.

A major problem arises from the fact that knowledge production and knowledge use are vastly different kinds of activities, with different objectives, traditions, methods of procedure, time frames, assumptions, and criteria of worth.[74] Traditionally, the researcher has been primarily interested in promoting the growth of knowledge without being particularly concerned about its applicability. The concern of the policy maker, on the other hand, is with achieving immediate policy, planning, or administrative goals and he or she is likely to be interested only in research that is relevant to his or her sphere of responsibility.[75] The preoccupations of the policy maker obviously create problems for the researcher in terms of selection of issues and the speed with which findings can be presented. The problems are clearly exaggerated if one's view of research utilisation is confined to the problem-solving model of research. While there is certainly a role for research and evaluation in the problem-solving context, particularly if a concern for use permeates the study,[76] a greater appreciation of the fact that research and evaluation findings have their major impact in influencing the decision maker's perception and understanding of policies and practices would serve to limit problems in this area.

A further difference between the approaches of the researcher and the policy maker arises from the fact that research assumes a rational view of events and has traditionally based its procedures on an empirical and sometimes positivist mechanistic representation of reality. Policy decisions, on the other hand, are complex political activities, involving negotiation, compromise, and response to pressures and lobbies from a wide variety of sources that must be fitted into pre-existing belief patterns and value systems.[77] While researchers may make recommendations for action or reform in their reports, the final decision about action is something that emerges from the political process. In reaching a decision, the recommendations of the researcher may be of value, but the policy maker's perspective is likely to be more broadly based and to take into account what has been described as 'soft' knowledge, that is knowledge that is 'nonresearch based, qualitative and couched in lay language'.[78] Furthermore, the policy maker, particularly if a politician, is likely to be more sensitive and attuned to the views of the various interest groups that will be affected by the decision. In this situation, research and evaluation findings are to be seen as nothing more than inputs to a debate, though perhaps a different type of input than the views of interested parties; they should not be regarded as a determining force in a non-democratic naively rationalistic process. The political process is the deciding factor, not the research or evaluation data or even the individual decision maker.[79]

As well as the intrinsic problems discussed above, further problems in the use of research arose in the 1960s and 1970s. These arose partly because the expectations of policy makers regarding the contributions of research to policy were not met.[80] The theoretical knowledge which social scientists could provide in constructing programmes for the amelioration of social problems (for example poor academic achievement) was generally found to be inadequate. Even when not inadequate on this score, social scientists could not provide the necessary information regarding design and implementation activities. Furthermore, studies provided inconclusive findings or the findings of the same study were interpreted in different ways. All this led to a growth in uncertainty about the degree of authority warranted by research.[81]

All the problems in the interface between policy and research do not arise from the inadequacies of research. For example, if the researcher has lost some authority, so too has the decision maker. While certain individuals are recognised as occupying positions of authority in the legislative and executive branches of government, their decision making is increasingly constrained by the views of other stakeholders in the system (for example teachers and parents). This means not only that the decision maker has to take into account a variety of sources of influence and conflicting values but that research also has to be sensitive to the priorities and values of stakeholders other than the identified decision maker.[82] The loss of authority of the decision maker, which is complemented by an increase in the role of other interested parties, does not diminish the role of research, unless research is viewed as a private communication between researcher and decision maker. Indeed, given the fact that many more points of view compete for a say in decision making, the more disinterested findings of research, if relevant and understood, can become all the more important in the political process.

If the expectations of policy makers for research were not met in the past, this was due in part to the fact that their expectations were unrealistic. Often they sought specific answers to specific problems without appreciating the variety of modes in which research can influence policy or the variety of factors influencing their own decisions. At other times, they may have been interested only in the tactical use of research, seeking information that would support or legitimate policy positions. Indeed, one may ask to what extent a policy maker wants his or her judgment tested. Does he or she really want people to evaluate the effectiveness of policy decisions? Many policy makers (particularly politicians) see themselves and their reputations as intrinsically tied up with their decisions, which, after all, are the solutions which they have reached after an appraisal of social problems. Given this kind of commitment, it may be difficult for the policy maker to remain impartial towards the findings of a presumably objective evaluation. A way round this would be for the policy maker to associate himself or herself with the identification of problems rather than with their solution.[83] This would leave room for research and evaluation, and politicians might not only protect but enhance their reputations.

These problems serve to illustrate the need for greater knowledge and understanding of research on the part of those working in the policy arena, a lack of which may, in the past, have militated against a more effective application of the findings of research to policy. Past failures may also have been due to a lack of contact between researchers and decision makers.[84] Researchers must take some of the blame for this; their dissemination procedures are not always effective, with the result that research findings do not reach the policy maker, at least not in an intelligible form.[85] Overly technical language may be interpreted by policy makers as jargon. Sometimes reports come to policy makers through newspaper reports, suffering distortion in the process. While newspaper reports can provide a useful information service on research to the public, such reports can hardly be regarded as adequate as a basis for policy decisions.

Much of the communication between the researcher and the policy maker will no doubt continue through existing systems of publication and dissemination. However, consideration might also be given to procedures which might contribute to an improvement of the situation. One procedure would involve the setting up of a body which would serve all government departments which at present are involved in the formation and execution of social policy, particularly in the areas of education, health, welfare, and justice. The body would serve to co-ordinate the functions of different departments in research, policy, and planning.[86] An alternative procedure would involve the appointment to administrative and policy-decision-making posts of people with research experience. Such action seems particularly necessary in countries such as ours which do not have a long tradition of social research or possess government structures which are particularly sensitive to such research.

Whatever procedures might be adopted to improve communication and mutual understanding between policy makers and researchers, it would be wrong to expect that research in the future will ever provide simple answers to social problems. Since the problems are enormously complex, one would expect solutions to be equally so. Thus, the use of research information in policy is not necessarily going to make decision making any easier. Indeed, if we have learned anything from the history of educational research, it is that research, by drawing attention to new facets of problems, can have the overall effect of making decision making more difficult. But if the increased complexity and alternate ways of framing, exploring, and resolving problems that research can bring to the policy-making process more accurately reflect reality, then policy makers should have a sounder basis for policy making.

Notes to Chapter 7

1. S. O'Connor, *A troubled sky: reflections on the Irish educational scene 1957–1968* Dublin: Educational Research Centre, 1986, p. 1.
2. G. Psacharopoulos, 'The planning of education: where do we stand?' in *Comparative Education Review* (1986), Vol 30, pp. 560-73.
3. G. FitzGerald, 'Investment in education' in *Studies* (1965), Vol 54, pp. 361-74.
4. Here we may note that there have been relatively few studies of Irish education from an economic point of view. This is surprising given the importance which economic studies have assumed in educational policy making and planning in other countries. While it is true that government policy of the 1960s and the major research study of the period, *Investment in education* (1965), owed much to a manpower-planning approach, there is no evidence that plans were ever based on precisely worked-out models of a mathematical, econometric, or linear-programming nature. Neither was much attention paid (in published policy or research at any rate) to an

economic evaluation of alternative strategies and programmes to achieve policy objectives. Despite a bow to manpower planning needs in policy statements, in retrospect much of the actual educational expansion of the 1960s and 1970s seems to have been the result of an increasing popular demand for education to which policy makers, planners, and schools responded.

5. K. Kennedy, 'The role of social science in relation to public policy' in *Proceedings of the Royal Irish Academy* (1973) Vol 73, pp. 647-68.

D. O'Doherty (ed), *The role of the social sciences in policy making: a science policy perspective* Dublin: National Board for Science and Technology, 1981.

Institute of Public Administration, *Research in Ireland: the relevance of Rothschild?* report of a seminar held at the IPA, Dublin, 1972.

6. V. McDonald, 'Policy making in the Department of Education: is it effective?', unpublished masters' dissertation, Trinity College Dublin, 1985.

7. C. H. Weiss, 'The many meanings of research utilization' in *Public Administration Review* (1979) Vol 39, pp. 426-431.

R. F. Rich, 'Uses of social science information by federal bureaucrats: knowledge for action versus knowledge for understanding' in C. G. Weiss (ed), *Using social research in public policy making* Lexington, MA: Heath, 1977.

8. J. B. Cousins and K. A. Leithwood, 'Current empirical research on evaluation utilization' in *Review of Educational Research* (1986) Vol 56, pp. 331-64.

M. W. Patton, *Utilization focussed evaluation* Beverly Hills, CA: Sage, 2nd edition, 1986.

C. H. Weiss, 'Knowledge creep and decision accretion' in *Knowledge Creation Diffusion Utilization* (1980) Vol 1, pp. 381-404.

9. D. Gil, *Unravelling social policy: theory, analysis, and political action towards social equality* Cambridge, MA: Schenkman, 1973.

10. A. Majchrzak, *Methods for policy research* London: Sage, 1984.

11. Problems relate to the position adopted by the researcher and his or her detachment in carrying out research (as against involvement and commitment to having an impact on society), the value of different kinds of evidence, and the reluctance of some researchers (particularly marxists and phenomenologists), for moral and political reasons, to become involved in policy-related research.

12. J. K. Hemphill, 'The relationships between research and evaluation studies' in R. W. Tyler (ed), *Educational evaluation: new roles, new means. The sixty-eighth yearbook of the National Society for the Study of Education* Part II. Chicago: NSSE, 1969.

13. The idea that there are at least two ways in which evaluation differs from educational research still persists, however. Firstly, much evaluation activity involves a judgmental component as well as a descriptive one. For example, in the Joint Committee on Standards for Educational Evaluation, *Standards for evaluation of educational programs, projects, and materials* (New York: McGraw Hill, 1981, p. 12), evaluation is defined as 'the systematic investigation of the worth or merit of some object'. By contrast, traditional

educational research sought to avoid such judgments. Secondly, while research tends to have its origin and seeks justification in the existing corpus of scientific knowledge and is carried out with the purpose of expanding that corpus, evaluation has focussed on practical problems which have been defined in terms of real-life situations arising out of the needs of decision makers and demanding a short-term response. This means that account has to be taken of such factors as cost, ethicality, political feasibility, and the immediate utility of findings (D. Stufflebeam and W. J. Webster, 'Evaluation as an administrative function' in N. J. Boyan (ed), *Handbook of research on educational administration* New York: Longman, 1988). Recently, it has been argued that all 'practical' research, not only evaluation, should take account of such factors (M. Scriven, 'Evaluation as a paradigm for educational research' in E. R. House (ed), *New directions in educational evaluation* London: Falmer, 1986).

14. L. Joyce, 'Developments in evaluation research' in *Journal of Occupational Behaviour* (1980), Vol 1, pp. 181-90.
15. B. Alvarez, 'A review of educational research in Ireland, 1960–1980' in *Irish Journal of Education* (1984), Vol 18, pp. 23-48.
16. P. H. Rossi, J. D. Wright and S. R. Wright, 'The theory and practice of applied social research', in *Evaluation Quarterly* (1978), Vol 2, pp. 171-91.
17. D. Mulcahy, *Curriculum and policy in Irish post-primary education* Dublin: Institute of Public Administration, 1981.
18. G. F. Madaus and J. Macnamara, *Public examinations. A study of the Irish leaving certificate* Dublin: Educational Research Centre, St Patrick's College, 1970.
19. *Buntús Gaeilge, Reamhthuarascáil ar thaighde teangeolaíochta a rinneadh sa Teanglann, Rinn MhicGormain* Dublin: Department of Education, 1966.
20. Alvarez, 'A review of educational research'.
21. *Investment in education. Report of the Survey Team appointed by the Minister for Education in October, 1962* Dublin: Stationery Office, 1965.
22. J. Harris, *Spoken Irish in primary schools: an analysis of achievement* Dublin: Institiúid Teangeolaíochta Eireann, 1984.
23. T. Kellaghan, G. F. Madaus, P. W. Airasian and P. Fontes, 'The mathematical attainments of post-primary school entrants' in *Irish Journal of Education* (1976), Vol 10, pp. 3-17.
24. R. Breen, *Education and the labour market: work and unemployment among recent cohorts of Irish school leavers* Dublin: Economic and Social Research Institute, 1984.
    R. Breen, B. J. Whelan and J. Costigan, *School leavers 1980–1985* Dublin: Department of Labour, 1986.
    D. Hannan, *Schooling and the labour market: young people in transition from school to work* Shannon: Shannon Curriculum Development Centre, 1986.
25. J. N. Johnstone, *Indicators of education systems* Paris: UNESCO, 1981.
26. A number of limitations of official statistics for use in policy-oriented research have been identified (see J. Blackwell, *Information for policy* Dublin: National Economic and Social Council, 1985; National Economic and Social Council, *Statistics for social policy* Report No 17, Dublin: NESC,

1976). Firstly, statistics are usually collected as a by-product of some administrative procedure. A researcher, or even a policy maker, might choose to collect other statistics. Secondly, statistics are usually presented in summary form in terms of totals or averages while a major concern for policy might relate to a sub-set of the population, such as those living in a particular part of the country. Thirdly, statistics usually describe inputs to services rather than outputs. Fourthly, there is sometimes a lack of consistency from year to year in the statistics that are published. This may render impossible the study of trends over time. And finally, statistics in Ireland, with the exception of those obtained in the Household Budget Survey are obtained separately for individual social services which means that one cannot examine in the statistics interconnections which may be crucial to policy between, for example, education, housing conditions, employment, and use of medical services.

27. S. G. Kelly and P. McGee, 'Survey of reading comprehension' in *New Research in Education* (1967), Vol 1, pp. 131-34.
28. Alvarez, 'A review of educational research'.
29. R. C. Geary and E. W. Henry, 'Education and socio-economic class: a statistical analysis of 1971 Irish census data' in *Irish Journal of Education* (1979), Vol 13, pp. 5-23.
30. D. Hannan, R. Breen, B. Murray, D. Watson, N. Hardiman and K. O'Higgins, *Schooling and sex roles: sex differences in subject provision and student choice in Irish post-primary schools* Dublin: Economic and Social Research Institute, 1983.
    T. Kellaghan and M. Hegarty, 'Participation in the leaving certificate examination, 1961-1980' in *Irish Journal of Education* (1984), Vol 18, pp. 72-106.
31. T. Kellaghan and G. F. Madaus, 'Trends in educational standards in Great Britain and Ireland' in G. R. Austin and H. Garber (ed), *The rise and fall of national test scores* New York: Academic Press, 1982.
32. G. Payne, R. Dingwall, J. Payne and M. Carter, *Sociology and social research* London: Routledge and Kegan Paul, 1981.
33. P. H. Rossi, J. D. Wright and S. R. Wright, 'The theory and practice of applied social research' in *Evaluation Quarterly* (1978), Vol 2, pp. 171-91.
34. Harris, *Spoken Irish in primary schools*.
35. D. T. Campbell, 'Factors relevant to the validity of experiments in social settings' in *Psychological Bulletin* (1957), Vol 54, pp. 297-312.
36. T. Kellaghan, *The evaluation of an intervention programme for disadvantaged children* Slough, Berks: NFER Publishing Co, 1977.
37. T. Kellaghan, G. F. Madaus and P. W. Airasian, *The effects of standardized testing* Boston: Kluwer-Nijhoff, 1982.
38. D. H. Greenberg and P. K. Robins, 'The changing role of social experiments in policy analysis' in *Journal of Policy Analysis and Management* (1978), Vol 5, pp. 340-362.
39. OECD, *Review of national policies for education. Ireland* Paris: Organisation for Economic Cooperation and Development, 1969.
40. P. M. Blau and O. D. Duncan, *The American occupational structure* New York: Wiley, 1967.

41. V. Greaney and T. Kellaghan, *Equality of opportunity in Irish schools* Dublin: Education Co., 1984.

42. V. Greaney and T. Kellaghan, 'Factors related to level of educational attainment in Ireland' in *Economic and Social Review* (1985), Vol 16, pp. 141-56.

43. M. Lewis and T. Kellaghan, 'Vocationalism in Irish second-level education', unpublished manuscript, Dublin: Educational Research Centre, St Patrick's College, 1987.

44. D. K. Cohen and M. S. Garet, 'Reforming educational policy with applied social research' in *Harvard Education Review* (1975), Vol 45, pp. 17-43.
T. Husen and M. Kogan (eds), *Educational research and policy: how do they relate?* Oxford: Pergamon, 1984.
L. Joyce, 'Political problems in evaluation research – can they be resolved?', paper presented at European Group of Public Administration Conference, Leuven, 1985.
M. W. Patton, *Utilization focussed evaluation* Beverly Hills, CA: Sage, 2nd edition, 1986.

45. M. S. Smith, 'What works works' in *Educational Researcher* (1986), Vol 15(4), pp. 29-30.

46. L. J. Sharpe, 'The social scientist and policy-making in Britain and America: a comparison' in *Policy and Politics* (1975), Vol 4, pp. 10-18.

47. Husen and Kogan (eds), *Educational research and policy*.

48. Weiss, 'The many meanings of research utilization'.

49. R. F. Rich, 'Uses of social science information by federal bureaucrats: knowledge for action versus knowledge for understanding' in C. H. Weiss (ed), *Using social research in public policy making* Lexington, MA: Heath, 1977.

50. OECD, *Review of national policies for education. Ireland.*

51. Kellaghan, *The evaluation of an intervention programme for disadvantaged children.*

52. O. Egan and M. Hegarty, *An evaluation of the Youth Encounter Project* Dublin: Educational Research Centre, St Patrick's College, 1984.

53. E. Suchman, *Evaluative research* New York: Russell Sage Foundation, 1967.

54. T. D. Cook and W. R. Shadish, 'Program evaluation: the worldly science' in *Annual Review of Psychology* (1986), Vol 37, pp. 193-232.

55. J. Macnamara, *Bilingualism and primary education* Edinburgh: Edinburgh University Press, 1966.

56. Ireland, *White Paper on educational development* Dublin: Stationery Office, 1980.

57. The study, which was unpublished at the time of the NESC report, was later published as T. D. Swan, *Reading standards in Irish schools* Dublin: Educational Co., 1978.

58. NESC, *Statistics for social policy* (Report no 17) Dublin: NESC, 1976.

59. NESC, *Economic and social policy 1980–1983: aims and recommendations* (Report No 53) Dublin: NESC, 1980.

60. Cook and Shadish, 'Program evaluation: The worldly science'.

61. C. H. Weiss, 'The many meanings of research utilization' in *Public Administration Review* (1979), Vol 39, pp. 426-31.

62. M. W. Patton, *Utilization focussed evaluation* Beverly Hills, CA: Sage 2nd edition, 1986.
63. C. H.Weiss, 'Measuring the use of evaluation' in J. A. Ciarlo (ed), *Utilizing evaluation: concepts and measurement techniques* London: Sage, 1981.
64. Cohen and Garet, 'Reforming educational policy with applied social research'.
65. Cook and Shadish, 'Program evaluation: the worldly science'.
66. T. D. Cook, J. Levinson-Rose and W. E. Pollard, 'Misutilization of evaluation research' in *Knowledge Creation Diffusion Utilization* (1979), Vol 1, pp. 477-98.
67. H. Friis, 'Government and research: commissioning and monitoring. A review of the findings of Rothschild and other studies with reference to Ireland' in *Research in Ireland: the relevance of Rothschild?* report of a seminar held at the Institute of Public Administration, Dublin, 1972.
68. Alvarez, 'A review of educational research'.
69. J. Lee, 'Society and culture' in F. Litton (ed), *Unequal achievement: the Irish experience 1957–1982* Dublin: Institute of Public Administration, 1982.
70. R. F. Rich, 'Uses of social science information by federal bureaucrats: Knowledge for action versus knowledge for understanding' in Weiss (ed), *Using social research*.
71. Weiss, 'Knowledge creep'.
72. Husen and Kogan (eds), *Educational research and policy*.
73. Weiss, 'Knowledge creep'.
74. Cook et al, 'Misutilization of evaluation research'.
75. C. H. Weiss and M. J. Bucuvalas, 'Truth tests and utility tests: Decision-makers frames of reference for social science research' in *American Sociological Review* (1980), Vol 45, 302-313.
76. Patton, 'Utilization focussed evaluation'.
77. A. Steinmetz, 'The ideology of educational evaluation' in *Educational Technology* (1975), Vol 15(5), pp. 51-8.
78. N. Caplan, 'A minimal set of conditions necessary for the utilization of social science knowledge in policy formation at the national level' in C. H. Weiss (ed), *Using social research*.
79. Cook et al, 'Misutilization of evaluation research'.
80. Cohen and Garet, 'Reforming educational policy'.
    Greenberg and Robins, 'The changing role of social experiments'.
81. T. D. Cook, 'Postpositivist critical multiplism' in R. L. Shotland and N. M. Mark (eds), *Social science and social policy* London: Sage, 1985.
82. Cook, 'Postpositivist critical multiplism'.
83. D. T. Campbell, 'Reforms as experiments' in *American Psychologist* (1969), Vol 4, pp. 409-29.
84. Kennedy, 'The role of social science in relation to public policy'.
85. D. H. Greenberg and P. K. Robins, 'The changing role of social experiments in policy analysis' in *Journal of Policy Analysis and Management* (1986), Vol 5, pp. 340-62.
86. S. O'Buachalla, 'Irish demographic issues and educational planning' in *European Journal of Education* (1982), Vol 17, pp. 71-79.

8

The Ideational Base of Irish Educational Policy

DENIS O'SULLIVAN

In this chapter I wish to advance a kind of analysis of Irish education that has not been previously attempted in a systematic manner. My intention is to focus on the character of Irish educational ideas as they are manifested in official reports, public debate and controversy, policy statements, professional deliberations, practice or proposals for practice, and policy-related research studies. The validity of the conclusions emanating from such diverse sources is not the immediate concern of my analysis. Rather, I am advocating a cultural withdrawal from the educational system for the purpose of penetrating our public understanding of it, while asserting that this understanding be acknowledged as a social construction. My prime concern is with the cognitive and ideological repertoire of concepts, ideas, propositions, issues and forms of discourse employed to engage the phenomenon that is Irish education. I seek to consider the adequacy of this repertoire, its establishment and legitimation, content and exclusion, maintenance or alteration, as well as its social and ideological base. For the purpose of focusing and coordinating the analysis, I intend to concentrate on an ideal frequently appealed to in educational discourse, equality of educational opportunity.

While the approach spans a number of perspectives it is broadly sociological. It has affinities with the general analysis of educational ideas[1] and recent critical discourse on the ideological underpinnings of educational practice in Ireland[2] and elsewhere.[3] There are elements of the approach in Tussing's comments on

I would like to thank Professor Damian Hannan and Dr Thomas Kellaghan for their comments on an earlier draft of this chapter.

agenda setting and evasion in educational debate[4] and in Mulcahy's consideration of official deliberations on the post-primary curriculum.[5] None of these studies, however, aspires to the general overview of educational ideas aimed at in this chapter. In all, three broad propositions about Irish educational thought are advanced: that it is conceptually and analytically weak, paradigmatically insulated and ideologically sanitised.

Analytical Constructs

Concept

A feature of each child's socialisation is the progression from an awareness of particular persons, objects and emotions familiar through daily contact to the incorporation of categories which reach beyond the child's known and existing experience. This significant development introduces such basic concepts to the child as father, mother, drink, food, anger, joy in the sense that, for instance, their own father is now known as a member of a general category of fathers, characterised by the concept of fatherhood, or the familiar smiles of their mothers are recognised as a pattern of facial expressions which have an established cultural meaning. Later in life more complex concepts like motivation, cause, effect, proof are introduced and regularly used in schooling in coming to terms with the humanities and sciences, and elsewhere in the flux of social, occupational and bureaucratic activity.

A number of points need to be made about this repertoire of concepts. Most fundamentally, it represents the set of filters through which the world is progressively known and internalised. It helps to make sense of the buzzing mass of stimuli by establishing a structure through their differentiation and integration: not alone does the concept of father associate those who qualify but it sets them apart through the concept of mother, for instance, from all those who are mothers in society. It, therefore, influences our perception of reality, what we really select from experience and how we organise and inter-relate it. Concepts are cultural and historical phenomena and can be seen to vary between cultures and over time. Colour concepts, for instance, may be more elaborate in one culture than in another where the darkness/brightness of objects might suffice. Concepts can vary in significance: the relational concept of cousin remains in modern times but the obligations and prescriptions associated with it are greatly diluted, and what remains differs between urban and rural areas. Concepts can be rendered meaningless as charity and theft might be in total communism.

It follows, therefore, that, theoretically at least, it should be possible to interpret experience in the light of a totally novel set of concepts. There is, after all, nothing absolute about our conceptual inheritance. To deviate, however, from what is accepted may well result in a disruption of social life, lack of comprehension, and perhaps the labelling of the innovator as genius or schizophrenic. One wonders, for instance, how 'sexism' or 'racism' would have been received by previous generations as categories for critically integrating certain features of social relations. Culturally prescribed concepts are invested with considerable power; they define boundaries of normality and demand allegiance for the purpose of meaningful human contact. To analyse why certain concepts dominate at any given time and the processes by which they change requires a consideration of the social interests involved, particularly in the case of concepts central to the key institutions of society.

Concepts operate at various levels of complexity. A great number of people, perhaps the majority, never find it necessary to go beyond the unreflective use of concepts in their daily life. Others build their careers and professional knowledge around the study of concepts like thinking, feeling, heat, light, intelligence and planets. What is used at one level in an operational way may be comprehended and labelled more diversely in the scientific study of the relevant phenomenon. In place of the operationally defined concept of group, for instance, sociologists, in their discourse and analysis, demand three concepts – social category, collectivity and group – which make finer distinctions and points of demarcation possible. Similarly, a botanist will describe even the most commonplace of flowers by a Latin name which establishes its taxonomic status.

The concepts we use, therefore, influence how and with what level of innovativeness and complexity we comprehend and understand reality.

Paradigm

The dictionary meaning of paradigm is given as a model or a pattern. This simplicity belies the complexities and controversy identified with its use in the realm of knowledge and ideas. Within the social sciences it has become an indispensable concept in analysis. Yet, it is in relation to the development of scientific knowledge — Thomas Kuhn's *The structure of scientific revolutions*[6] — that the most influential consideration of paradigm exists.

A succinct definition of paradigm is unlikely to do justice to Kuhn's formulation. One reviewer claimed to have identified 22 different meanings for it in the text.[7] In a postscript to the 1969 edition, Kuhn sought to clarify the concept by pointing to two uses:

> the entire constellation of beliefs, values, techniques, and so on shared by the members of a given community. . . . [and] one set of elements in that constellation, the concrete puzzle solutions which, employed as models or examples, can replace explicit rules as a basis for the solution of the remaining puzzles in normal science.[8]

Normal science itself refers to 'research firmly based upon one or more past scientific achievements, achievements that some particular scientific community acknowledges for a time as supplying the foundation for its further practice'.[9] These achievements are such that they have successfully attracted adherents from competing modes of scientific activity and yet remain sufficiently open-ended to allow for a variety of problems to await resolution. Before that state of normal science or paradigmatic-based research is established there are intense debates about appropriate methods, problems and standards of solution among competing schools of thought.

A paradigm's regulatory power over the nature of enquiry reaches the identification of meaningful problems, the facts worthy of consideration as data, the integration of discoveries, and the theory and methods of data collection to be followed.

> one of the things a scientific community acquires with a paradigm is a criterion for choosing problems that, while the paradigm is taken for granted, can be assumed to have solutions. To a great extent these are the only problems that the community

will admit as scientific or encourage its members to undertake. Other problems, including many that had previously been standard, are rejected as metaphysical, as the concern of another discipline, or sometimes as just too problematic to be worth the time. A paradigm can, for that matter, even insulate the community from those socially important problems that are not reducible to the puzzle form, because they cannot be stated in terms of the conceptual and instrumental tools the paradigm supplies. Such problems can be a distraction.[10]

In the social analysis in this chapter this regulatory dimension of paradigm is central in that it alerts us to the mental sets operating to include and exclude specific problems, solutions, methods and data as meaningful and worthy of consideration.

Ideology

While many of the current meanings given to ideology can be said to have been anticipated in the writings of a variety of thinkers throughout history, it has become conventional to trace its recent use to 'that group of savants in the French revolution who were entrusted ... with the founding of a new centre of revolutionary thought. . . it was to this group that the term "ideologues" was first applied'.[11] In modern usage, ideology can have any of the following meanings:

1. A stated set of ideas pertaining to political options relating to systems of government, or to major societal institutions such as the economy, the church, education or the family. This is the meaning that is used most commonly in public debate;
2. The underpinning justification together with its repertoire of perceptions, categories and rationalisations of a particular social category (occupational, social, religious, etc.), its beliefs, theories or practices;
3. As used in Marxist scholarship, the Frankfurt school and most recently in radical pedagogy to denote, in its softest form, the socially interested meanings imposed on phenomena.

It is this third use of ideology which is most applied in recent theorising on the link between education and society. In the deployment of Marxist ideas in educational analysis during the 1970s, a deterministic vision of the link between education and society prevailed. The relations of production were seen as the prime influence on education, with schools serving the interests of those who controlled production. Schools acted as agencies of socialisation, it was argued, transmitting, not merely the required skills, but more particularly the personal traits and habits required to facilitate an unreflective adaptation to a world of work. Among the earliest exponents of this position were Bowles and Gintis.

> The structure of social relations in education not only inures the student to the discipline of the workplace, but develops the types of personal demeanour, modes of self-presentation, self-image, and social-class identifications which are crucial ingredients of job adequacy.[12]

Furthermore, socialisation throughout the process of education subverted the proclaimed ideal of equal educational opportunity and helped to reproduce inherited position whereby working-class children got working-class jobs and middle-class children got middle-class jobs.

> Different levels of education feed workers into different levels within the occupational structure, and, correspondingly, tend toward an internal organisation comparable to levels in the hierarchical division of labour. . . . [And later,] predominantly working-class schools tend to emphasise behavioural control and rule following, while schools in well-to-do suburbs employ relatively open systems that favour greater student participation, less direct supervision, more student electives, and, in general, a value system stressing internalised standards of control.[13]

Differential socialisation in schools, Bowles and Gintis assert, corresponds to the differential socialisation among the social classes. The irony of this is that working-class parents are seen to be supporting schools in making their own children working-class. In the wider sense they are propping up a system which discriminates against themselves and their children in reproducing inequality. For Marx himself, their failure to recognise this is one example of their false consciousness induced by the dominant ideology, that realm of meanings and ideas which support and legitimate the capitalist system.

Strangely, given the socially neutral image of schooling, Althusser lists schools as crucial ideological state apparatuses, others being the family, law, church and unions, transmitting the required capitalist ideology.[14] As a Marxist structuralist, Althusser stresses the force of existing social formations incorporating dominance and unequal power. His theory acts as a useful antidote to simplistic notions about effecting social change. However, he sees no possibility of change through the educational system and, overall, his theory suffers from its passive view of individuals and neglect of human agency. The tension between human agency and structure in shaping social change is well captured in Marx's famous statement in the *Eighteenth Brumaire of Louis Bonaparte*:

> men make their own history, but they do not make it just as they please; they do not make it under circumstances chosen by themselves, but under circumstances directly encountered, given and transmitted from the past. The tradition of all the dead generations weighs like a nightmare on the brain of the living.[15]

While structuralists like Althusser emphasise the constraints of the latter part of this statement, recent educational writing in the Marxist tradition has attempted to reinstate the human agency of the earlier part.

Throughout *Ideology and curriculum*, Apple emphasises the existence of resistance and struggle in opposition to capitalist interests. He recognises the significance of ideology:

> Certainly, we must be honest about the ways power, knowledge, and interest are interrelated and made manifest, about how hegemony is economically and culturally maintained. But, we also must remember that the very sense of personal and collective futility that may come from such honesty is itself an aspect of an effective dominant culture.[16]

Nevertheless, he asserts:

> The notion of reproduction can lead to an assumption that there is (perhaps can be) no significant resistance to such power. This

is not the case. The continuing struggle for economic rights by
workers, the poor, women, blacks, native Americans, latinos,
and others, serves as a potent reminder of the possibility and
actuality of concrete action.[17]

In Giroux, who intellectually expands the more creative and
action-based ideas of Freire, we find the most advanced attempt
to articulate a theoretical space between dominating humanity and
resisting humanity, between the structuralist and culturalist
positions.

> Human agents always mediate through their own histories and
> class or gender-related subjectivities the representations and
> material practices that constitute the parameters of their lived
> experience. This is true within the parameters defined by the
> school, the family, the workplace, or any other social site. What
> is needed to offset the one-sided theory of ideology provided
> by many structuralists is a more fully developed theory of
> mediation and reception. Such an approach would link agency
> and structure in a theory of ideology so as to treat dialectically
> the role of the individual and group as producers of meaning
> within already existing fields of representation and practice.[18]

One therefore needs to treat individuals and social formations
as both the producers and product of ideological discourse and
practice.

In the form of social analysis being embarked upon in this chapter
the strength of the phenomenon of ideology is not so much its
passive interpretation, as political credo or position or as
occupational raison d'etre, useful as these may be. It is through
its active interpretation that ideology alerts us to the need to
interrogate human subjectivity and material products as they are
embodied in educational policy and its effects.

In Figure 1 an attempt is made to show how these three constructs
− concept, paradigm and ideology − interrelate with one another
and interface with society. By deploying this conceptual schema
I hope to advance a constructive critique of Irish educational
thinking, mindful that much has been achieved but nevertheless
sensitive to the limitations imposed by inadequate and ill informed
analytical constructs in articulating and advancing educational
policy.

FIGURE 1
The Conceptual Schema

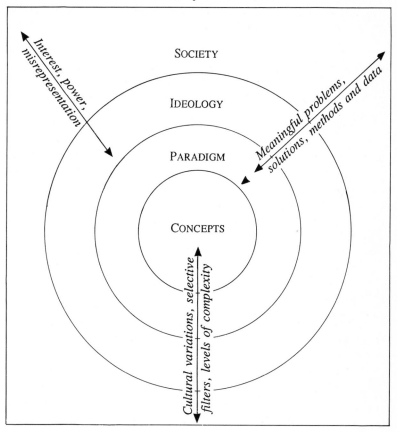

A Note on Methodology

Methodologically, the analysis in this chapter does not fit neatly into any of the research designs to be found in standard textbooks on educational research. The notions of subjects, measurement, data, control groups and cause − effect are all present, but their definitions, use and role are made diffuse by the nature of the analysis. The following characteristics of the analysis are relevant: it is a societal study involving an assessment of ideas, and it is both qualitative and interpretive.

While the analysis pertains to educational ideas in Irish society, the attempt throughout is to focus on those individuals and social groupings who make policy. Once one moves beyond the government, relevant ministers and the civil service, the membership and even the relative significance of policy-making groups is debatable. Church and religious bodies and, in recent times, teachers' organisations and economic and industrial interests can claim membership. Parents' interests represent an emerging force that is not considered in the analysis through lack of published data; this gap is likely to be filled by the National Parents' Council. With regard to those whose task it is to generate ideas — the academic community — their incorporation into the policy-making sector has never been satisfactory. Most frequently, their involvement was tokenist, as in the membership of official committees and commissions, and beset by mutual suspicion. In this analysis the ideas of those academics who have publicly contributed to debate on educational policy and who have been incorporated into the deliberations of educational bodies and associations are given prominence.

In attempting to establish a yardstick by which to assess Irish educational ideas, the conceptual schema outlined above is not deployed in a vacuum. The appeal, albeit implicit in a number of instances, is to comparative method. The point of reference throughout the analysis is to practice and experience in other educational systems, be it in formal educational debate, publications and deliberations of interested groups and in the mass media. Because of the qualitative nature of the analysis, one is comparing the extent to which educational ideas underpinning policy are made explicit, their level of elaboration, the diversity of paradigm, and the recognition of interest and misrepresentation.

The analysis raises the question as to what is to be considered as evidence. There are no ready sources of data. There are few insights into the process of policy making of the kind one might get from political autobiography. The analysis relies heavily on what is said and left unsaid and by what is studied and ignored by the policy-making sector, and on the direction of actual policy. It may well be that beneath the surface of public debate within the policy-making sector, there is a complex world of educational ideas. But we must wait some indication of this before its existence can be considered. In the meantime, interpretation must rely on what is available as evidence, however imperfect that may be. Further revelations may well force a modification of the interpretations offered here.

Equality of Educational Opportunity

Wittgenstein's off-quoted assertion that 'the limits of my language are the limits of my world'[19] has a particular poignancy when considered in the light of the restrictive vocabulary of Irish educational debate. The major interventions, controversies and debates during the past two decades — the expansion of educational provision, the redirection of the content of the curriculum, second-level structural reorganisation and first-level pedagogic change — all share an educational vocabulary of conceptual fragility. This takes a variety of forms: an absence of sharp conceptualisation, the use of concepts at an unelaborated common-sense level, and an unfamiliarity with or failure to acknowledge the existence of relevant conceptual discourse elsewhere.

Equality of educational opportunity was presented by Seán O'Connor in his influential *Studies* article 'Post-primary education: now and in the future' in 1968 as a prominent objective for what he referred to as recent developments in Irish education.[20] It was an appropriate ideal to select. Dr Hillery's widely-quoted policy statement on proposals for change in post-primary education in 1963 concluded that 'the whole plan is a move in the direction, not only of a better coordination in our entire education system, but of equality of educational opportunity'.[21] George Colley, who succeeded Dr Hillery as Minister for Education, was to use the same appeal in 1966 in his letter to the authorities of secondary and vocational schools requesting their co-operation in the pooling of post-primary facilities at local level.[22] Though equality of educational opportunity was the concept most utilised to orchestrate moral responses to differential educational attainment, it lacked elaboration as a principle in its own right during this formative period in educational policy making.

It was not that the concept of equal educational opportunity could not bear analysis. Without going into the philosophical ramifications of the concept, which could helpfully range back to Aristotle's principles of justice, there existed a number of fundamental policy issues pertinent to the deployment of the concept in Ireland.

What dimensions of equality of educational opportunity were to be the focus of intervention?

What impediments to equal educational opportunity were to be considered suitable for intervention, the range of impediments being influenced by the dimension of equality of educational opportunity in focus?

What social principles were to operate? In particular, how was equal educational opportunity meant to relate to other social processes like social mobility, life chances, power and economic change?

Dimensions of Equal Educational Opportunity

The free education scheme and the expansion of educational facilities had a major impact on the landscape of Irish post-primary education in terms of pupil numbers, the intellectual and aspirational profile of pupil intakes, the erosion of the religious representation amongst post-primary teachers, and the public cost of education. Yet, this major intervention did not benefit from a scrutiny of the ideal of equal educational opportunity to which it was directed. Upon analysis, however, it is possible to conceptually place the focus of this intervention.

In discussions on the possible dimensions of equal educational opportunity, James Coleman is often credited with having shifted the emphasis of debate from equality of access to equality of effect.[23] Equality of access demands that no pupil should be denied access to educational institutions or courses of study on the basis of irrelevant considerations. It represents a predictable liberal response to pupils who are denied education because of fees or the absence of social contacts. This was developed in an internal memorandum drawn up in connection with what came to be known as the 'Coleman Report', *Equality of educational opportunity*.[24] Five dimensions of equality of educational opportunity were considered, three related to equality of input and two to equality of outcome. Input included financial investment in schools as well as differences between schools in terms of teachers' skills and morale. Were schools in certain areas or schools attended by racial or social minorities less well endowed in this regard? Outcomes relate to the results of schooling, the effects on pupils. Given similar intakes do schools differ in their ability to realise the potential of pupils? Where there are differences between school intakes because of early advantage, what are schools doing to compensate for these environmental impediments to equality of results? Clearly, equality of effect is a demanding interpretation of the requirements of equality of educational opportunity. Indeed, where pupil intakes differ in attainment Coleman was later to assert that it was 'wholly unobtainable', if considered at the individual level.[25] But, even if considered in terms of particular social groups, there is no denying that it places schools in a demanding compensatory role, a role that was emphasised in a host of compensatory programmes in the United States throughout the 1960s.

Three foci of equality of educational opportunity then emerge: access, input and effect.

In his 1963 policy statement, Dr Hillery gave prominence, as one of the two weaknesses of our post-primary education system, to the fact that

> there are still areas of the country which have neither a secondary nor a vocational school within easy daily reach of potential pupils and where under the existing system such is not likely to be available in the foreseeable future.[26]

The free education scheme itself was announced to the National Union of Journalists on 10 September 1966 by the Minister for Education, Donogh O'Malley.[27] This innovation was directed, he said, at 'the basic fault of our present educational structure ... the fact that many families cannot afford to pay even part of the cost of education for their children'. The scheme he was drawing up, he asserted, would ensure that 'in future, no boy or girl in this state will be deprived of full educational opportunity − from primary to university level − by reason of the fact that the parents cannot afford to pay for it'. Both of these statements can be considered as high points in the public exposure of the plight of children handicapped by economic circumstances and geographical location which was common at this time in Dáil debates and politicians' statements.[28]

In 1965 the OECD-sponsored report *Investment in education* identified significant variations in educational participation by occupational group and geographical area.[29] While just over half the 13-17 age group was found to be in full-time education in counties such as Tipperary and Waterford, Donegal's rate was somewhat less than a third. Occupationally, there was a marked contrast between the participation rates of students from professional and white-collar families and those from skilled, semi-skilled and unskilled manual-worker families, with the contrast becoming more marked the higher the age group and educational level. While the *Investment in education* survey team were careful to point out that they did not have data on income differences between families, they later concluded that children of parents of certain social groups, including those with lowest income, were found to have a higher probability of failing to maintain their position in entry to post-primary school and to university and other third-level institutions.

It seems clear that inequalities in access to educational provision were the object of attention though it must be acknowledged that the comments of the National Industrial Economic Council on *Investment in education* made some efforts to extend the concept.[30] To suggest that the focus was on the access dimension, however, runs the risk of crediting policy makers of the era with a greater intentionality in policy and planning than appears to have been the case. What is being manifested seems nearer to practical social information rather than to theory, and to some unstated notion of 'fairness' or 'unfairness' rather than to individual rights or justice. The dimension of knowledge least in evidence is that which is consciously known at a discursive level. This would involve a more elaborate classification of phenomena based on key attributes, an appreciation of their inter-relationships, a more reflective approach to popular categories and an attentiveness to the impact of social interests.

For the focus of the free education intervention to be identified as the access dimension of a particular explication of the concept of equality of educational opportunity, it would require that the intervention be treated at a level of discourse which goes beyond the practical and recipe level.

To suggest that such a form of discourse was not applied is not to deny the merit of the free education scheme, long regarded as one of the more flamboyant strokes in Irish politics.[31] What is asserted is that the resulting inadequate understanding of the nature of the intervention effectively isolated it, and inhibited the pursuance of a coherent programme of (or even policy commitment to) equal educational opportunity. It was as if policy makers were operating at the level of pedagogical and social folk medicine − the educational equivalent of the folk healer and the herbalist − proposing improperly understood antidotes for inadequately defined illnesses: there may be favourable effects but one may go bald in the process of curing acne, or spend one's life burning down houses to savour the delights of roast pig. The implication for policy was that expanding equal educational opportunity to encompass other dimensions, their feasibility and costing as well as their social implications − a pre-requisite for any long-term planning towards equal educational opportunity − never informed the consciousness of policy makers. Nor did, with some minor exceptions, the issues which the access dimension gives rise to: the problem of selection and what form of educational knowledge and credentials students were entitled to have access to. The emphasis on the throughput of students was very much a consequence of this. Quantitative measures of education predominated: level of formal education reached rather than internal processes of schooling. Not surprisingly, the interventions to follow − the raising of the school leaving age to fifteen and circular 10/67 on the yearly promotion of pupils were quantitative measures. The manner in which both of these interventions 'resolved' the problem of educationally delayed pupils and terminal leavers from primary school in a fashion typical of quantitative intervention is worth pursuing; it highlights the implications for planning of inadequate conceptualisation.

The extent of educational delay in Irish primary schools was quantified by *Investment in education* in 1965. It was found that in fourth, fifth and sixth standards two-fifths of the pupils had been delayed for at least one year, with about one in ten delayed for about two years or more. With the minimum school-leaving age set at fourteen, pupils delayed for two years or more would be entitled to leave full-time education without having completed their primary school course.

Pupils who terminated their full-time education with their exit from the primary school came to be known as primary school terminal leavers and were to receive some attention in the latter part of the 1960s. Hyland recorded a drop in the number of terminal leavers from 18,000 to 10,000 between the school years 1964/65 and 1966/67.[32] Rudd found that, despite the introduction of free education in September 1967, the percentage of primary school leavers becoming terminal leavers merely dropped from 15 per cent to 13 per cent in the school year 1967/68. This 13 per cent, according to Rudd, represented a 'hard-core, those whom the administrative and economic changes were not affecting'.[33]

By examining the educational careers of a sample of terminal leavers Rudd was able to reveal that their educational attainment was even lower than was immediately evident. She presented the following as an approximate breakdown of the leaving attainments of her terminal leavers sample:

20 per cent left from sixth standard or below
20 per cent left having registered less than half the required attendances in sixth class
25 per cent left having registered more than half but less than 85 per cent (average) of the attendances in sixth class
15 per cent left having made 85-100 per cent attendances in sixth class
20 per cent left having completed sixth and made some progress in a subsequent year.[34]

Furthermore, when the attendance records of the pupils in this sample for the primary school grades second to sixth were examined it was found that whereas 68 per cent had average attendances in second class, the percentage decreased gradually to 62 per cent in third class, 59 per cent in fourth class, 55 per cent in fifth class and 31 per cent in sixth class.

Therefore, not alone did terminal leavers fail to receive any form of post-primary schooling, but a sizeable proportion could not be considered to have completed the primary school course; in fact, even though officially in attendance at primary school, their attendance records almost from the beginning of their school careers were drastically inferior to those of the average child. It seemed clear from this data that what was emerging was not fundamentally a matter of leaving full-time education without exposure to post-primary schooling, but rather one of educational underachievement. It pertained to the effects of schooling, to pupil performance, rather than to pupil access to educational programmes. In fact it would be argued that the two interventions mentioned − circular 10/67 on pupil promotion and the raising of the school leaving age to fifteen − 'solved' the problem of terminal leaving. Circular 10/67 of March 1967 directed that 'the normal procedure should be that a pupil is promoted to a higher standard at the end of each school year'.[35] Semi-automatic promotion would ensure that few pupils would reach the minimum school leaving age while still in primary school, and the raising of the school leaving age from fourteen to fifteen further confirmed this. The access problem had been confronted for terminal leavers in that it became the norm for pupils to receive some post-primary schooling. The failure to recognise the performance problem which underpinned terminal leaving was, however, beginning to fester.

A study of teachers' perceptions of the progress of their pupils in Irish primary schools was to confirm the suggestions of educational underachievement in Rudd's study of terminal leavers. Its authors stated:

> The first thing that strikes one about the findings is the relatively large number of children (25%) whose progress was regarded by teachers as unsatisfactory. The number of pupils who were regarded as having difficulty in at least one subject (66%) was even larger still.[36]

The link between underachievement and those destined to become terminal leavers was established by Greaney and Kellaghan in the first report of a longitudinal study of Irish school children: they found that average verbal achievement scores were significantly lower than those of pupils who entered secondary or vocational schools, and that almost half were rated by their teachers as having made unsatisfactory progress.[37]

It would appear that for each pupil cohort progressing through the educational system, a significant minority continues to be lost to the system with doubtful levels of basic skills such as literacy and numeracy. Breen estimates, on the basis of those who leave post-primary schooling having never sat a public examination and those who are unable to obtain a D grade in group certificate English and mathematics, that about 10 per cent are leaving school with deficiencies in basic skills.[38] The proliferation of adult literacy programmes in Ireland during the past decade suggests that the experience of living has not corrected these deficiencies.[39]

Had the well meaning expansionist policies of the 1960s been better informed with regard to the varieties of inequalities in education and the unreflecting goodwill focused beyond access issues, then surely the vigour and optimism of the era would have ensured some erosion of these basic deficiencies at an earlier age of schooling.

Some awareness of inequalities of input between types of post-primary schools can also be inferred during this formative period. As early as 1958, J. J. O'Meara, professor of classical languages at UCD, had called for an enhancement of status for vocational schools.[40] This was to be repeated in 1963 in Dr Hillery's statement to the press[41] and in the *Second programme for economic expansion*.[42]

Dr Hillery, in his 1963 policy statement, saw 'the bringing of the vocational stream throughout the country to a parity of standard and evaluation with the secondary school stream' as constituting 'a very important educational and social reform'. Later that year this was to be reaffirmed by the first part of the *Second programme for economic expansion*. In fact, Randles concluded that the improvement of the vocational system could be considered a dominant feature of educational planning in the 1960s.[43]

It was, nevertheless, possible to contain these assertions and innovations within established paradigms relating to the social evaluation of the diverse forms of knowledge and abilities, and to the role of central government in the financing of educational institutions. It fell to Dale Tussing, a visiting American professor, to play the role of 'cultural stranger': his response to the 1980 *White Paper on educational development* contained illuminating breaches of native paradigms.

> At the top are the fee-charging schools, both Catholic and Protestant, which despite the fact that they are selective in their admissions procedures and charge fees, continue to receive sizeable state grants. Then come the secondary schools that pursue selective admissions procedures which, perhaps surprisingly, are aided no differently from those schools accepting all-comers. Below them come the rest of the secondary

schools with university graduates for teachers, still addressing a middle-class or aspiring middle-class clientele essentially seeking academic instruction towards desirable white-collar occupations. Most of the comprehensive and community schools fit into this stratum as well, taking their character from the dominant secondary school pattern. At the bottom, serving mainly the lower third of the income distribution are the vocational schools. This discussion describes social stratification in second level only at its grossest and ignores the subtle differences within the various categories, e.g. as between Presentation and Christian Brothers' schools on the one hand, and Loreto and Dominican schools on the other, or as between prestigious Dublin Protestant secondary schools and some of the more plebeian Protestant schools around the country.[44]

Whatever reservations one might have about the actual classification system employed, Tussing was raising in public debate what in the past had been implicit. There can be few parents who are unaware that certain schools have a social tone or ethos about them which may be desirable or undesirable. Such a tone is most frequently identified with the socio-economic background of the traditional clientele of a school and is considered to confer benefits or disadvantages on its pupils, by way of influence, association or reputation. Differences in the socio-economic composition of student bodies in urban primary schools and across boarding schools in Munster have been documented;[45] tone, ethos, tradition, and reputation are less amenable to quantification. Both factors are elements in the community input into schools and are appropriate for inclusion in any consideration of equality of input.

Tussing was even more specific with regard to financial input in an address to the Irish Vocational Education Association in 1983. Distinguishing between public and private benefits of education, and arguing that the state should not be expected to pay for a level of education beyond the point of public benefit, which he took to be that of the compulsory level, he added a further refinement:

Education to a higher standard through the application of more resources to certain pupils creates a private benefit, just as does education beyond the age of compulsory schooling. Therefore, I have to question continued large-scale state aid to fee-charging secondary schools ... this support for fee-charging second-level schools, through capitation grants and payment of incremental teachers' salaries, constitutes a device by which the state contributes to the perpetuation of elitism and class stratification through the school system ... in my opinion, no further cuts in second-level finance in the free sector are appropriate before there are significant reductions in state support to the fee sector.[46]

When considered alongside Tussing's concern for a particular social principle, the pragmatic character of the indigenous objection (that to cut subsidies to the private sector would simply result in a greater influx into the public sector)[47] is highlighted:

In the present instance, I do not believe the argument: the parents of these privileged children can and will pay more. But even if it is true, so be it; we will then have a decline in privilege and in the school system's contribution to its perpetuation.[48]

Questioning the funding of schools was even further removed than differential status from the conventional agenda of educational issues. It had been taken for granted in providing financial support to schools that the state should take no interest in the admissions policy or whether the school was fee paying or not. The ideological debate on this in countries such as the United States and England involved sharply divided points of view about what in Ireland did not seem to constitute a meaningful issue. Such questions were outside the Irish frame of reference on the funding of schooling. Changes in level of grants or the introduction of new types of grants such as those for school building or equipment, were devoid of consideration of principle and seemed to owe their origin to economic or political pragmatism.

Despite Tussing's intervention, a factor fundamental to differential status − the social stratification of knowledge − remained obscured. The functional distinction between the two types of post-primary schools derives from the knowledge and skill they were initially entrusted to transmit. Yet, bodies of knowledge and skill vary in the status accorded to them, and, delineated into areas of expertise, they become the basis for occupational positions. These occupations, in turn, refer to their knowledge and skill base as the source of their distinctiveness and as a legitimation for differentials of income, power and status.

The links between the vocational and secondary sectors of post-primary schooling and different occupational levels have always been clearly drawn. For boys the vocational school led to manual occupations of varying levels of skill, while for girls they led to secretarial and typing positions. Secondary schooling was the traditional route to white-collar and professional occupations. This was recognised by pupils and presumably by parents, and was reflected in a range of studies from the 1960s. Hannan's finding among adolescents in County Cavan in 1965 is typical:

> Both males and females receiving a secondary education aspire almost equally and almost exclusively to non-manual occupations (87% and 97% respectively). Great sex differences, however, do exist in the case of those receiving a vocational education. Over 50% of the girls aspire to non-manual occupations, while this is true of only 5% of the boys.[49]

The pattern of these aspirations should scarcely surprise. They were after all wholly consistent with the knowledge, skills, personal attributes and dispositions peculiar to each type of school until the 1970s, when the vocational school curriculum was extended. By that time the functional link between vocational schools and the lower-status occupational sectors had been institutionalised. The concern of politicians and commentators regarding the lower status of the vocational school, however, ignored this process by which the sector's lower status was established. To focus on the lower status of the vocational school was to engage the symptom: it was like trying to clear spots rather than cure measles. The underlying malaise, the hierarchy of knowledge and occupations in the distribution of economic reward and prestige, remained unquestioned.

Raven[50] and Hutchinson[51] claim that in Ireland there existed a tendency to deny the existence of status differentials across occupations or at least to question the extent of the differentials. Despite their research which demonstrated that the distribution of status across occupational levels was similar to other Western societies the local argument seemed to be, according to Raven, that while such differentials might well exist in other societies, they did not constitute a significant feature of the Irish social structure. Not surprisingly, therefore, social mobilisation in Irish society has tended to be based on broad social categories, like the parish or the community. Long before it became a fashionable concept, the total community was being used by Muintir na Tíre, founded in 1931 by Canon Hayes, as the unit of organisation. Significantly, he had already decided to move away from the initial idea of mobilising on the basis of agricultural commodity interests − a sectional interest.[52]

To organise on the basis of socio-economic position is to be accused of fostering social division and disharmony. As Talbot noted, 'the co-operation of the whole community rather than the collaboration of a single class produces a truly Christian order and helps to break down class antagonism'.[53] The paradigm of society inherent in this suspicion is a consensual one. It considers social order to be founded on the basis of a common set of values and interests. Conflict between social and economic interests is seen as a social aberration, and capable of being resolved with goodwill and common sense. Accordingly, the theory that there exists an inherent and inevitable conflict of interests between those at different levels of the economic structure is rejected.

Ideologically, the consensual paradigm helps to retard the development of opposing paradigms, such as conflict-based ones, and this limits the range of social interpretations and actions. In this instance, explanations and policies relating to status differentials between vocational and secondary schools are confined to funding, standards, and public awareness; the structure of occupations or knowledge is unrecognised as a possible explanation. This need not be a wilful or prejudiced exclusion. To employ a particular paradigm can be to act in good faith. Its consequence, nevertheless, in the Irish context under discussion, is to restrict understanding and vision. The act of ideological interrogation must then be to highlight the restrictive nature of particular paradigms, and to encourage the development of analytical constructs which will facilitate an appreciation of multiple paradigms, their interests and effects. The nearest we have come in Ireland to confronting either traditional paradigms or ideologies was far removed from education, in the debate on the proposal to amend the Constitution in relation to abortion, and to a lesser extend during the lead up to the referendum on the possibility of legalising divorce. Characteristically, the former in particular was regarded as 'divisive'. Yet, what was involved was a realisation that a consensus did not exist relating to fundamentals of human life, personal freedom and society. To claim that such a realisation is divisive is to simply acknowledge that individuals realise they differ in paradigm and ideology, i.e. they have different understandings of socially important issues, and of whom they benefit in terms of their structural location within society.

The substantive issue of differential status between vocational and secondary schools also provides a number of instances in which ideological debate is neutralised. In Europe similar problems with dual or tripartite post-primary schooling led to the establishment of comprehensive schools. Sweden had begun on the development of a single post-primary structure after the second world war; France began innovations in the late 1950s, and a decade later England and Wales, under a Labour government, were in the throes of comprehensivisation. Intense ideological debates accompanied these educational innovations. Some saw the changes as ushering in a new and more equal society where barriers between occupational groups would be broken down, and elitism and privilege in education abolished. Others saw it as a dangerous utopianism, an attempt at social engineering, imposing unwanted structures and undesirable Fabian ideas on society.

While the first comprehensive schools in Ireland, as in England, were built to serve isolated areas, inadequately served by post-primary schooling, the official legitimation of the new type of schooling in the subsequent debate differed dramatically from the European experience. When Dr Hillery first announced it in 1963 he sought to justify the direct state provision of the post-primary school building:

> While this involves important and perhaps fundamental educational principles, the considerations which give rise to it in my mind are, I may say, at least as much social as educational. In that regard it has been well said recently that education, social and economic needs so far from conflicting, actually add force to each other.[54]

Leaving aside the consensual nature of the final assertion, it might appear that Dr Hillery was opening up a national debate on the philosophical underpinnings of comprehensive schooling. Nothing could be further from the truth; when placed in context, it appears to refer to geographical impediments to educational opportunity, and to a growing economic need for skilled personnel. In the Dáil,

Dr Noel Browne asked the Minister to explain the educational theory behind the proposal. Dr Hillery's reply could well stand as the nearest a Minister has come to outlining the rationale of the position since Dick Mulcahy's 'oil-can man speech' as Minister in 1957: 'to do what is possible is my job and not to have the whole matter upset because of some principle or ideal'.[55]

Not that the Minister was subjected to much prodding. Public attention centred on the possible location of the schools and the lack of information and consultation. Yet, the Minister had indicated that the type of school he had in mind operated in Sweden and was planned for France. Would it not have been possible for educators to familiarise themselves with comprehensive debates in these countries and to initiate an informed discussion on this basis? While a number of newspaper features dealt with comprehensive schooling at the time, it was not until February 1970 that an extended educational treatment appeared: a series by Father Thomas Morrissey in the *Irish Independent*.

Dr Hillery's dismissal of principles or ideas was not an isolated rejection. In 1961, he found it necessary to apologise for the inclusion of a social objective when introducing a Bill to extend provision for local authority scholarships:

> The scheme is not just a piece of social welfare. Its primary object is educational. It is directed towards bringing forward, for the benefit of the country as a whole, the best talent that the country is producing, and that from whatever economic level in which such talent is to be found.[56]

Nor was this anxiety unique to Dr Hillery. In 1966, the Minister for Education, George Colley made a similar disclaimer when explaining the comprehensive school idea.

> I feel I should begin by explaining what I mean by comprehensive education .... it is necessary, because of the misconception which many people have about it, to state as precisely as possible what comprehensive education is. Negatively, it is not anything ideological or political. Positively, it is a system of post-primary education combining academic and technical subjects in a wide curriculum, offering to each pupil an education structured to his needs and interests and providing specialist guidance and advice on the pupil's abilities and aptitudes.[57]

So remote was the Irish mind from a consideration of social ideals that even a decade later a noted educationalist in commenting on this period failed to comprehend that the comprehensive ideal demanded a unitary educational structure for all children.[58] Bilateralism was indeed to be questioned and later challenged both by the Minister and his Department and on financial rather than educational grounds. The treatment of comprehensive schooling in Irish debate, in fact, represents an informative case study of how gate keepers (in this case educational) can selectively filter ideas from abroad which might threaten the native paradigms and ideologies.

Overall, it is clear that equal educational opportunity, despite its frequent citation as an ideal, was never confronted as a concept demanding analysis and elaboration. The appeal to equal educational opportunity as a guiding principle was no more than an appeal to an unexplicated sense of 'fairness' and used to emotional rather than intellectual effect. This failure to intellectualise equal educational opportunity led to a crude understanding of its implications for planning, as we have seen in the treatment of access to educational opportunities.

When what amounted to input dimensions of equality were considered − as with school financing and differential status between vocational and secondary schools − the debate operated within a circumscribed range of issues and possibilities. Explanations foreign to the paradigm such as the differential status of bodies of knowledge and occupations in society at large were not encouraged. Ideologically, this dominant paradigm serves to protect the interests of those who benefit from stratified knowledge and occupations by suppressing any questioning of its role in what in this instance is perceived as an educational problem. And when innovations, such as the comprehensive school idea which originated from a social as well as an educational critique, were imported into Irish educational discourse, there was a conscious effort to jettison all elements of social reconstruction. In effect, therefore, by specifically attempting to avoid ideology (considered as social critique or reconstruction), Irish educational planners have acted ideologically, i.e. in the interests of those social groups who benefit from existing social and educational structures.

Equality of effect never appears to have been incorporated into the political understanding of equal educational opportunity. This seems to have been the case despite the sensitivity to this element of equality among the educational committee which in 1968 recommended the establishment of the Rutland Street Pre-School Project.[59] The nearest one comes to a recognition of school outcomes in the context of equality is in the response to those who experience impediments to educational achievement. And this response, as we shall see below, once again operates within a particular paradigm of aetiologies, explanations and interventions.

Impediments to Equal Educational Opportunity

What impediments to equal educational opportunity are to be considered? The list of possible impediments is wide-ranging — financial, geographical, gender, ability, cultural, educational, social structural, and generational. As we have seen, in recent times the consensus is that financial and geographical impediments to access to schooling, or to the ability to benefit from education are unacceptable. Thus the ability to pay fees or buy books or the inaccessibility of appropriate educational programmes all constitute suitable foci for concern and possible intervention. Empirical and moral assertions are involved. It is being claimed that financial and geographical situations cannot of themselves be regarded as pertinent to the capacity to benefit from schooling, and furthermore that financial and geographical impediments offend against 'fairness'.

Ideas on gender as a factor in educational opportunity have experienced considerable change. Traditional beliefs, grounded in sex-role differentiation in the family, workplace and social and political arenas, were reflected in the structures of schooling. Access to different learning opportunities depended on gender. This took the form of inadequate provision for technical, higher mathematical and scientific subjects in girls' schools, with domestic science unavailable in boys' schools. Access might be impeded, formally or informally, to such courses where they were available. At the level of performance, variations were explained in terms of constitutional differences between male and female. Ideologically, the allocation of social roles and theories of male and female constitution were integrated into Catholic apologetics. While the structural legacy of this tradition is still in evidence, it is clear that there has been a significant shift of opinion in relation to role allocation; and theories of male and female psychology which question the validity of gender as a legitimate basis for exclusion from learning opportunities, or as a satisfactory explanation for differential school effects at the level of performance or disposition, have emerged.[60]

Why the change? Access to the media, particularly newspapers, helped to propagate the ideals of the women's movement, some of whose leading lights were themselves journalists. Membership of the European Community demanded changes in legislation (occupational and financial etc) which discriminated against women. The establishment of the Equal Employment Agency served to monitor and act on instances of discrimination.[61]

A crucial factor remained largely invisible. Attempts to eliminate sexual discrimination could be, and were, socially contained within existing structures, in a way that would have been impossible with many other forms of discrimination. Contrasted with the establishment of an equitable taxation system for farmers, the self-employed and the wealthy, for instance, sexual discrimination is a much safer, more manageable topic which can be and has, to date, been robbed of its ideological force in Irish society.

Hannan et al's widely publicised study of sex differences in subject provision and student choice in Irish post-primary schools illustrates this weakness.[62] Arguing for a greater uptake by girls of such non-traditional options as science and technological subjects on the grounds that it would provide greater access to better-paid occupations with opportunities for promotion, the study, in effect, operates within a paradigm of unexplored and taken-for-granted aspirations, reward criteria and understandings of success and happiness. Its aim, fundamentally, relates to how curricular choices at school might help girls to compete more effectively according to the existing rules by which status, wealth and power are allocated. It is difficult to avoid the feeling at various points in the report that to aspire to the more 'human' professions of teaching and nursing, to occupations with limited promotional opportunities or to have low achievement motivation is to be regarded as socially pathological. There is much to be commended in the broadly based educational experience of girls. The fact that this has vocational weaknesses given the dominance of male criteria of worth in human activity may suggest the need to challenge these criteria rather than the curricular choices of girls, a policy option that remains excluded by the manner in which the problem is defined.[63]

No supporter of equal educational opportunity would deny that the ability to benefit from educational programmes is a precondition of any application of the ideal. As Minister for Education, Jack Lynch had advanced the opinion as early as 1957 that children in one type of school might be better in a different discipline. In the 1960s teacher leaders expressed concern that unsuitable students entering senior secondary school courses might lead to falling standards.[64] Dr Hillery was to be far more specific on this topic:

> You cannot raise the school leaving age and give the matter no more attention. Raising the school leaving age carries implications ... it implies vast expenditure of state money which we cannot afford to spend lavishly and indiscriminately so there is an implication that there will have to be some guidance of the pupil towards a type of post-primary education most suited to his abilities, and some consideration of our programme for the needs of the country ... I do not think that anybody would say that everybody in the community should have an academic education and I do not think anybody really believes that the selection of the type of education should be determined by one's financial position.[65]

What has come to be increasingly discussed, however, in sociological commentaries is the extent to which ability can be considered as a static variable. The view was put forward with increasing force in the 1960s that ability to benefit from schooling was capable of being environmentally inhibited; and that to accept the manifestation of ability on the point of entry to post-primary education, for instance, as some absolute measure of the child's capacity to benefit from schooling is to ignore the socially constituted element in ability and the reality of environmental variations in the experience of pupils. In consequence, the ability to gain access to an educational programme, or to benefit from its content, is capable of being perceived as a product of an unequal opportunity to realise the required ability. Ability, therefore, where there is a suspicion of impeded development or unrealised potential, becomes an object of moral concern requiring either positive discrimination in the form of compensatory programmes, educational priority areas and home start schemes, or more fundamental changes in the social structures which support these impediments. This scenario is further complicated by the problematising of the content of schooling, particularly during the 1970s. What constitutes ability to benefit from schooling, after all, is dependent on what demands schools make on pupils in both hidden and official aspects of the curriculum.

Kathleen Lynch has asserted that Irish educational researchers assume ability to be a static variable and singles out Dr Thomas Kellaghan, head of the Educational Research Centre, for special consideration.[66] Dr Kellaghan has responded to similar arguments and is not the most appropriate target for such criticism.[67] The fact that the stability of IQ test scores increases with age has led to ability being treated, for practical research purposes, as if it were static. This is a potential source of confusion. Yet, the rationale of the Rutland Street intervention programme for disadvantaged children, of which Dr Kellaghan was director, was that measured intelligence could be augmented using well planned educational and social strategies. In fact, this is a much more environmental interpretation of ability than is to be discerned among educational practitioners, politicians and the general public, who see the potential for intervention in cultural attributes and school response and progress rather than in cognitive ability.

The operational definition of ability in the important longitudinal study *Equality of opportunity in Irish schools*[68] — performance on the Drumcondra verbal reasoning test administered at the age of eleven years — however, is confusing. Little is made of the fact that 42.9 per cent of students from professional/intermediate professional homes compared to 9.9 per cent from unskilled homes scored at 108 or greater on this test. Specifically, the position taken on the contribution of innate ability, home environment and primary school experience to this variation in measured ability at age eleven remains unclear.

Internationally, cultural factors figure prominently in the attempts to identify features of a child's background which impede the ability to benefit from schooling. In Ireland, the earliest contribution to public consciousness in this area was Liam Ryan's 'Social dynamite', published in *Christus Rex* in 1967, and subsequently serialised in *The Irish Times*.[69]

'Social dynamite' reported on a study of one hundred school 'dropouts' from a corporation housing estate in a provincial city in Ireland. It proved to be a highly incisive anthropological account of the culture of the area, recording a high incidence of unskilled workers, low and precarious salaries, overcrowding and large families, a value system which had little regard for planning or schooling, and an adolescent career pattern which lead predominantly from primary school to work or unemployment. Written in a highly readable style, this evocation of the cycle of deprivation was frequently referred to in the media and reached a wide audience. So also did the solutions, largely of a cultural and a service nature, offered — community centre, social workers, a more varied primary school curriculum, and the need for a more understanding attitude from middle-class outsiders. The theoretical basis of the article — the definition of the situation — was largely ignored. The working-class teenagers defined secondary schooling as something for those who had brains and money, as an alien institution, and their educational careers, in consequence, excluded secondary school experience. Thus, the teenagers' definition of the educational situation is realised by their own actions. Ryan was to develop this theory at a more structural level later.

Whether such attributes constitute deficits, differences, or flawed lifestyles was hotly debated elsewhere, with implications for the nature of social intervention and educational change.[70] Leaving aside these largely rhetorical labels, two opposing schools of thought emerged. The standard compensatory approach was that pupils whose formative experiences differed from those of the general society in such a way as to impede school progress deserved the opportunity to make up for these experiences. On the other hand, those who saw compensatory education as a form of cultural imposition questioned the right of educators, legislators and academics, as representatives of another set of cultural responses, to seek to change a child's lifestyle. The point has also been forcefully argued in England[71] that the research on the unequal representation of students from lower socio-economic groups at higher levels of the educational system reflected variations in educational and occupational aspirations across the socio-economic spectrum, rather than instances of inequality or discrimination. The inference is that students act freely and without pressure in accepting or rejecting the educational system. This raises more complex questions on the impact of parents and background in general upon children's aspirations and cultural responses to schooling; the manoeuverability of children, their rights in relation to their parents' culture and the problem of voluntarism in decision-making, i.e. how free are people in reality to choose the range of options which theoretically exist in a democratic society?

While the label of social class had been employed in the early demographic and political arithmetic studies of participation in education during the 1950s and 1960s, it was the material dimension that had been stressed, to the extent that social class became synonymous with salary and occupational status. It was later with social class, in the Marxist sense of a relationship with the means of production and Weber's coordinates of social stratification, that social and economic structures of society gained attention. Particularly pertinent to our analysis was the assertion that cultural features of a child's background can only be comprehensively understood in terms of stratification and the broad structure of society.[72] Cultural differences were not to be seen as mere idiosyncrasies: according to this view, to advance equal educational opportunity in any fundamental way was to engage the structures of society and the distribution of status, resources and power.

In Ireland, responses to cultural impediments to educational opportunity have been almost exclusively corrective.[73] The assumption has been largely that of the compensatory ideal where the intention is to change children's cognitive efficiency and/or aspects of their cultural responses, and those of their parents. This is to be found in the Rutland Street Project and in proposals such as the Irish National Teachers' Organisation policy document, *The educational needs of disadvantaged children*.[74] The fact that educational disadvantage is unequally distributed across the social classes is well recognised. There is also the acknowledgement that those features of lifestyle which inhibit educational progress are, in part, a function of the socio-economic background, though there would be disagreement as to the relative influence of environment and heredity on cognitive factors. What remains neglected is any consideration of the structural basis of disadvantage which is reflected in a circumscribed world of opportunity, social relations, ambition, experiences, values and even freedom. The assumption seems to be that disadvantage can be greatly ameliorated within the disadvantaged area and without any significant repercussions for society at large. A rare exception was Liam Ryan's reflections, in 1979, on his 1967 study, 'Social dynamite'.

Ryan's comments came in an interview with T. P. O'Mahony in the *Sunday Press* and, though the emphasis is narrowly on financial status rather than on a more comprehensive understanding of stratification, they represent a pithy exposition, in layman's language, of the structural basis of cultural disadvantage:

> If I were rewriting 'Social Dynamite' today I think I'd stress the economic side of it more than I did. I have come to realise more and more that for a poor person, his whole style of life and attitudes and outlook are linked considerably more than I thought then to his income. I have changed my mind about the significance of economic factors.
>
> People in deprived areas cannot change their attitudes and outlook unless their financial situation changes. In many ways their whole style of life is a strategy for survival. In other words, you cannot teach a housewife better management skills or higher levels of aspiration while she is still poor.
>
> While she is still poor and struggling with immediate problems her lifestyle and her mentality are largely conditioned by that fact. In the light of this I would advocate more and more today an incomes policy rather than a service policy in dealing with the poor and the deprived... The mentality, attitudes, outlook and aspirations of the poor cannot be changed independently of their income.[75]

Elsewhere, the school itself was not ignored in the identification of possible impediments to equal opportunity. Ability grouping, teacher expectations, evaluation procedures and school ethos were considered in terms of their partiality to students from middle-class background. Factors such as these, it was argued, could put pupils of equal capacity to benefit from school at a disadvantage. Ultimately, it could be held that the yardstick of educational achievement — what knowledge pupils were expected to master in schools — needed to be scrutinised given the facility of middle-class students to master it with greater ease than working-class pupils.[76] The general issue as to what selection from the vast corpus of knowledge is to be considered suitable for transmission to pupils becomes a factor to be considered in assessing impediments to opportunity to gain educational credentials. Specifically, what constitutes a suitable curriculum for working-class children, with the desire for relevance to be balanced against its potential curtailment of social mobility, constitutes one of the great and least-articulated problems in modern education.

As in the case of structural factors, these considerations not alone remain unaddressed in relation to Irish education but go unrecognised as meaningful issues. While attention to the curriculum has been sustained over the past fifteen years or so the approach to content and pedagogy has been largely functionalist, guided by such worthy considerations as continuity, relevance, integration, discovery and participation, but concerned essentially with fitting pupils into a society that is allowed to remain unproblematic. Similarly unexplored is the proposition that a social bias is incorporated in the school curriculum which facilitates unequal achievement. Significantly, many of the curriculum developments are located within the vocational sector or serve prospective early leavers and academically weak pupils and involve diluted versions of mainstream curricula: the contention that the effect is at once to ease the problem of behavioural control in school and to restrict access to high-status credentials remains unconfronted.[77]

Generational impediments to participation in education is an emerging source of concern that is responded to in the idea of lifelong learning[78] and one that has been recognised at an early stage in Ireland. Both the Interim and Final Murphy Reports on adult education were aware that the educational opportunities available to the older generation compare unfavourably with those available to the younger generation.[79] The Kenny Report is more specific:

> More than a third of the present adult population have left school before fourteen. In equity, and in the interests of the economy and social stability, they must be encouraged to participate in education and provided with more opportunities to do so.[80]

How widely diffused this recognition is remains a matter of speculation though paid educational leave (PEL) was conceded in principle in the National Understanding of 1980.

Once beyond such impediments as geography and financial status which the access dimension makes salient, the debate on impediments to equal educational opportunity becomes particularly hazy. This is accounted for only in part by the complexity of the topic and seems to derive in the first instance from the failure to confront equal educational opportunity as an ideal that demands equal outcomes among significant groupings in society. Unelaborated and uncritical references to underachievement, unrealised talent and disadvantage predominate. With the exception of considerations of gender and, to a lesser extent, generation the discourse remains locked in the categories and explanations of the 1960s. The treatment of both culture and gender as impediments to achievement is similarly narrow: once again we find that those explanations or interventions which involve a questioning approach to social and economic structures go unconsidered.

Equality, Mobility and Social Structure

Looking at the link between education and society and attempting to identify since the formative 1960s an awareness of its complexity and social significance is a barren exercise; seeking evidence of social principles or philosophies of justice which take cognisance of a stratified society and its implications in terms of resources and power is frustration itself.

A number of debates have been generated by the education–society link. The philosophical debate concerned itself with the aims of education, general and vocational models of education being its most public foci of attention.[81] The transition from school to the outside world and how this might be facilitated has been the concern of curriculum innovators and is reflected in projects such as the community-based learning programmes.[82] The specific transition to the world of work has been a much more contentious issue with the involvement of career guidance teachers, employers, interest groups, trade unions and agencies such as AnCO and the Youth Employment Agency. Paradigmatically, what these considerations of the school and society linkage have in common is that society is seen either as a monolithic undifferentiated structure or in terms of an unproblematic stratified society.

The strength of the local paradigm is well illuminated during the earlier period under discussion in reactions to an address given by Professor Eoin Mac Tiarnáin at the Conference of Convent Secondary Schools in 1960. In Ireland, Professor Mac Tiarnáin detected a degree of class differences and an acceptance of the doctrine of class difference so shocking that I am compelled to refer to it in unjustifiably strong terms and call it a caste system.[83]

and he drew attention to what he saw as 'a lack of native virile philosophy'. He was clearly viewing Irish educational reality from an American paradigm which incorporated a sensitivity to unequal social structures and an awareness of the reproduction of these inequalities through education. The indications from both the response of the meeting and a subsequent commentary are that the issues being raised by Professor Mac Tiarnáin were redefined in terms of the native paradigm. The focus of the response was free education, state funding and accusations of an inactive Minister for Education rather than unequal social structures.[84]

Indicative also of the strength of the local paradigm were the reactions of an Irish educationalist to the American educational system at this time. Dr T. Ó Raifeartaigh, secretary of the Department of Education, had visited American educational institutions in 1960 and subsequently recorded his reactions in *Studies*. Far from commenting on disparities in equality between American and Irish schools, or on the heightened awareness in the United States at this time of how inequality in the social structure impinges on educational performance, Dr Ó Raifeartaigh was impressed by operational aspects such as its decentralised character, subject methodologies, mechanical aids and parental involvement.[85]

Upon inspection two principles seem to impinge on the manner in which educational opportunity operates in Irish society. These are meritocracy, which relates to the basis on which social and economic resources will be distributed, and sponsored mobility, a norm by which upward social mobility is organised. Following Young,[86] meritocracy is denoted as ability plus effort equals merit; and is contrasted with aristocracy where adult status is ascribed, due to one's position at birth, rather than achieved. To the extent that one can systematise the unspecific, Greaney and Kellaghan are largely correct in interpreting ministerial statements on educational opportunity since the 1960s as manifesting the meritocratic principle.[87] This principle can be criticised in terms of ideology, efficiency and equity.

Ideologically, one can reject the idea of a stratified society where occupations carry unequal status and reward as unacceptable, thus making the principle by which socially and economically more desirable positions are distributed redundant. It has also been argued that ability as recognised and accredited in the educational system is no guarantee of occupational competence.[88] Meritocracy as it operates educationally may be inefficient in matching individual talent and occupational requirements. The concern for equity has been outlined in the previous section, the argument being that what is demanded as indicators of ability and effort in the educational system is socially biased in favour of the middle class.

Despite the existence of these criticisms in educational debate elsewhere, in Ireland Kathleen Lynch's sustained questioning of meritocracy is exceptional.[89]

In a paper published in the *American Sociological Review* in 1960 and given an extended readership by its inclusion in *Education, economy and society*, Turner drew attention to folk norms which define upward social mobility and sought to establish links between these and the structure of the school system.[90] He distinguished between two 'ideal type' folk norms, sponsored mobility and contest mobility.

Contest mobility he defined as a

> system in which elite status is the prize in an open contest and is taken by the aspirant's own efforts. While the contest is governed by some rules of fair play, the contestants have wide latitude in the strategies they may employ. Since the prize of successful upward mobility is not in the hands of the established elite to give out, the latter are not in a position to determine who shall attain it and who shall not. . . . [With sponsored mobility, on the other hand,] elite recruits are chosen by the established elite or their agents, and elite status is given on the basis of some criterion of supposed merit and cannot be taken by any amount of effort or strategy. Upward mobility is like entry into a private club, where each candidate must be sponsored by one or more members. Ultimately, the members grant or deny upward mobility on the basis of whether they judge the candidate to have the qualities they wish to see in their members.

This dichotomy was established to help illuminate some of the differences between the educational systems in the United States and England. Its ideal type character also needs to be stressed. There is no merit in attempting to straitjacket Irish experience to the typology in every detail. What it does represent in its overall emphasis as well as in certain of its details is a tension often manifested in policies which pertain to equality of educational opportunity. In considering the four main distinctions to be drawn between the two norms of sponsored and contest mobility it is possible to demonstrate the manner in which the Irish system leans in the direction of sponsored mobility.

Firstly, the overarching objective of contest mobility is to give elite status to those who earn it while the purpose of sponsored mobility is to maximise the talent of society by sorting each person into an appropriate niche. This latter emphasis on the needs of society and in particular those of our expanding economy is found consistently in the ministerial statements of both Dr Hillery and Mr Colley as quoted earlier in this chapter and is reflected in the development of the career guidance service. There is a sense in which this emphasis dilutes the individualism of the meritocratic principle by exalting the knowledge and skill requirements of society.

Secondly, since under contest mobility society at large establishes and interprets the criteria of elite status they must be highly visible and require no special skill in their assessment. Material prosperity and mass popularity are ideal in this respect. On the other hand, intellectual, literary and artistic excellence which can only be evaluated by those trained to assess them are a means by which elites recognise potential recruits suitable for sponsorship. The centralised character of Irish education makes the unitary currency of mobility possible while the traditional reference groups of what has been a predominantly rural society − the Church and the professions − exalt formal qualifications rather than entrepreneurial ability or commercial success.

Thirdly, contest mobility abhors premature evaluation and tends to delay judgement whereas in sponsored mobility early selection, which allows for a long period of socialisation, is desirable to ensure that anticipated vacancies in the elite will be filled. In Ireland, while formal selection is not a public feature of schooling differentiation by post-primary school[91] and stream[92] functions to channel students to different occupational levels with considerable predictability.

Fourthly, sponsored mobility is most likely to operate where there is a single elite, a clear social hierarchy and where the elite possesses a monopoly of elite credentials. The centralised character of Irish education is again functional with the university system, in particular, operating a controlling effect, through matriculation requirements, as to what is to be recognised as high status knowledge.

Nowhere are these features of the leaning towards sponsored mobility explicated; nor is the manner in which they might be diluting or impeding the meritocratic principle considered.

With increases in unemployment and a greater dependency on social welfare payments, the 1980s saw a rethinking in some quarters of the basic principles of Irish social structure.

Some, like Laurence Crowley, the accountant who oversaw the liquidation of many companies since the onset of the recession, argued along the following lines in 1982.

The atmosphere still in this country rather suggests that industrial unemployment is temporary. I don't agree .... people will say 'remember the good old days in the early 80s when only 170,000 were unemployed'. There are two vital elements here. One is how we value people and the other is what we define as work... We have tried hard to encourage manufacturing industry that people have begun to judge their own value on how well they can fit into that industrial system and now it will expand using less and less people; creating wealth certainly but eliminating job opportunities all the time. Our new age demands that we find a new value for ourselves outside of the system of the creation of wealth. So what will people do? How can we get an opportunity to earn our bread? This is the second vital area, the redefining of what constitutes worthwhile enterprise — what we mean by the word work... I would like to define work as any activity which contributes to the betterment of the society we live in. Today it is still defined as an activity which contributes financially to our society... We must look for new wealth creating enterprises, sure — but we look to use that wealth, to share that wealth to start job creating enterprises .... stop thinking about getting wealth and employment from the same enterprises. Start thinking about the creation of wealth and the creation of employment separately. This involves the transfer of wealth from the new world of technology to a new world of work. Between the two — financial wealth enterprises and the social wealth enterprises — we can build a new busy country. I look forward to small local enterprises, locally organised and controlled, run on a business-like basis doing real work.[93]

A number of research reports on incomes, social structure and social welfare from the Economic and Social Research Institute (ESRI) and the National Economic and Social Council (NESC) raised fundamental questions about equity, income distribution and social mobility.[94] So also did social analyses and policy statements from religious and church groups.[95]

Little of this seemed to impinge on educational thinking. Indeed NESC reports on education involved ideationally — sterile demographic and economic analyses rather than any fundamental consideration of the implications of reduced employment prospects for schooling.[96] Despite the growing levels of unemployment, employers still spoke about preparing young people for the realities of work[97] and educational programmes on the transition from school to work were initiated. The Industrial Training Authority (AnCO), the national body for Coordinating the Education, Recruitment and Training of personnel for the hotel, catering and tourist industry (CERT), the Council for Development in Agriculture (ACOT) and the vocational education committees (VECs) provided a wide range of training programmes. No doubt these programmes helped to prop up and protect the social structure by occupying the time of young people, helping them to give direction and meaning to their days and giving them some confidence in the existing employment system. Clearly, they also felt their attendance at training courses would increase their competitiveness on the job market. Yet, it has been argued that the success of these programmes (in the sense of gaining employment) needs to be treated with some caution given the practice of recruiting to these programmes the better qualified school leavers who are likely to have a higher chance of employment independently of their attendance.[98] Either way, what is at issue is the identity of those who are to be employed not the overall employment rates. Far more responsive to the employment situation were the community-based programmes of

AnCO and the Youth Employment Agency (YEA), both now integrated into FÁS. These include projects aimed at improving the environment, restoring places of historical interest, developing recreational facilities, carrying out surveys, and working with young people.

What is significant about these projects is that, like Laurence Crowley's redefinition of work, they create new categories of paid employment. It can indeed be argued that they are in a rudimentary way redefining work and its function within society. While they are generally perceived as no more than transitory stop gaps, there is every possibility that such projects would be seen as supplying the traditional functions of work (for example self-esteem, status conferring, personal satisfaction) in future years. And the distribution of wealth may be far more divorced from whatever socially important services are provided than occurs at present.

The only attempt to provide some educational response to the belief that full employment is an outmoded ideal is the North Mayo/Sligo based education for development project of the Irish Foundation for Human Development.[99] It represents an important case study in conflicting educational paradigms.

The Irish Foundation for Human Development is a non-government body, 'concerned with study and action programmes relating to the essential nature of the individual, his relationships with other individuals, the environment and the community'. The Foundation incorporates three independent centres, the centre for the person, the centre for human relations and potential and the centre for community, environment and technology. It is this latter centre which oversaw the work of the the North Mayo/Sligo project. In an excellent external assessor's report, Jim Callan analysed the course, consequences and problems of this project with considerable sensitivity and understanding.[100] It is worthwhile quoting at length selectively from the initial portions of his report.

> It is one of the assumptions in this report that a major problem which the North Mayo/Sligo project experienced at every level was a clash of ideological perspective between the perspectives of the people in the area as to their social, industrial and educational needs and the perspective of personnel from the Irish Foundation for Human Development who sponsored and directed the project.

It is important to identify how local industrialists and educationalists perceived their needs and, consequently, their expectations from the educational project concerned with changing the existing situation in schools. These needs are identified here within the context of school to working life.

From the minutes of seminars conducted with local interested bodies and selected economic and social experts a distinct cleavage emerged. Jim Callan contrasted what he referred to the 'efficiency' perspective and the 'job' philosophy. He elaborates as follows on these approaches:

By the so-called 'efficiency' perspective I mean those participants who perceive the existing problems in terms of making the present relationship between schools and work more efficient. From this perspective the problem is primarily one of developing effective strategies and techniques within the existing frame of reference so that full employment can be achieved. This concern with the philosophy of full employment — jobs for everyone — is reflected in the contribution from a political economist who 'was not altogether optimistic of the possibilities of creating the number of jobs required to give full employment by 1981 — he predicted a slowing down in the creation of service jobs and the likely resumption of emigration to the European mainland'.

Likewise, a senior economist with the Industrial Development Authority (IDA) pointed out that 'there has not been any significant shortage in the Irish labour market of any skill — so that even if pupils had skills, the question was would there be enough jobs; in his opinion, there would not be enough jobs; having regard to the population growth and the growth rate of the economy, it was inevitable that emigration would commence again and the best that could be done with school leavers was to equip them (by education and training) to take up jobs in the EEC countries' ....

Callan summarised the situation as follows:

The issue of information on job opportunities, the development of skills required by industries, the concern with job creation represent the context in which people in the region saw the contribution and role of the school in the transition from school to work.... [And:] The critique which teachers give of the educational system is similar to the one which industrialists give to the economic system and job market. Neither question the underlying assumption or orientations of those systems. The changes that are needed are not of any radical nature: improvements can be made by means of more expertise, better techniques, the establishment of better mechanisms and communication channels between existing bodies, organisations and institutions.

The alternative perspective was put forward by the representatives of the Irish Foundation for Human Development. Best known nationally was Dr Ivor Browne whose ideas on the need to find new ways of thinking about work, job creation and human development have been widely propagated.

> We cannot find answers to this frightening problem while we continue to ask the wrong questions. The dilemma is made worse by the way in which we are construing reality... Since the nation's wealth is produced by less than one sixth of the population, the distribution of that wealth for the survival of all seems to be more relevant than job creation. We can't have enough jobs. What will we do with our time? How will be live? We have to find alternatives for those ousted from jobs. [101]

Here we see the argument returning in the same sharp focus to the terms in which Laurence Crowley discussed the same situation. Dr Browne draws the following significant inference:

> Most important of all is to make an act of faith in the basic goodness of people. If, having denied them the opportunity of getting a job ... we secure them in human dignity, people will respond by engaging, on their own initiative, in a wide variety of activities that are life enriching.
>
> These would include gardening and other food production, crafts, small industrial undertakings, arts, educational and a host of cultural activities ... The job is not the only way of life, it was not in the past and will not be in the future. [102]

No doubt he was thinking, among other things, of the fact that an aristocracy had for many generations lived a life without 'work' supported as they were by material inheritance and finding many (one assumes) self-enhancing ways of passing their time. Jim Callan continued as follows: 'their alternative way of understanding work and its place in one's life is quite different from the dominant understanding of that concept, which equates work "with the notion of a job" for which one is paid'. With regard to the success of the project in communicating with schools and in making suitable contributions in the area of imaging, creative expression and movement, Jim Callan concluded: 'the story of this project is about good intentions but poorly communicated, good ideas but time ran out for satisfactory execution of them. It's also about mis-trust, lack of clarity, non-creative contributions and the fear of taking risks'.[103] However, he asserts that 'the project's underlying orientation is still valid. Radical alternatives to our schooling system are required which require tentative and exploratory work. This is what the Foundation basically embarked on. There is value in it being further explored.'

With the exception of this project, however, liberal functionalism, which developed during the expansionary period under discussion, persists as the only salient paradigm for linking school and society. Educational expansion was expected to at once advance equal educational opportunity and provide for the skill needs of the economy. Fundamental questions about this remained not merely unanswered but unposed. The principles by which talent would be labelled as such, recognised and harnessed, the social hierarchy, the nature of work and its rewards and the division of labour await recognition as meaningful problems in Irish educational debate. And this remains so despite the raising of many critical issues about Irish social structure by social researchers and religious and church groups in recent years.

Conclusion

What we have seen in previous sections is a sampling of impoverished educational thought in Ireland. Given the frequent appeal by politicians to the concept of equal educational opportunity it was decided to use this concept as the focus for organising the analysis. Yet despite its frequent use as a justification for developments, the concept was found to be unarticulated and unduly crude in its use. Three issues arising from the concept of equal educational opportunity were used to facilitate the current analysis − the dimensions of and impediments to the achievement of the ideal as well as the social principles which were to operate in pursuing it. When politicians and educators spoke of equal educational opportunity during the formative 1960s, it was access to educational programmes which seemed to concern them. Some politicians were also concerned about such input dimensions of equality as status and investment differentials between vocational and secondary schools. Equality in the effects or outcomes of schooling was never a serious concern though there was a recognition that being reared with 'unsuitable values' inhibited school progress. This is, of course, a post hoc categorisation imposed on concerns and innovations which at the time appear to have been stimulated by a vague sense of 'fairness' and 'folk educational theories'.[104] In consequence, the limitations and problems associated with the access dimension − the emphasis on quantity rather than quality of education, on the throughput of students rather than on actual educational progress and the issue of pupil selection for different kinds of schooling − are trivialised or obscured.

Concern and action about the status differentials between secondary and vocational schools were contained within the only salient social paradigm of the time. The idea of questioning or even acknowledging the stratification of knowledge and status positions was far removed from established thinking. More remote again was the suggestion of a link between such stratification and the differential status among types of post-primary schools. In a country where the norm was to speak of the funding of schooling as if all schools had similar financial resources, and where differential status among secondary schools was officially invisible, it took someone outside the native paradigm of suitable questions, hypotheses and interventions to place these realities on the educational agenda. Ideologically, those who benefited from a social paradigm which allowed social and economic stratification to go unquestioned were ruffled, and eventually a minor change in the funding of schools outside of the 'free education' system was introduced. The comprehensive school had of course been the response in a number of European countries to the problems associated with dual or tripartite post-primary systems of schooling. In importing the idea to Ireland it was robbed of its social objectives, and its ideological connotations were repudiated at ministerial level without any indication of serious consideration.

When considering impediments to equal educational opportunity we found that while the list of possible impediments was wide-ranging and the debate intensive internationally, the Irish response was narrow and selective. The only development on the access impediments (geography, finance) recognised during the 1960s were domesticated versions of gender and cultural factors. While their emergence varied, gender and culture were locally recognised as important factors with selective input from abroad. Nevertheless, they both operated within acceptable social paradigms. Educational intervention directed at gender impediments urged changes in the subjects studied by girls as well as in their career orientations but paid scant attention to the broader question of the reward structures of occupations traditionally aspired to by girls. Politicians' understanding of cultural impediments was crude and non-specific; among many educational researchers the emphasis was unduly on what could be measured empirically. As with gender, both thought within a narrow range of questions and options almost completely unaffected by such international issues as cultural invasion, structural linkages and voluntarism in social choices. Not surprisingly, therefore, responses to cultural impediments, particularly since the failure to act nationally on the implications of the Rutland Street Project's evaluation[105] are mere token gestures, well publicised but unlikely to make an impact.[106]

A pleasant exception is the early recognition of generational inequality which may well come to be more widely acknowledged as unemployment and redundancy create a need for retraining.

During the educational innovations of the 1960s equal educational opportunity was spoken of with no consideration of the implications for society apart from the expectation that more opportunities in education would unleash socially beneficial talent. This expectation was a reflection of the theory of human capital which proclaimed the merits of investing in the education and training of human beings for the greater productivity of a country. This theory, of course, assumes that the aspirations of individuals coincide with the productivity needs of society, and takes no account of how salary, status and values influence the desirability of occupational types irrespective of the economic demand for them.

The link between schooling and society became more explicit

with the institution and expansion of the career guidance service
and with the development of curriculum programmes aimed at
preparing students for the world of work. As with the official
response to differential status between vocational and secondary
schools, society was seen as unproblematic: it was taken for granted
that schools should prepare young people for the demands and
expectations of the work place, whereas the possible defects of
work (for example, dehumanising, boring and repetitive, lack of
autonomy, or low wages) were ignored. Once again we find an
innovation which fails to break out of the native paradigm and
leaves unquestioned the nature of work in Irish society. Even more
surprising is the failure of a more critical paradigm to seriously
impinge on educational thinking in recent years with a deepening
of the recession and a greater number of people relying on social
welfare. Outside of education there has been a questioning of
fundamentals of social structure such as the meaning of work, the
unreality of full employment and the distribution of wealth. Yet,
the commercial, educational and training institutions continue to
speak of the need for vocational preparation as if no employment
crisis existed. More training courses and longer schooling will of
course influence the identity of those who gain permanent
employment but they will have little impact on job creation. At
best, some kind of compensatory training for those who leave
school early with minimal qualification or none may make the social
distribution of unemployment somewhat less pronounced among
children of working-class parents.

How is this lack of facility for ideas, unease with values or
paranoia in the face of ideology to be explained? Clearly, many
factors, some a legacy of our intellectual history, are involved.
A number of suggestions can be grouped under the broad topic
of how we talk about education, how making sense of education
is orchestrated in Ireland. There is, for instance, the localism of
so many contributions on education from elected representatives.
This is the case with such recurring issues as building grants,
extensions, sanctioned teachers, and the provision and route of
the school bus service. One of the central responses to Dr Hillery's
announcement in 1963 of his plan to build a number of
comprehensive schools was the question of their location and how
they would influence existing schools. Similarly, negotiation and
the advocacy of local interests dominated the subsequent

community school issue. One can add to this list debates on the location of new universities and technological colleges, decentralisation, parental involvement and, in recent years, financial cutbacks and closures. The most striking example of localism was the TD who favoured compensatory education but felt that any benefits given to one sector of his constituency would have to be given to all.[107] Indeed, educational ideas in society at large in Ireland are locally inspired[108] with, perhaps, a legitimatory borrowing from abroad, rather than following from some fundamental principle or ideal. Another factor to consider is the atheoretical character of educational thinking in Ireland. The emphasis is on issues − in many instances quite unrelated issues − such as computers in schools, class size, sex education, health education, development education, music and art in education, transfer from primary to secondary schools and examinations and evaluation. However valid and worthy these issues, Irish educational thinking seems to depend on them if it is to exist, and there is the constant challenge, particularly to new Ministers for Education, to find a new issue which can be identified with them and provide a direction for their term of office. Consequently, it is difficult to identify either ideologically left or right in educational thinking within the political parties and, not surprisingly, it is not easy to distinguish between their policies. One scarcely needs to add that this is not a healthy context for a democratic society if it is to develop thoughtful and reflective educational thinking and policy.

Related to these localist and atheoretical issue-based characteristics is the use of slogans in Irish educational thought. Slogans replace principles in that slogans provide a moral loading but they differ from principles because they are not derived from a social theory or vision. It is not uncommon, therefore, for contradictory slogans to co-exist in the same appeal for educational action. Slogans are grounded in appeals of a high moral loading which are considered self-evident, beyond dispute and not demanding justification to anyone educationally, economically or socially alert. Typical examples would be 'equal educational opportunity', 'cherishing all the children of the nation equally', 'community schools' and 'discovery learning'. By means of uncontentious appeals of this nature many diverse viewpoints are capable of being attracted. Though written in relation to a different context the following quotation is particularly relevant to educational ideas in Ireland:

> For slogan systems do not die from explicit rejection but through lack of attention ... When the general slogans in the system fail to capture the imagination, no longer command loyalty, and creative disciples fade away, the system dies.[109]

The absence of ideological cleavages in educational thinking among political parties in Ireland provides a breeding ground for slogans.

Finally, I wish to look at how we formally generate educational ideas and at how we arbitrate and provide reflection on our educational issues. In directing the realm of educational thinking representative commissions drawing from a range of interested parties including independent experts, have been mostly used. Commissions of this nature in modern times have reported on a wide range of issues including curriculum, youth, transition from primary to post-primary schooling, examinations, adult education and in-service education from the Council of Education in the 1950s to the Curriculum and Examinations Board (CEB). No one can deny but that these have made their own contribution to whatever educational development and progress we have experienced. It can be argued, however, that it is not the best strategy for generating fundamental policies. The National Economic and Social Council (NESC) model whereby a representative body responds to a specialist report has a lot to commend it. A critical addition is that specialists need to be involved not only in the analysis of a given problem but also in helping to define what the problem is. The articulation of any problem − the nature of the questions to be asked, the perspectives to be utilised and the methodologies of critique to be employed − frequently define the kind of answers one is likely to receive. Our statement of educational problems is informed by the native paradigms we have inherited. For this reason, one of the problems with commissioned research or side committees utilised by, for instance, the CEB is that they have their research and discourse problems given to them. Accordingly, there is a very real possibility that the process of analysis will be conceptually or ideologically muddied at the earlier point of defining the nature of the problem.

In this regard the *Investment in education* recommendation, that an educational development unit should be established within the

Department of Education in Dublin, was far reaching and significant. The report recommended that a new post of assistant secretary be established, the occupant of which would be responsible to the secretary of the Department for long term planning work:

> for considering policy matters in general and, in particular, to be responsible for directing the findings of the professional staff of the development unit into the administrative system of the Department.[110]

The development unit would be staffed by professional personnel and the report specified that the head of this unit 'should have an independent, inquiring, critical, creative mind, a thorough acquaintance with educational theory and practice and an appreciation of the need for a quantitative approach where this is applicable. He should have the virtue of detachment to a very high degree and a lack of commitment to the status quo'.[111] Working under this head of the development unit would be a first class statistician, a full-time economist, an inspector of schools, an expert in quantitative methods and decision-making processes and a sociologist. They stressed the need, however, for the presentation of the results of the professional work of the development unit to remain in the hands of the professionals right up to the point at which they enter the administrative machinery of the Department and that they would consult periodically with the advisory committees consisting of the representatives of the government department responsible for economic programming, the National Industrial Economic Council and the Director of Statistics.

This recommendation made in the latter part of 1965 was timely and was acted upon a year later when Seán O'Connor, then assistant secretary of the Department of Education, was appointed head of this newly-formed development unit in 1966. Gifted though he was as a thoughtful administrator, Seán O'Connor was not the most appropriate person to head the development unit. A career civil servant with a great commitment to changing the status quo, he lacked the firm background in educational studies which the *Investment in education* team had envisaged. What is highly informative in this regard is the report of the OECD investigation team that looked at certain aspects of Irish educational organisation and policy in June 1966 in preparation for their confrontation meeting which was held on the 19 and 20 October, 1966.[112] Among the people they met was Seán O'Connor and, in his capacity as head of the Development Branch as it had come to be called, he discussed with them issues pertaining to the operation of the branch. He indicated that he was concerned specifically about 'the problems of the planning and control of the work programme of such a group of highly qualified individuals'. He anticipated that 'this branch would necessarily require people whose high qualifications in a variety of disciplines might also be expected to produce strong differences in points of view' and he asked any delegates present who had experience of such a situation to let him have their comments on this matter in their own educational context. The response from a number of the delegates is informative and worthy of quotation:

> The delegate of Denmark explained the procedure in his own country and in Sweden to maintain close touch between the experts' work and practical action. In Sweden, the Minister asks a group of experts to submit proposals on the particular problem he has to solve. The experts' report is then sent to the various bodies, institutions or persons interested in the problem. The Minister himself is then in a position to present a report to the Government or Parliament which takes account of the view of the experts and the comments of the persons involved in the activity concerned. In Denmark, under such conditions, a committee is established with its membership usually comprising of both experts and those responsible for action; the resulting report sent to the Minister is usually in a form permitting immediate practical application.[?]

They warned, however:

> there is the danger with this procedure that new ideas might be diluted by the immediate considerations of the members of the Committee who were engaged in the activity under consideration, but at the same time it can be taken for granted that the Committee's recommendations will normally be accepted.

In the light of Mr O'Connor's concern for control of the unit, the following point made by Mr Embling of the United Kingdom is particularly significant. He 'pointed out that it is not possible or desirable to exert a simple control over the expert survey and research work for planning. The more qualified the expert group engaged in planning work, the more difficult and complex become the responsibilities of those who supervise them, but this circumstance should, in compensation, result in a more sophisticated and effective programme. The very divergences which arose among such a team could encourage creativeness. Thus, there was every advantage of recruiting experts of high calibre, even though they may proceed more slowly.' It can be argued that the leadership of the Development Branch demanded someone in sympathy with this approach to ideas, who would stimulate and lead rather than seek to control a highly qualified and motivated group of specialists. That recommendation of *Investment in education* in 1965 suitably modified to modern conditions and understandings still has a great relevance for educational planning. Re-activated, it could well obviate the possibility of someone writing a critique of the kind I have written about the Irish educational system twenty years hence.

Notes to Chapter 8

1. For example J. Evetts, *The sociology of educational ideas* London: Routledge and Kegan Paul, 1973.
2. K. Lynch, 'Dominant ideologies in Irish educational thought: consensualism, essentialism and meritocratic individualism', paper read at Educational Studies Association of Ireland Annual Conference, University College, Galway, 20-22 March, 1986.
   T. Fleming et al, *Priority areas in adult education* Dublin: Aontas, 1986.
3. Centre for Contemporary Cultural Studies, *Unpopular education* London: Hutchinson, 1981.
4. Dale Tussing, 'Accountability, rationalisation and the White Paper on educational development', paper given to Statistical and Social Inquiry Society of Ireland, Cork, 13 March 1983.
5. D. G. Mulcahy, *Curriculum and policy in Irish post-primary education* Dublin: Institute of Public Administration, 1981.
6. T. Kuhn, *The structure of scientific revolutions* Chicago: University of Chicago Press, 1962.
7. M. Masterman, 'The nature of a paradigm' in I. Lakatos and A. Musgrave, (eds), *Criticism and the growth of knowledge* Cambridge, Mass.: Cambridge University Press, 1970.
8. Kuhn, *Scientific revolutions* p. 175.
9. *Ibid* p. 10.
10. *Ibid* p. 37.
11. S. Hall, 'The hinterland of science: ideology and the 'sociology of knowledge' in Centre for Contemporary Cultural Studies, *On ideology* London: Hutchinson, 1978.
12. S. Bowles and H. Gintis, *Schooling in capitalist America* London: Routledge and Kegan Paul, 1976, p. 131.
13. *Ibid* p. 132.
14. L. Althusser, *Lenin and philosophy and other essays* London: New Left Books, 1971.
15. K. Marx, *Selected works* 1973 edition, London: Lawrence and Wishart.
16. M. Apple, *Ideology and curriculum* London: Routledge and Kegan Paul, 1979, p 161.
17. *Ibid* p. 160.
18. H. Giroux, *Theory and resistance in education* London: Heinemann, 1983.
19. Quoted in P. L. Berger and B. Berger, *Sociology. A biographical approach* Harmondsworth: Penguin, 1976.

20. S. O'Connor, 'Post-primary education: now and in the future' in *Studies* (Autumn 1968).
21. P. J. Hillery, 'Policy statement on post-primary education', 20 May 1963, in OECD, *Reviews of national policies for education, Ireland* Paris, 1969.
22. G. Colley, 'Statement to the authorities of secondary and vocational schools' (1966) in OECD, *Reviews of national policies for education, Ireland* Paris, 1969.
23. J. S. Coleman, 'The concept of equality of educational opportunity' in *Harvard Educational Review* (1968), Vol 38, pp. 7-22.
24. J. S. Coleman, et al, *Equality of educational opportunity* Washington, DC: US Government Printing Office, 1966.
25. J. S. Coleman, 'What is meant by "an Equal Educational Opportunity"?' in *Oxford Review of Education* (1975), Vol 1, pp. 27-29.
26. Hillery, 'Policy statement'.
27. D. O'Malley, Address to the National Union of Journalists, Dún Laoghaire, 10 September, quoted in the *Sunday Press*, 11 September, 1966.
28. E. Randles, *Post-primary education in Ireland 1957-1970*. Dublin: Veritas Publications, 1975.
29. OECD, *Investment in education* Dublin: Stationery Office, 1965.
30. National Industrial Economic Council (NIEC), *Comments on 'Investment in education'* Dublin: Report No. 16, 1966.
31. B. Farrell, *Chairman or chief?* Dublin: Gill and Macmillan, 1971.
32. W. Hyland, 'Effect of retardation on national school pupils' in *Oideas* 2 (1969), pp. 50-55.
33. J. Rudd, *Report: national school terminal leavers* Dublin: Germaine Publications, 1972.
34. *Ibid* p. 25.
35. D. O'Sullivan, 'National school terminal leaving and school delay' in *Studies* Spring (1973), pp. 63-74.
36. T. Kellaghan *et al*, 'Teachers' assessments of the scholastic progress of pupils' in *Irish Journal of Education* (1969), Vol 3, pp. 95-104.
37. T. Kellaghan and V. Greaney, 'Factors related to choice of post-primary school in Ireland' in *Irish Journal of Education* (1970), Vol 4, pp. 69-83.
38 R. Breen, 'Equality in education', address to the Irish Vocational Education Association, 1985.
39. D. O'Sullivan, 'Adult continuing education in the Irish Republic: a research synthesis' in *International Journal of Lifelong Education* (1989), Vol 8 forthcoming.
40. J. J. O'Meara, *Reform in education* Dublin: Mount Salus Press, 1958.
41. Hillery, 'Policy statement'.
42. Ireland, *Second programme for economic expansion Part I*, Dublin: Stationery Office, 1963.
43. Randles, *Post-primary education*.
44. Tussing, 'Accountability'.
45. D. A. Lynch, 'A study into the relationship between occupational groups and school factors and patterns of transfer from primary to post-primary schools in Cork city', unpublished MEd thesis, Department of Education, University College, Cork, 1974.

D. MacCárthaigh, 'Adaptation and socialization of male pupils in boarding schools of Munster', unpublished MEd thesis, Department of Education, University College, Cork, 1980.

46. Dale Tussing, 'Irish educational policy reconsidered', address to Irish Vocational Education Association, 17 May 1983.

47. J. Sheehan and J. Nolan, *A report on the financing of Catholic secondary schools* Dublin: Council of Managers of Catholic Secondary Schools, 1982.

48. Tussing, 'Irish educational policy'.

49. D. Hannan, *Rural exodus* London: Chapman, 1970.

50. J. Raven, 'A note on occupational prestige in Ireland' in *Social Studies* (1974), Vol 3, pp. 435-436.

51. B. Hutchinson, *Social status and inter-generational social mobility in Dublin* Dublin: Economic and Social Research Institute, 1969.

52. P. Commins, 'Rural community development: approaches and issues' in *Social Studies* (1985), Vol 8, pp. 165-178.

53. D. Talbot, 'The image of Muintir na Tire' in *Rural Ireland*, (1965) pp. 21-25.

54. Hillery, 'Policy statement'.

55. P. J. Hillery, reply to Dr N. Browne, TD in *Dail Reports* Vol 203, Col 684, 11/6/1963.

56. Quoted in Randles, *Post-primary education* p. 70.

57. G. Colley, 'Our future in education' in *Sunday Press* 9 January 1966.

58. Randles, *Post-primary education* pp. 306-307.

59. T. Kellaghan and S. Ó hUallacháin, 'A pre-school intervention project for disadvantaged children' in *Oideas* 10 (1973), pp. 38-47.
S. Ó hUallacháin and T. Kellaghan, 'A project for disadvantaged pre-school children' in *Oideas* 3 (1969), pp. 28-32.

60. D. Hannan et al, *Schooling and sex roles* Dublin: Economic and Social Research Institute, 1983.

61. J. Levine, *Sisters* Dublin: Ward River Press, 1983.

62. D. Hannan et al, *Schooling and sex roles*.

63. D. O'Sullivan, 'Pedagogues under threat — paradigms rule OK' in *Bulletin of the Sociological Association of Ireland* April 1974, No.37.

64. Randles, *Post-primary education*.

65. P. J. Hillery, in *Dáil Reports* Vol 214, Cols 711-721, 18/2/1965

66. K. Lynch, 'Dominant ideologies'.

67. V. Greaney and T. Kellaghan, 'Factors related to level of educational attainment in Ireland' in *Economic and Social Review* (1985), Vol 16, pp. 144-156.

68. V. Greaney and T. Kellaghan, *Equality of opportunity in Irish schools* Dublin: Educational Company, 1984.

69. L. Ryan, 'Social dynamite' in *Christus Rex* (1967), Vol 21, pp. 7-44.

70. H. Entwistle, *Class, culture and education* London: Methuen, 1978.

71. J. Murphy, 'Class inequality in education', *British Journal of Sociology* (1981), Vol 32, pp. 182-200.

72. P. J. Squibb, 'Education and class' in *Educational Research* (1973), Vol 15, pp. 194-208.

73. An exception is P. Archer, 'An evaluation of educational intervention programmes' in Irish National Teachers' Organisation *Educational disadvantage* Dublin: INTO, 1984.
74. Irish National Teachers' Organisation, *The educational needs of disadvantaged children* Dublin: INTO, 1979.
75. *Sunday Press* 30 December 1979.
76. G. Whitty, *Sociology and school knowledge* London: Methuen, 1985.
77. T. Crooks and J. McKernan, *The challenge of change* Dublin: Institute of Public Administration, 1984.
    E. Doyle, List of alternative programmes/projects currently in operation in JMB Schools (Voluntary Schools), June 1984.
    Ireland: National dossier on European Community Pilot Projects, 1979-1982. *Preparation of young people for work and facilitation of their transition from education to working life* Dublin: Department of Education, 1984.
78. T. Faure, *Learning to be* Paris: UNESCO, 1972.
79. Committee on Adult Education, *National Adult Education* Survey (Interim Murphy Report). Dublin: Stationery Office, 1970.
    Committee on Adult Education, *Adult Education in Ireland* (Final Murphy Report). Dublin: Stationery Office, 1973.
80. Commission on Adult Education, *Lifelong learning* (Kenny Report). Dublin: Stationery Office, 1984, p. 32.
81. Mulcahy, *Curriculum and policy.*
82. Ireland: National dossier.
83. Quoted in Randles, *Post-primary education* p. 53.
84. *Ibid* pp. 56-57.
85. T. Ó Raifeartaigh, 'Education in the U.S.A.' in *Studies* (Spring 1961), pp. 57-74.
86. M. Young, *The rise of the meritocracy 1870-2033* London: Pelican Books, 1961.
87. Greaney and Kellaghan, *Equality of opportunity.*
88. I. Berg, *Education and jobs* London: Penguin Books, 1976.
89. K. Lynch, 'An analysis of some presuppositions underlying the concepts of meritocracy and ability as presented in Greaney and Kellaghan's study' in *Economic and Social Review* (1985), Vol 16, pp. 83-102.
90 K. Turner, 'Modes of social ascent through education: sponsored and contest mobility' in Halsey, A.H., Floud, J. and Anderson, C.A. (eds.) *Education, economy and society* New York: Free Press, 1961.
91. Greaney and Kellaghan, *Equality of opportunity.*
92. D. Hannan and M. Boyle, *Schooling decisions: the origins and consequences of selection and streaming in Irish post-primary schools* Dublin: Economic and Social Research Institute, 1987.
93. L. Crowley, text of address in *Evening Echo* 23 November 1982.
94. National Economic and Social Council, *Universality and selectivity. strategies in social policy* Dublin: NESC, 1978
    National Economic and Social Council, *A review of industrial policy* Dublin: NESC, 1982.

D. B. Rottman et al, *The distribution of income in the Republic of Ireland: a study of social class and family cycle inequalities* Dublin: Economic and Social Research Institute, 1982.

C. T. Whelan and B. J. Whelan, *Social mobility in the Republic of Ireland: a comparative perspective* Dublin: Economic and Social Research Institute, 1984.

95. S. J. Healy and B. Reynolds, *Ireland today. Reflecting in the light of the gospel* Dublin: Justice Office, Conference of Major Religious Superiors, 1985.

96. National Economic and Social Council, *Educational expenditure in Ireland* Dublin: NESC, 1976.

National Economic and Social Council, *Population projections 1971-1986: The implications for education* Dublin: NESC, 1976.

National Economic and Social Council. *Education; the implications of demographic change* Dublin: NESC, 1983.

97. C. Power, Paper on the second-level school curriculum. Statistical and Social Inquiry Society of Ireland, Cork, 13 March 1981.

98. R. Breen, *Education and the labour market: work and unemployment among recent cohorts of Irish school leavers* Dublin: Economic and Social Research Institute, 1984.

99. Irish Foundation for Human Development, Report on the North Mayo/Sligo Pilot Project 'Education for development' (1982) in Ireland: National Dossier on European Community Pilot Projects, 1979-1982 (1984).

100. J. Callan, The North Mayo/Sligo Project 'Education for Development' 1978-1982. The Final External Evaluation Report (1983) in Ireland: National Dossier on European Community Pilot Projects, 1979-1982, 1984.

101. Quoted in Callan 'Final external report'.

102. *Ibid.*

103. Callan, 'Final external report'.

104. S. O'Connor, *A troubled sky: reflections on the Irish educational scene 1957-1968* Dublin: Educational Research Centre, 1986.

105. T. Kellaghan, *The evaluation of an intervention programme for disadvantaged children* Slough: NFER, 1977.

S. Holland, *Rutland Street* London: Pergamon Press, 1979.

106. L. Mackey, 'The role of positive discrimination in education, unpublished MEd thesis, Department of Education, University College, Cork, 1987.

107. S. Ó Buachalla and J. MacAirt, 'Poverty and educational provision in Ireland' in *Irish Journal of Education* (1979), Vol 13, pp. 54-61.

108. O'Connor, *A troubled sky.*

109. B. P. Komisar and J. McClellan, 'The logic of slogans' in B. Smith and R. H. Ennis (eds), *Language and concepts in education* Chicago: Rand McNally, 1961.

110. OECD, *Investment in education* p. 353.

111. *Ibid* p. 354.

112. OECD, *Reviews of national policies for education: Ireland.* Paris, 1969.

Index

275